Browning Ross: Father of
American Distance Running

Browning Ross: Father of American Distance Running

Jack Heath

ISBN: 1511888253
ISBN 13: 9781511888257
Library of Congress Control Number: 2017909859
CreateSpace Independent Publishing Platform
North Charleston, South Carolina

This book is dedicated with gratitude to the Ross, Knoblock, and Heath families; in memory of Browning and Sis Ross.

Foreword

BROWNING ROSS WAS THE FIRST runner I ever met. We met when I entered a classroom at Gloucester Catholic as a freshman to sign up for the track team he coached on March 7, 1974. As I waited in line to sign up, I read a small, promotional signup poster placed on the wall by the upperclassmen on the team, "Coach Mr. Browning Ross 1948 and 1952 Olympic Teams and Gold medal winner at the 1951 Pan Am Games." It was the first time I heard his name.

Browning, always humble, never talked about his running accomplishments, so this was as much as I knew about his competitive history for a few years. I was most impressed by the fact that he was my coach, and he was a nice and very patient man. It was also eye-opening that Browning in his 50's, was still running and still faster than anyone on the team. At 14 I had never thought of the possibility of anyone running past high school or college and I was fascinated that it was a possibility.

I would soon find out through other runners, coaches, and writers about Browning's life story and accomplishments. Besides coaching us he wrote and published a running magazine called the Long Distance Log, he officiated the Penn Relays and our meets, to put on races every weekend, and he seemed to be the only coach we saw that ran with his team.

One day after hearing another fascinating anecdote from his past- it might have been a story about Jumbo Elliott and John Joe Barry in Villanova, meeting Emil Zatopek or Haile Selassie's lion face to face, winning ten diamond rings at Berwick, or jogging with Muhammad Ali- I asked why he hadn't written a book about his fascinating life.

"Who would read it?" he asked. Then he thought for a second and a big smile spread across his face and his blue eyes twinkled. "My wife Sis would probably read it to see her name in print."

I always wished Browning had written that book but I knew he was too humble and too involved in the present and every facet of running to bother writing about himself.

Years later I tried to interview him for an article for American Running magazine and true to form he deflected every question about himself with humor. It is said the "Greatest Generation" never bragged about what they had done or what they had been through during World War II. Browning extended that silence to his accomplishments.

Tom Osler was a friend of Browning's for over 40 years. He was present at Browning's founding of the Road Runners Club of America and said, "Olympians and running champions aren't as rare as you might think. There are actually a good many people who have been Olympians and many were quite unremarkable except for their running accomplishments. Browning Ross was different. He was a two-time Olympian and one of the dominant runners of his era at a wide variety of distances but what sets him apart are his contributions to running.

What George Washington was to this country Browning Ross was to running. Two of his contributions, single-handedly publishing the Long Distance Log, the first national running magazine, and starting the Road Runners Club of America kept running alive in this country until the running boom of the 1970's when running became a mass participation sport. He also gave back to the sport by putting on probably close to a thousand races. Browning did all of this with a tremendous sense of humor and humility that encouraged so many other people to run-- including myself."

This book is an attempt to tell his story.

1951 British Games Mile Roger Bannister outside lane, Browning Ross inside lane.

Pioneers Meet

"The Road goes ever on and on
Down from the door where it began.
Now far ahead the Road has gone,
and I must follow if I can,
pursuing it with eager feet
until it joins some larger way
where many paths and errands meet.
And whither then? I cannot say"
— J.R.R. Tolkien, The Fellowship of the Ring

ON MAY 12, 1951, BROWNING Ross the 27-year-old American, from Woodbury, New Jersey, wearing number 7, toed the inside line in the first lane of the starting line in the British Games Mile race in White City Stadium in London.

Many of the 47,000 boisterous track fans in White City stadium had waited out a rain delay to see 22-year-old favorite son Roger Bannister of Great Britain run against a field of five invited world-class milers in what was billed as the "Bannister Mile"-- the biggest mile race of 1951. The spectators did not realize they were also about to witness the only competition between two runners who would someday be the most influential distance running pioneers in their respective countries.

Ross was invited because he had run the Steeplechase in the 1948 Olympics in London. He was also the 1951 Pan Am Games 1500-meter gold medalist and silver medalist in the 3000-meter Steeplechase (tied for first with Curt Stone). He also had one of the fastest American mile times in 1951.

Bannister, a student from a working-class family at the University of Oxford and at St. Mary's Hospital Medical School, London, had run the mile in the Penn Relays a few weeks before, taking the lead after two and a half laps and winning in 4:08.3, with his last lap a blistering 56.7. Bannister said after his Penn victory that he felt ready to run a mile in 4 minutes, 5 seconds.

Bannister would also win this race in 4:09.2, and of course go on to run the first sub-four-minute mile three years later. Bannister thought enough of the British Games Mile to mention Ross and the race in his book "The Four Minute Mile". London papers described the race as "loud as a championship football match at Wembley Stadium, Ross took the lead for the first lap. At the second lap, the field was still closely bunched only six meters apart when Bannister took off and pulled way to the roar of the crowd."

Bannister would also become a physician and a major proponent of running as a part of a balanced life-long fitness in Britain and around the world.

Ross and Bannister would also both run in the 1952 Olympic Games in Helsinki. Browning Ross would go on to impact every facet of American distance running for the next 47 years. He would win close to a thousand races at various distances, coach track and cross-country at every level, found the first National American Running Magazine, the Long Distance Log and also found the Road Runners Club of America which was modeled after the Road Runners Club of Britain.

This is the life story of Browning Ross, the Father of American Distance Running, before and after the British Games.

Henry Wood, the Lenape, and the Colonel

HARRIS BROWNING "BROWNIE" ROSS WAS born in Woodbury New Jersey on April 26, 1924. Frank and Olive Ross's first- born son was delivered in Underwood Hospital by J. Harris Underwood, one of two Jefferson Hospital doctors who had set up competing hospitals blocks from each other in downtown Woodbury, N.J It is said that Dr. Underwood delivered a little over 10,000 babies in his career, roughly equivalent to the population of Woodbury today. Woodbury, a two-mile square town located just thirteen miles from Philadelphia was already 240 years old in 1924 and was best known for its most famous resident, 82-year-old Colonel George Gill(GG)Green.

Fittingly, Browning was born in an Olympic year. The first winter Olympics have held in Chamonix France in 1924, and the summer Olympics were held in Paris.

Finland's Paavo Nurmi was the world's greatest runner that year, breaking world records in the 1500 and 5000 meters 3 weeks before the Olympics. Nurmi won 5 gold medals in the 1924 Olympics despite Finnish officials not entering him in his best event the 10,000 meters. His feat of winning Olympic gold medals in the 1500 and 5000 meters 42 minutes apart is still considered by many the greatest Olympic performance of all time.

1924 was also a year that marked a changing of the guard as American President Woodrow Wilson and Russian Premier Vladimir Lenin passed away, and the last emperor of China abdicated.

Future Presidents Jimmy Carter and George H.W. Bush were born that year, and another leader of the past was rediscovered as Egyptian King Tutankhamen's sarcophagus was found after thousands of years. Cultural icons Charles Lindbergh, Charlie Chaplin and Babe Ruth dominated the daily newspapers and newsreels of 1924; while Gershwin's "Rhapsody in Blue," the half jazz, and the half-classical masterpiece was performed for the first time.

When Browning took his first steps, the nation was five years into a fourteen-year prohibition.

Browning and other Woodbury grade school students were taught about how Gill became a millionaire by producing the first mass produced medicinal elixirs in the country, and how their production led to a massive job and building boom in Woodbury starting in 1872.

But they also learned about Woodbury's long history before Green-- how their hometown was founded in 1683 by Henry Wood, a Quaker from the Northwest of England, who had left Great Britain due to religious persecution. Wood was incarcerated in England for practicing as a Quaker and left his home to set up a community in New Jersey where he and his family could practice their religion freely.

Wood and the Quakers befriended the native Lenape Indians and acquired much of their land including Woodbury from the Indians despite a difference of opinion.

The Quakers thought they were buying the land while the Lenape, unfamiliar with the concept of anyone owning land thought they were leasing their land to the Quakers as an act of friendship.

Woodbury school children were taught the legend of how the early Woodbury settlers faced starvation when Woodbury's food supply became exhausted, and the Quaker men set out to find food. When their return was delayed, the women were saved from starvation by an Indian maiden who floated across Woodbury Creek to deliver food supplies to them.

From these tenuous beginnings, Woodbury earned the name the "garden patch of Philadelphia" during the Revolutionary War. The Lenape had long before identified Woodbury's sandy loam soil along the Delaware River as perfect for farming.

In 1793, one of the nation's first abolition societies, The Gloucester County Abolition Society was founded in Woodbury. The spirit of tolerance flowed through Woodbury and became a part of its citizens DNA.

In the 19th century, two unrelated major events helped bring Woodbury to prominence.

First, a seventy-five-year-old dam broke across Woodbury Creek just south of the city in 1831 opening up the Creek and Woodbury for sloops and small ships, which brought Philadelphia goods and commerce to the town. New Jersey historian John Cunningham wrote, "A Woodbury town orator enthusiastically proclaimed that the tide which had run out 75 years ago has finally run back".

As a result, a railroad station was built in Woodbury to accept trains from Camden five times a day, further strengthening Woodbury's connection to Philadelphia.

During the Civil War, much of the produce raised in southern New Jersey farms passed through Woodbury on the way to market in Philadelphia to feed the Union Army.

Second, in 1862 President Abraham Lincoln, fearing the Confederacy was making headway in the Civil War, asked for 300,000 new Union volunteers for a new 12th Regiment of New Jersey. This new regiment was trained and "mustered" at newly formed Camp Stockton, located in Woodbury. Among the major influx of soldiers and residents stationed at the new Camp was Colonel George Gill "GG" Green.

After the war, Green bought the rights to two small patent-medicines-- "Green's August Flower" and "Dr. Boschee's German Syrup" from his father, Lewis M. Green. He married and moved to Woodbury in 1872.

Green scoffed at other so-called cure-alls common at the time as "snake oil," but touted his own elixirs as a cure for indigestion and stomach pain of dyspepsia and chest discomfort.

In one of the first examples of successful American mass advertising, Green created a marketing campaign involving mass mailings of free samples.

Ten million samples of Boshees Syrup and 2.4 million samples of August Flower, were mailed out along with the distribution of five million of his almanacs, and postcards advertising the two products.

With all of the samples and mail leaving the city, Woodbury became the 7ᵗʰ biggest post office in New Jersey despite its small population.

Green became a millionaire in an age when annual income was typically only a few thousand dollars a year. Green also plowed much of the profits back into Woodbury creating hundreds of local jobs and a massive building boom in downtown Woodbury. In 1880, he built many ornate buildings in Woodbury including hotels and Woodbury's Opera House on Broad and Centre Streets. (Browning would later move his family to Centre Street in Woodbury, 3 blocks from the Green Opera House). Green also built and opened the Woodbury glass works in 1881 to supply glass bottle and vials for the medicines. The glass works along with a box factory to box the hot selling products led to a massive employment surge in Woodbury.

Greens patent medicine business quickly declined after the passage of the Pure Food and Drug Act in 1906-- the same year Coca-Cola removed trace amounts of cocaine from its formula.

Their popularity soon faded in the early 20ᵗʰ century throughout the United States, and by 1916, both of Greens products were discontinued. In an expose done by Colliers Magazine at the time the ingredients were said to mostly contain laudanum, a tincture of opiate (legal at the time) believed to be highly addictive. The elixirs also contained low levels of cyanide and morphine and alcohol.

Later analysis by pharmacists claimed that the active ingredients in Greens two patent medicines might have actually exacerbated the conditions of the maladies treated by the elixirs, such as stomach distress while masking their symptoms.

Colonel George Green died in Woodbury on February 26, 1925, a year after Browning was born. Browning and thousands of other Woodbury youth played basketball on the second floor of one of Green's buildings which survived into the 21ˢᵗ century.

From Apple Orchards to a National Championship

FRANK ROSS WAS ONE OF the many railroad workers who moved to Woodbury, New Jersey to work on the railroad in the 1920's as a telegraph operator. Frank was born and raised in South Seaville, New Jersey, a significant stop on the West Jersey and Seashore line, located about 30 miles from Cape May New Jersey, with his parents and 2 brothers.

South Seaville was also a significant Methodist camp. Frank worked on the nearby West Jersey and Seashore line as a switchman. Frank soon met and married Olive "Dusty".

Olive was born in Newport News, Virginia. She was adopted by a Methodist minister and his wife (the Littleton's). The Littleton's raised Olive in Kennett Square, Pennsylvania near Longwood Gardens.

Soon after marrying, Frank Ross and his bride moved to Woodbury. Frank continued working for the Railroad, as the line extended into Woodbury.

Twenty-three-year-old Olive Ross and husband were so appreciative of Doctor Underwood delivering a healthy baby boy that they named their son Harris Browning Ross in honor of the doctor. He would grow up to attend Woodbury schools and answer to his middle name Browning or "Brownie". Within days of Browning's birth, Olive received letters of congratulations from her girlfriends, "So you went and had a baby without telling us. Good luck to mom, dad, and baby Ross!"

A brother, Forrest "Babe" Ross would follow Browning two years later. The Ross's Methodist faith was a strong influence on Brownie and Babe. The Woodbury Daily Times reported in June of 1928 that "Mrs. Frank H Ross and little sons Forrest and Browning of Queen Street are the guests of Ministers, the Rev. and Mrs. Paul Reynolds of Vienna, Md. and Rev. and Mrs. George A Cooke of Lewisville Pa. for the balance of the month."

By all accounts, Browning grew up with a sense of humility and a love for the disenfranchised. His sympathy for the underdog may have arisen from knowledge of his own family roots. Browning's daughter Bonnie explained, "Dad's mom Olive was found abandoned in a drawer in Newport News and raised by a Methodist Minister. Ironically, he was known to personally be a kind man, but was defrocked for preaching virulently anti-Catholic sermons."

Browning was brought up as a Methodist, but in a more tolerant religious atmosphere than his mother had seen, fitting the climate in Ross's new hometown of Woodbury.

As young boys, both Browning and Babe were interested in all the sandlot sports being played in town, football, basketball, baseball, wrestling, tennis, and track. And of course, the boys would all play pick-up basketball games upstairs in the old Green Opera House.

However, Browning and Babe were most interested in running. Browning's neighbor Don Sanderson, a future mayor of Woodbury remembers, "Browning and Babe's dad Frank wasn't interested much in sports. I frequently saw him in a suit, but their mom, Olive was a good runner who we heard had won ribbons as a school girl. I think that's where the Ross brothers got their love of running.

Sanderson remembers Browning running through apple orchards and through his property to his home on Queen Street at least four times a day. "Babe sometimes ran with him, but Browning never missed a day. Browning looked fast-- he had strong, powerful form, ran up on his toes.

I actually thought Babe had a smoother form, but Browning had a determination when he ran that you could see in his eyes. I think that's what made him great." Sanderson said, "We were all kids together but even then you could see the focus in Browning's eyes. Both boys were great runners at Woodbury, who earned college scholarships after the war, but Browning always had that laser-like focus and desire for running and that's what made him an Olympian."

When asked about their school days seventy years later Babe concurred and said, "We weren't training for anything we just liked to run."

Sanderson, "Their father Frank served in the First World War as a Cavalry Man, and I remember one year when he rode a horse and led the Woodbury parade."

"When the Second World War started, there were blackouts in town, there weren't many cars, but the cars on the road had their headlights blacked out and the streetlights were turned off. There was also rationing of meat and a lot of other items. Running was actually a pretty good way to get around."

A Catholic Star Herald interview in 1989 described how Browning got his childhood start in running, "It all started back in the 1930's when Ross was a grade school boy. Neighbor George Benjamin, a New Jersey State Track Champion introduced a new game to the neighborhood kids, foot races around the block and Browning discovered running was something he liked to do."

Browning provided more detail about Benjamin's influence to Bob Shryock, a columnist for the Woodbury Times, "Browning recalled getting a gentle push into track from George Benjamin Jr. in fifth grade.

"He was a great person, a terrific guy," says Ross of Benjamin. "He was the one who got a bunch of us started in track when my house was near West End School. He definitely had a bearing on the direction I took because he was kind of the track star at Woodbury High and the kids knew it, and we looked up to him. He organized unofficial neighborhood meets for us just to get us started on track. He was a very friendly guy, always upbeat. He was the one that got me going."

Browning saved a newspaper clipping of a Shanahan Catholic Track Club track meet where he and Benjamin were Shanahan teammates. Eighth grader Ross won the 880-yard run, and Benjamin won both the shot and discus.

Benjamin won a track scholarship to Temple University and then gave up a job at DuPont to enter the military in 1943. Browning was serving overseas in the Navy when he received word that his mentor was killed in action December 21, 1944, in the Philippines. Benjamin was awarded the Congressional Medal of Honor for his heroism, fighting a Japanese machine gun position with only a pistol and then calling in vital tactical information while dying.

Browning's classmates interviewed 70 years after Browning's 1943 graduation from Woodbury High, concur that Browning was a likable friend with a great sense of humor whose primary focus was on sports—especially running.

Classmate, Norma Snyder-Beard lettered in hockey, basketball, and tennis and graduated from Woodbury High in 1944 and recalled 70 years later, "Brownie Ross was a friend of mine from the 1940's. We became friends when we both helped out with the summer playground program for kids in Woodbury. I think it was 1944. The program was 6-8 weeks of playground activities held mostly in the courtyard by the school.

Brownie and his friend, John Residence, rode down to the shore on motor scooters later that summer to visit us at the beach at Stone Harbor, NJ. They stayed for a few days with my family. Besides swimming, I remember Brownie went out running on the beach every day.

Brownie was very laid back and not very mechanically inclined. One time I heard some noise while we were inside eating dinner. Brownie was out front sitting in his car which had stalled out. I went out to help him start his car. The engine was flooded and I got it started."

"When the Gloucester County YMCA opened, Brownie wrote a story about me swimming for the Woodbury Times that started with this paragraph: "Norma Bear, a Woodbury housewife is hooked on swimming. The way she describes it, it is like eating peanuts, once you start you just can't stop."

"Ironically I remember Brownies' families' garden behind their house on Queen Street and one of the things they grew was peanuts."

Don Sanderson had similar memories, "Frank Ross had a huge garden and Babe would help him in the garden and sell some of the flowers and things they grew. I don't think Browning had any interest in the garden or in

Frank's other hobby—photography but Babe was interested in photography too.

Babe Ross recalled, "My dad was very interested in photography and sent away for a Leica camera from Germany. I was also interested in photography, and I also delivered flowers that he grew. One time I remember delivering some flowers to a woman in Woodbury and there was a bee hiding in the flowers that flew into the lady's house that bought them. She said, "I'll pay you for these flowers if you catch that bee and take him out of here!"

Peggy Yeiter Balistreri was another classmate and friend of Browning. Interviewed decades later she remembered Browning running nearly every day but also remembers most of her classmates doing some daily walking and running to get where they had to go. "If you wanted to get somewhere you walked, or ran if you wanted to get their faster. I remember Browning telling me where he'd be and sometimes I'd run to meet him. There weren't as many cars available then. A lot of us would go to Almonesson Lake in the summer. It was a popular hangout.

Balisteri also remembered Browning's love of a variety of sports, "I always remembered that Browning was never a drinker, and got along with everyone in the school. I never saw him have any disagreements with anyone. Of course, he was really into sports at school."

"I remember one time in school teasing him about trying out for and being good at most of Woodbury's sports including cross country, wrestling, and track. I asked him if he was going to try tennis next. He said, "I might!"

"Most of all I remember he was exactly the same when he came back from the war. My brother was a manager for the Woodbury track team and when he came back from the war it really affected him-- he was never the same. Browning was the same person after the war and after the two Olympics too."

Don Sanderson recalled, "Woodbury was a great place to grow up in the 30's and 40's. There were two movie theaters. You could walk to nearby lakes in Almonesson or Westville in the summer. Grossman's Deli used to roast fresh peanuts and vent the exhaust onto Broad Street so you would have to stop in and buy a bag of peanuts to take to the movies."

Coincidentally, Almonesson was also the birthplace of Olympic four-time gold medalist Mel Sheppard. Sheppard was born in 1883 spent the first nine years of his life in Almonesson. "What I remember most is swimming in Almonesson Lake," Sheppard wrote in his autobiography, SPIKED SHOES, AND CINDER PATHS, which was published in serial form in Sports Story magazine in 1924, the same year Browning was born. Sheppard won the first of his three gold medals in 1500 at the Olympic Games in London in 1908. Growing up only 3 miles away from Almonesson in Woodbury, Browning would run also his first Olympics in the second London Olympics forty years later.

In 1931, when Browning was 7 years old, one of Woodbury's two movie theaters, the Rinalto earned a mention in the New York Times. "Woodbury's local police sentenced three schoolboys, charged with having broken the lock of the theater's exit door to see a movie, to receive ten lashes each and pay a $5 fine. The officer then descended from the bench and administered the flogging himself with a borrowed strap."

At the start of the Second World War in 1942, Americans were encouraged to start "victory gardens" to grow their own vegetables. Woodbury students took time off from school and were assigned to work on nearby farms. Woodbury's athletic teams added newly formed Army teams to their scholastic schedule along with their traditional South Jersey High Schools. The Ross family were already known for their large garden and Browning was starting to attract attention for his athletic accomplishments at Woodbury's schools.

Through his six years at West End Primary School, and his two years at Woodbury Junior High, Browning continued to play sandlot sports and continued to run with Babe for the pure joy of running. As a Woodbury Freshman, he remembered the first time he thought about the sport of track was when he heard a commotion in his back yard and came out to see his classmate and neighbor unsuccessfully attempting to "pole vault" over a clothesline with his mother's clothes prop.

Browning recalled that he vowed to stick to only running events if he went out for track after watching the debacle. His first sport as a freshman at Woodbury was Cross Country. Running the 2 ½-mile distance for Coach

Benjamin Geist, Browning became Woodbury's number one runner half way through the season when he beat Senior Jim McGuinness, one of the top milers in South Jersey at the time.

Browning Ross, back row center cross-country team photo.

Edward Phetteplace, a writer for the Sports Times of New Jersey, wrote about meeting Browning as a freshman.

"Back in 1939, a small, wiry towheaded Woodbury High freshman, attired in the lingerie of a gym suit and sneakers... was noticed by passersby...running out Delaware Street, veering his course which took him across the surroundings of Bell Tract Lake... then along the back of the Woodbury Creek... finally completing his course at the rear entrance of the High School. Waiting at the completion of the course was "Cap" Paine, Woodbury's track and field coach. Cap was all smiles as he stood three in admiration with his stopwatch, then turning to this writer he remarked, "Say Phetty did you ever see anything like that kid?... did you see those legs... that natural stride...and what stamina.. he wasn't even breathing hard after running five miles."

"What's his name?" I asked. "That's Browning Ross, he's only a freshman," said the elated Cap. The name did not have much meaning at the time. But today Browning Ross is considered one of the top-ranking distance runners in the nation."

Browning won a number of dual meets in cross-country in the latter half of his freshman season but had his heart set on baseball instead of track. After he was cut from the team by Coach Guest, he turned his attention to track.

He soon found himself trying multiple events and scoring in the pole vault (with a real bamboo pole) long jump and discuss and all of the running events.

Ross soon realized he had foot-speed equal to any of the sprinters on the team but also great endurance from his year-round running with Babe. Track season also saw Browning come under the wing of Cap Paine. He would share a close, lifelong relationship with Paine much as he would later form with Jumbo Elliott at Villanova. He also managed to frustrate Browning while potentially saving his life.

**Browning Ross High School Yearbook Track
picture, with Coach Cap Paine on right.**

Coach Cap Paine was the Woodbury High Physical Education teacher, and also coached football, basketball, and track. Paine, an excellent motivator, had been a multi-sport star at Ursinus University. Paine later recalled how he had sent "cream puffs" to his own football team under the guise of a thoughtful gift from a rival team and coach. The ruse worked, firing up his Woodbury football team to victory a day later.

Bonnie Ross, "Cap failed dad in Phys Ed class, (although he would later call Browning probably the best athlete he had ever coached) delaying his graduation by a year, probably to keep him out of the beginning of the War." When US troops entered World War 2 in January of 1942, the war was not going well for the United States. At least 5,200 Americans perished in the Bataan Death March. The Marines suffered over 4,000 killed or wounded in Guadalcanal. There were a lot of casualties from South Jersey in the first year of fighting in World War II.

Browning traveled to Warinanco Park in Roselle, New Jersey his senior year for the New Jersey State Cross Country Championships.

The dean of New Jersey track and cross- country writers Ed Grant was present at the meet and still had vivid memories of the race almost seventy years later.

"In those years (1942) there was one race and a single Champion for the entire state. The race was held in Elizabeth, NJ and the heavy favorite was a boy named John Serrie from Bayonne. He had an outstanding track season the spring before and was dominant in cross- country races that fall. Someone pointed out a boy named Browning Ross from Woodbury to me.

He was small and had on canvas basketball shoes. No one in North Jersey gave him much of a chance. The race went off and Browning Ross kicked his ass. He won in 13.29 and he would, of course, go on to win the indoor National Mile Championship as well as the State Mile Championship the next spring. By then everyone knew his name."

Three weeks later Browning ran in the National Scholastic Cross-Country Championships featuring the top runners in the country and finished third, only ten yards behind winner Lloyd Blethen of Dover Maine and four yards behind Arthur Sullivan of Brooklyn.

In the 1940's many of the major high school track meets in New Jersey produced a high-quality hard paper program in advance of the meet listing competitors, their competition numbers, and their events. Browning exhibited a keen interest in track by filling in the event results with every place and time in the meets. He kept all of these programs.

Browning also started to enter road races his junior year. Most of the races were held in Philadelphia or South Jersey. Some dated back to the early 1900's like the YMCA Camden Street Run.

Most road races were sponsored by athletic clubs like Shanahan Catholic and Nativity Catholic Club and started and finished at the organization's clubhouse. There were frequently hundreds of spectators lining the course and the races received front page sports coverage in Philadelphia and New Jersey newspapers.

Almost all of the races were handicap races with the best runner assigned the scratch or last starting position and the other entered runners assigned time handicaps by the race directors in advance of the race. The races were of various distances, most often from four to six miles, and often featured large crowds of spectators.

Gloucester, NJ's Dave Williams, four years older than Browning, was the dominant runner in the Philadelphia, South Jersey and Delaware area winning most of the fastest time prizes of the races he entered.

In March of 1942 Browning, 17, earned front page of the Philadelphia newspapers by winning a major race, a 5-mile street run in West Philadelphia in 27:04. Browning also managed to win some time prizes and was often second to Williams in many road races. In a front-page Courier Post preview of the Camden YMCA Street Run, the paper noted it was the oldest race in South Jersey, and also stated: "Outstanding in the list of entries without a doubt is Dave Williams whose home is in Gloucester but runs under the colors of Shanahan and Georgetown University. Dave comes naturally to running as his father George competed many times in the same race years ago. At the present time, Dave is probably the outstanding runner in the East if not the country. And he has certainly made his mark in the Camden "Y" run. Last year as a scratch man starting five minutes after the first runner he managed to win the race becoming the first scratch man to ever win the "Y" race." On December 6, 1942, the Courier Post featured a full-page picture of Williams beating Ross by two yards in the Camden YMCA four-mile street run with the headline "S.J. Harriers Steal Show in Camden Y Street Run."

"Williams who represented Shanahan Catholic Club placed third in the National 10,000 meters National Championship in Newark Delaware, and also tucked away the Middle Atlantic AAU 10k on Thanksgiving. Williams has been undefeated for two years while performing for his alma mater Gloucester Catholic." (Williams, a sophomore at Georgetown, actually wore a "G" for Georgetown on his singlet in the race picture. His alma mater Gloucester Catholic did not have a track or cross-country team when he graduated in 1937). "Browning Ross, Woodbury High senior was also carrying Shanahan's colors and was second by two yards. His actual time was 23 minutes, 45 seconds. Ross is unbeaten in scholastic competition and is interscholastic and state champion"

Browning also finished second to Williams in the twenty-fifth annual six-mile Nativity Catholic street run. He was finally able to beat Williams, who was suffering from a cold, in the Shanahan Catholic five-mile race in 25:26.

Browning won a one-mile Middle Atlantic AAU indoor championship at Camden's Convention Hall in March on a small concrete track. Williams edged Browning a few days later in the Mitchell AA Camden County 4 ½ mile cross-country run with Babe finishing third.

In the beginning of April 1943, Williams edged Browning again in the Ontario (Philadelphia) four and a half-mile street run on time. "Ross, who started 30 seconds before Williams, held the lead until the last mile. Then Williams, the only scratch man in the field drew abreast. Entering the last quarter mile, Williams drew ahead and stayed there until 50 yards from home. Here Ross opened a driving finish and beat him to the line by five yards. Dave Williams and Browning Shanahan teammates were developing into fierce competitors and fast friends.

On February 27, 1943, Browning won the Indoor Interscholastic mile championship in New York in 4:37.5, making him National Indoor Mile Champion. The same day Dave Williams won the AAU 2-mile Championship for Georgetown, in high winds at the University of Pennsylvania.

In 1943 Woodbury dominated in Group III, the big school division at the time. (Today Woodbury is among the smallest schools in the small school Group I division).

In addition to Browning, Cap Paine's Woodbury track team featured some other outstanding athlete's pole-vaulter Charlie Rambo, John Residence, hurdler Jim Leslie and of course Babe Ross.

A few years before, Roscoe Lee Browne had run the 800 meters for the Thundering Herd. Browne went on to set the national record in the 1,000 yards and of course also to world renowned as an actor.

On March 26, 1943, Browning finished the indoor track season by winning the AAU mile in 4:38.9. The Meet also featured a military obstacle course race which entrants had to navigate half the 293 yards with a 20-pound sack and a women's basketball throw. Women's events were a rarity in the indoor track meets, and Marion Twining competing for the Philadelphia Moose captured first with a throw of 88 and one-half feet.

Barry Ross, "My grandpop Frank Ross worked most of his life for the railroad. He got dad a job one or two summers for the railroad at the station in Cape May. It was a bridge that had to be opened for boats outside of town, dad had to hustle back to close it if he forgot after a boat passed."

Browning was undefeated on the track his senior year for Woodbury starting with the Eastern Indoor Track Championships, considered the National Indoor Mile Championship, in Madison Square Garden. He won the mile in 4:37.5 against the best high school milers in the country.

In outdoor track, Browning usually ran the mile. He set track or stadium records in virtually every mile he ran, usually in the 4:30's. Many of the race results made mention of Browning smashing record stadium records-- a statistic that is rarely kept today. Some of the stadium records he broke dated back to the 1920's and 1930's. Browning's Gloucester County (NJ) Mile Record lasted for 21 years.

Browning displayed his versatility by also often running the 880 and mile relay and occasionally the sprints. He also frequently entered and placed high in the long jump and pole vault. Woodbury also had an outstanding pole-vaulter Charles Rambo who combined with Browning and John Residence to sweep most of the running and field events they entered as seniors.

The 1943 Woodbury Yearbook had this inscription: "The 1943 Woodbury track team gained five championships: George School Invitational, Camden Suburban League, Gloucester County, South Jersey Group III, and New Jersey State Group III.

Co-captain "Brownie" Ross was, without a doubt, the star performer. He became the National Indoor Middle Atlantic AAU Indoor Mile Champion with a time of 4:38.9, and on February 27 at Madison Square Garden, National Interscholastic Mile Champion. Then Brownie added two more titles, New Jersey State Group III Mile Champion and Penn Invitation Mile Champion."

Browning graduated Woodbury in June 1943. 46 years later he would tell the Catholic Star Herald: "When I graduated Woodbury High in 1943, I never thought I'd go to college. A week after graduation I found myself drafted into the Navy, in the middle of World War II."

(Later, in his Woodbury yearbook Track team picture, Browning penciled across each runner's chest what branch of the service his teammates entered in World War II, and which high school teammates were killed in action.)

Before Browning reported to the Navy, he was invited to a major Fourth of July meet in Philadelphia the AAU track championships at Franklin Field, home of the Penn Relays. Before Philadelphia featured concerts on Independence Day, they hosted major track meets as the centerpiece to celebrate the holiday.

The Meet also featured color guards, bands, singers and a full battalion of troops. Browning was invited to run the mile, three-mile, and 880-yard run. Residence was invited to compete in the Pole Vault along with Jim Tuppeny, who later became the head coach of the University of Penn and Villanova and a lifelong close friend of Browning.

In front of a capacity crowd of close to 80,000 spectators, Browning won the mile in 4:31 in a race also featuring Dave Williams and New Jersey fellow state New Jersey track and cross-country state champion Phil Stilwell. Browning's future Villanova teammate George Guida and future "Irish Pipeline" recruiter for Villanova won the 220-yard race.

One of the most noteworthy aspects of the Meet was the three special women's events. Women's track events were also rare in outdoor meets, and this meet contained three-- a women's 440-yard relay sponsored by the Philadelphia Loyal Order of the Moose, a 150-yard dash, and a baseball throw. Dave Williams' father George was one of the head judges of the field events including the baseball throw.

Just as Browning's running career was reaching new heights he had to put everything on hold. He was told to report to the US Naval Training Center in Bainbridge Maryland immediately after his Independence Day track triumph in Philadelphia to start his wartime service with the Navy.

Browning Ross US Navy 1943.

Browning's Letters Home

"Only that traveling is good which reveals to me the value
of home and enables me to enjoy it better. Take the shortest
way 'round and stay at home". Henry David Thoreau

WHEN BROWNING ENLISTED IN THE Navy after graduating Woodbury in
the summer of 1943, World War II was in full swing on two fronts. General
Patton was leading the Allied advance against German and Italian troops in
Tunis, and the Australian mainland was under attack by the Japanese Airforce.
Almost everyone from the Woodbury class of 1943 joined some branch of the
service, enrolling in the recruitment offices in downtown Woodbury.

The enlistee's parents all put service flags in the window with a blue star designating their family members' active service. The Ross family would add a second star to their flag when Babe Ross joined the Army.

Browning enlisted in the Navy and spent the next three years away from home, stationed in naval bases at Bainbridge Maryland, Samson New York, Boston, and Norfolk, Virginia. He then left the United States aboard an LST (Landing Ship Tank) bound for the Mediterranean and North Africa. LST's were naval vessels created to support amphibious operations by carrying significant quantities of vehicles, cargo, and American landing troops directly onto foreign shores by sea during World War II.

During his three years in the Navy, Browning wrote and sent home close to 200 letters and postcards. He also kept a diary which functions both as a record of his time in the Navy and a reflection of the hopes, wishes, and frustrations of a 19-year-old South Jersey boy far from home and family, and distant from his favorite sport of distance running during those three years.

In his letters and diary entries during the war, Browning exhibits his irrepressible sense of humor, his love for his hometown of Woodbury, NJ and his family and friends at home. His writings also give testament to two of his major lifetime loves-- running and writing. In his letters, Browning wistfully misses the routine rhythm of events at home— especially the races that he loved to run that still go on without him. Years later Browning didn't have much interest in re-reading his letters. "I can't believe how obsessed I was with food in so many of those letters," he said. He did remember one postcard he sent home with particular amusement. "I really struggled in French Class for some reason and I was relieved to pass. My teacher Miss Baker told me "I passed you in French because I am secure in the knowledge that you will never use or mangle that fine language again." "As soon as I got to France during the war I sent her a postcard from where I was stationed in France to Woodbury High."

Browning, like most World War II Vets who served, rarely talked about his time in the War. He would deflect questions with "So you want to hear about the Big One, WW2 huh?" He would then usually change the subject to lighter matters. Browning's letters and postcards serve as a fascinating historical snapshot of World War II by an eyewitness as events are unfolding. Browning writes about momentous events occurring that affect him or his brother Babe in his letters; as well as the dull routine of trying to survive the monotony and drudgery of day to day war time life without a hope of coming home before the war is over.

In one of his first letters home in July of 1943, from the United States Naval Training Center in Bainbridge Maryland, Browning wrote:

"Dear Mother, Pop, Babe, and Gyp,

We passed the big inspection you get every Saturday with flying colors. So we got off. Boy, we had things shining in our barracks. Our pants, faces, and hats all had to be cleaned, shoes polished etc. If you have a *speck* of dirt on you, you're done for... ...I ran around the gym plenty today. I'll be in good shape with regular meals and hours. Madison Square Garden could fit into the gym here 2 or 3 times. It is about 4 times as long as Convention Hall in Camden, NJ. A lap and a half around it is ¼ of a mile. Send me about 3 wooden pencils Mother. We get five dollars next Tuesday. They call it the "flying five" because it goes so fast. We have to buy a book, Navy Manual, mattress and pillow covers, haircuts and shaving cream with it right away, you have $1.35 left from your pay.

In almost every letter home Browning talks about running and his attempt to get a workout in somehow-- the Navy often had other plans.

"I was talking to a Physical Instructor. He doesn't know if there is a Navy track team-- if there isn't one they can start one I guess. He thinks I can get into PI (Physical Instructor) school after boot training. He said most PI's are 20 years old (Browning was 19) and are pro athletes or college stars. I'll workout with the cross-country team (at Woodbury) when I come home in September."

Among the many inconveniences Browning mentions being away from home during wartime: "You can only make one phone call home and then you have to go to the back of a long line before making a second call or everyone will start to holler."

Browning mentions a bright spot in the tedium away from home in every letter-- movies almost every night. "We can see them even before they come to Woodbury. Last night was "Appointment in Berlin" and tonight is "What's Buzzin Cousin" which I am going to miss."

Browning would see much of Europe and Africa during his time overseas and would also watch according to his estimate close to a thousand movies, including "Buzzin Cousin" multiple times in wartime duty stations in the US and overseas. His location in his letters home was often censored by the War Department, but locations are spelled out in his personal diary which the expert speller perhaps intentionally playfully misspells as "My Dairy".

Here are some highlights of Browning's letters home in 1943, first from Bainbridge Maryland his first duty station.

July 23- "We have to learn 18 knots next week. Send me 3 wooden pencils, I still have the pen but I'm too lazy to fill it tonight. Saw "Presenting Lilly Mars" last night with Judy Garland and Tommy Dorsey. It will be in Woodbury soon, it was pretty good. I got your letter this morning, that makes me feel better. On back of his envelope: Sailors Mail, Rush Like Hell!

July 27- "Boy what a morning, we had to march when we could just about stand up. Some of the older ones had to drop out. We don't get much running except in formation in step but the rest of me is in shape. I'll read the Amateur Athlete magazine in the morning and send it back, put it with the rest in my bottom drawer. You can only make 1 call and then you have to go to the back of the line or everyone starts hollering. We saw the movie "Appointment in Berlin".

July 29- "Didn't get an interview for PI school; I'll try to go to the hospital school. Boy, I'm disgusted; wish I had gone in the Army now. You have to be 20 for PI Instructor, so that left me out. Then I argued a while, but it's no good-- at least I don't have to go to sea. Boy, this is a sick looking outfit. Now I'll just learn all I can in boot training and school and hope the war's over soon so I can get out of here to go to college so I can take up Phys Ed. Make Babe finish school and get drafted, he should never enlist."

July 30- "We got another shot this afternoon; it hurts and is a little fever-ish in my left arm. We'll get 3 more shots in a week. I think we ate goat meat today, ugh! I bought you compact-- leather with the Navy insignia. They inspect for dirty clothes in our locker."

August 3- (Bainbridge Maryland) "I got drafted for work detail today. We had to out and pour gravel into ditches, have to go back from 1 to 4. Have to make sure I'm not around when they hand that out again. They say we need "volunteers" and they point to you, you, you, you, etc. PS we got another haircut this week on the sides, here is my self-portrait."

August 4- "Boy was I mad last night. I was all signed up to go see Jimmy Durante on the stage here. And some guy got sick and I had to take his guard duty from 6:30 to 9:45 pm. I went to sick bay and go the treat-ment for athlete's foot and pills for a cold, it's almost gone but you might as well get all the medicine you can, it's all free. I hope the track meet re-sults are in your letter. I wonder if I could get some apples, plums or some fruit; somehow they go fast here. Is Babe running? He should, that would be good to run in the evening. I passed the swimming test last night 2 lap breaststroke, 2 side stroke, and 1 backstroke, tread water for 10 minutes and jump off a 10-foot tower."

August 5- SWAK (Sealed with a Kiss) and "Bad news!" written on the outside of the envelope. "Well, mother, you can't come down at all now. Some louse poured ink all over the work detail leaders' clothes. So, we have now we have two watches, 8 hours of watch a day, from 4 am to 8 am and 4 pm to 8 pm, and no canteen. Guys who smoke can't smoke anymore and we can't run the radio on. If one person does anything look what happens. All visitors have been canceled, the NJ guys were having people come to visit, and boy are they burned up! We have to get up at 5 am instead of 5:30. I guess I can't call anymore now, shucks. Send a bar of soap so I can wash my clothes."

(Another letter later sent that same day) "9 days of leave might be canceled until they find out who did it. The chief said he's waiting for someone to speak up. They found ink on our clerk Martins clothes. He might have done it to cover up what was done to our Master of Arms. It couldn't have been a boy ik because we were all out drilling. Martin, St. Mary and a few on special cleanup detail are all that's here besides the 4 guards. Martin handles the ink so that's against him; he could have done it easy. I'll let you know as soon as something happens."

August 6- "Well, we haven't found the guy who put ink on the clothes so no visitors. I feel weak from the shot yesterday. We drilled with wooden guns and marched and had a class on row boats. Send me some eats if you can."

August 7- "Can't go to the Canteen, at least we can write. Boy, guys around here are mad. We can wash and eat at least. Boy oh boy what luck. 5 more weeks and Boots will be over so I'll just have to go along until then. I'll be glad when boots are over. 3rd Regiment is having a track meet. I'll go to the gym tomorrow and run around and see if the 4th can have one. I'll show you how I handle the rifle with a baseball bat when I come home. They still haven't found the "ink man" yet. If only we could find the guys who put the ink on those two fellows' clothes, we would have it easy. This Chief believes if one sinks we all sink, I don't agree with him though. We have to scrub the movie floors after the movies. The Woodbury guys are all expert goldbrickers, all 12 of us."

September 23- "We saw Benny Goodman last night. They fit all they could over 15,000 Naval personnel in the concert hall. (Bainbridge VA). Gene Krupa played drums for him, they played everything."

A few days later Browning wrote. "I got a visit from Bill Brown and Green from Pitman in the barracks. They said," what's your fastest mile time? We have a bet on it." I said 4:31.

Green said it was 4:32 and Brown had said lower. They bet $1.50 on it. So, Brown then threw me a dollar and they left. Not bad! That's the fastest buck I've ever made. See running has already paid me dividends!"

Browning was soon transferred to Sampson New York by train. The train fitfully passed close to Woodbury, past South Jersey and Philadelphia so slow that Browning wrote he could "walk faster that the train was moving, or could run home to Woodbury and back and still catch the train". The only bright spot-- "Every few miles the Red Cross nurses boarded the train to take letters to mail and to bring cokes and snacks onto the train."

Browning took advantage of the trains' slowness to write and hand off half a dozen letters and postcards to the Red Cross. The reason for the slow movement of the train-- there had been a deadly accident Labor Day weekend, only a month before that had killed 79 people and injured 117.

Browning and his fellow midshipman often had to queue up and wait in line, sometimes in the rain, often for up to an hour for each meal. They found themselves often coming down with colds and worse. Browning kept track of the results from every race he was missing at home.

November 3- "Joe said Babe, Crane, Dave Williams and then Stillwell finished in the first four places in the race; and Babe got a gold medal yesterday. They are good medals. I'll practice and run in the Shanahan 5 Mile on the 19th. Dave will win plenty once he gets over his illness. Maise has Scarlet Fever in Bainbridge."

November 12- "Gulp of some medicine for my cough. I have 3 entry blanks for the Camden Y Run, and the Junior and Senior Mid-Atlantic AAU's- I should win that one. Tell Babe to get in shape to beat Stillwell and get in first 3 in Mid AAU Junior's Tell Babe to ask Cap to run him and Leslie in Nationals at Seton Hall. "

Jock Semple joined the Navy after Pearl Harbor at 39 years old and served as a PT Instructor. He was assigned to the Sampson Naval Training School where he was put in charge of all athletics activities, and as coach of the Sampson track team. He knew everyone who entered Sampson with a distinguished running background and quickly recruited Browning after he arrived. Browning and Jock became friends, but Browning and the other Sampson runners chafed at what they saw as Semple's preferential treatment in attending races.

November 15- "The Chief said there was a 2 ½- mile race today in Van Cortland Park and the AAU asked for a team from here to represent the Third Naval District. We could have run and gone home Sunday but they couldn't get the other three of the team to go. Two were in boot camp and couldn't leave and the other was Semple, a long-distance runner who didn't want to go because he ran 26 miles last Sunday. We could have had all expenses paid and I would have been home Saturday night. Boy, were we disappointed. Joe said Semple has been getting off every weekend to run and didn't like the idea of 2 1/2 miles because he would do lousy and might not get off as much. Semple only came in 8th in the 26-mile run and Joe said I could give him 2 minutes and beat him in 3 miles. He gets all his expenses and everything paid to run for the base and we can't. He's a Chief Petty Officer I guess that helps. Well anyway, they (the Navy) know we are here now."

November 25- "We tried to get to the Berwick Marathon (a 9-mile race in Pennsylvania that Browning would later dominate) 125 miles from here. Semple went yesterday to run for Sampson on all expenses paid. What a life he has-- he gets off every week because he's got a rating. We had school all day, a big turkey dinner and then church services and guard duty all night. It's his last year. We were stuck here taking written, semaphore and blinker tests."

November 29- (On Postcard) "I've got a cold today, nothing to do but sleep and read. We read everything we can. Semple got 11th in the Berwick Run. Philadelphia runners all beat him. I guess we're just unlucky never getting out to run ever. 26 cents to clean my blankets, I'll send one at a time so I won't freeze. Told Kelly Woodbury won and he nearly fell over. Snowing hard here."

December 2- (From Samson, NY) "Saw George Guida tonight he got in PI school. He had all the qualifications. He went to Villanova College. I read it was a good race Sunday- Joe, Babe, Dave Strickland bunched for 4 miles or so. I wish I could run in the Camden Y run this year. That's my favorite run. I'm running some every day, that and the physical hardening will keep me in shape for Shanahan Run. Maybe the war with Germany will be over in a few months. PS I've just been designated to help sweep out the barracks. Before lights go out, oh me!"

December 16- "I'm in sickbay. The kid who sleeps next to me was taken out on a stretcher all pains and stiffened up. The kid on the other side was taken out with Scarlet Fever. I sure have a good bunk! I have 102 degree fever, after being 100 yesterday I can't eat and couldn't sleep with a sore throat and sweating."

December 17- "My temperature is down to 101, still in bed in sick bay with cat fever or the flu, have to take a white capsule 3 times a day. I'm smothering in here it's so hot but it's good for you I guess, they want you to sweat... It would happen the week I'm supposed to come home. I really have the luck. I missed a week of school-- my book and clothes are back in the locker. I'm reading g old Readers Digests. The troop train will meet me to get some Christmas presents. Don't know what to get Babe for Christmas. It will be a week earlier for me. I listened to Fibber McGee and Molly and Burnes and Allen last night but now there's no radio, everyone's gone. It will be hard to sleep in my bunk after having this nice mattress. Maybe my luck will change once I feel better. There are good prizes in the Shanahan Run, 25 prizes, two-time prizes and 10 medals."

December 18- "Well I won't be home for another month. The Dr. examined me and said keep applying the same medicine, (2 pills) can't figure out why I can't get up. Temperature is normal. Dr. opened the window and turned off the heat. He wants it cold for those with temperatures. I have to stay here now I will get cold. The guy next to me coughed terrible, so I didn't get any sleep all night. There's two pretty good doctors here and this lousy one who keeps me here for nothing. You get a weekend off every so often and they take it from you, it burns me up. They moved the age of PI up to 21 years old now. I sure have got the worse luck in the world. I feel disgusted with everything. I was so mad I didn't know what do when I lost this weekend. I wouldn't come over here (sick bay) again if I'm dying, they don't cure you any better than sleeping in the barracks taking the pills during school where it's warm during the day. Don't let Babe join this outfit if you don't have a rating your nothing at all. I've lost a week already."

December 20- "Out of bed, feel woozy, I sent 16 Christmas cards out. When I get back I'll have my tonsils out some day at Underwood. Christmas is a holiday here. I'll go to church and call you if I don't get home. I should have gotten medical Corpsmen; it's a pretty good job."

(Another letter sent later that night)- "Dear Mother, Pop, Babe, and Gyp, Well I should be home tonight and here I sit 3 of us just finished washing dishes all day for 20 patients and 20 corpsmen and Wave nurses. What a job.

They make you laugh in here. They say let's go make our reservations with the undertaker now. Some are pretty sick when they come in. they think this doctor is a horse doctor, he's strict and nobody likes him because of that. I sent out 32 Christmas cards. Kinney got some for me tonight; we can't get out the door until we're discharged. Some cards to Mrs. Price at school, Dave Williams, and the Williams family in Gloucester. Our barracks got haircuts today, I missed that at least."

December 21- "Doctor made me stay home another day said I didn't look so well, Holy Mackerel! What do I have to do to get out of here? I'm missing a lot of school, this is lousy just sitting here waiting for work. Stillwell won 1st place time prize and 1st Shanahan prizes, whew! He beat Morgan. He said Dave went in the Army and left already. I should hear from him. Boy, it will nice if I get next week off, I think I should but does the Navy? What an outfit. Tell Babe to go in the Merchant Marines or the Army!!"

December 22- "Got out this morning and went back in school for 3rd period. I found Sunday's Inquirer Shanahan pre-race write up. It said I'd be there but didn't have much time to train. 2 months wait for a 48-hour liberty, what a place. I'll probably break a leg before I get home next time. All the officers and Ships CCO here get 7 days starting tomorrow. I don't think that's right, do you? I'll bet the line for the telephone will be a mile long but I'll wait. The movie tonight was Alaska Highway with Popeye and a news reel. I have guard 12 to 4 am, that's the worst guard. I can chase the mice around with a broom to stay awake."

December 23- "3 of us set up a Christmas tree in CPO recreation room. Is Dave in the Army? Make sure Babe runs in the high school meet. There are 3 prizes, why didn't they have that last year? We're off Friday afternoon until Monday. I don't see why we can't go home but that's the Navy!"

December 24- "Boy, what a Christmas present! I got 90 in Blinker and a 100 in Semaphore this morning I think I passed written and I was only in school 2 days this week. Lt. Beck wished us a Merry Christmas and Happy New Year and explained why we couldn't go home. It seems there is a war on and only 10% of us are allowed off base at a time for a protective measure. Going to movies to see "What's Buzzin' Cousin," the same old movie I saw last summer. Boy, how I would like to be home now but I'm better off than a lot now I guess. I have a lot of magazines and papers to read this afternoon. I'll lie in my bunk and take it easy no 5:15 wakeup. Ask Mr. Williams if there is a race January the 16th. I'll try to get in shape indoors after New Years. No school until Monday, hot dogs!"

December 25- "I tried to call you Mother from 2 to 6:30 couldn't get through all lines jammed up. Listened to President Roosevelt while I was waiting. Some guy got a fancy pair of pajamas and got a lot of raspberries. Listening to a touring ships orchestra playing fast swing, with piano player Johnny Noble and drummer Johnny Long. They said they'd give anyone who would sing along a *case of cigarettes*. They also had baskets of nuts and apples."

December 26- "Got up at 10 am again 2 days in a row, a record! Watchlist went up I'm on 12 to 4 am watch—- the "dog watch". I'm the downstairs watch and Ewald's upstairs so we can take turns sleeping on the steps, tricky! I just got a Life magazine so I'll lie on my bunk and read it."

Bonnie Ross: "Dad mentioned how hard it was to train on board ship when they were out to seas. He accidentally discovered a way to train. If you got a mild reprimand they would make you run on the ship carrying two full buckets of water. If you wanted to run, you couldn't but if you were being punished for a minor infraction you could run. So, dad would do something minor, just enough to get the forced running with buckets punishment to get a workout in."

In 1944 Browning decided to start a diary on Jan 1st and the following are his diary entries. He would resume writing letters home in April.

Jan 1- "I reported to the Naval Training Station in Samson NY."

Jan 4- "I was late for school and may lose my liberty for the weekend."

Jan 22- "Jock Semple came over to visit and made sure we are granted permission to run the race at Leghorn Bay."

Jan 23- "I got measured for a track suit to run some races for the Navy."

Feb 3- "I got first place in the Time Trials in Madison Square Garden in New York City. We (Navy) finished third in the mile relay to the Columbia Midshipmen and the Coast Guard. I stayed in a room in the Hotel Paramount." (Ironically, the Paramount is the hotel where Browning would found the Road Runners Club of America 14 years later.)

Feb 14- "Reported to Base Solomon in Md. My first duty was loading spuds on a truck all day. Babe got the second-place time in the rescheduled Mitchell AA run."

March 2- "I reported to Boston for duty. Watched the Sherlock Holmes movie "Pearl of Death" with Basil Rathbone on base."

March 8- "Went home on leave, ran the Woodbury cross country course."

March 10- "Went to a dance at Gloucester High."

March 20- "Got a letter from John "Jock "Semple about running on the Navy team for the Boston Marathon."

March 26- "Went to another dance at Gloucester High then back to the base where someone stole my dress jumper out of the dryer room, so I bought another one. Ran four miles and got permission to run in a 10-mile race in Boston."

April 1- "Finished second in the ten-mile run in Jamaica Plain, it was won by Farrar of the US Coast Guard."

April 4- "I ran 4 miles in South Boston."

April 6- "Got a rub down for a bad case of shin splints got a rubdown; I got a letter from Jock Semple about running in the Boston Marathon for the Navy team."

April 13- "I stood guard duty all day. Got a letter from Cap Paine. Tomorrow on duty until 11:30am then going up to Holy Cross and see Bud and take my track suit and do a workout there. Went to National AAU Boxing Champs at Boston Garden. I had a reserved ticket for $2.20 the Athletics Chief here gave me. A cop gave me a ticket right before that and I will give it to another sailor. A Philadelphia boy got to the finals, they had 7500 people there."

April 14- (On a Postcard from Holy Cross College) "Worked out with the Holy Cross track team, near froze. It's up on a hill, cold, windy but what a place. It's really nice. I ate in the school mess."

April 15- "Mother here's $5 to save, I won't need it. I nearly froze yesterday guarding the prisoners. I ran on the Holy Cross outdoor board track and lapped the Holy Cross Milers on 12 laps on the boards. Chief will call the BAA to enter me in the marathon. There are 55 entries in the Boston Marathon now, pretty good! A couple of them are from Mitchell AAU in Philadelphia. I found my scissors in the mattress cover; I'll get a haircut before the marathon."

April 16- "The Chief phoned in a Boston marathon entry for me and I filled out a liberty chit for the marathon."

April 17- "We took the German prisoners to church services-- Catholic, and Protestants. I wrote to Johnny Semple and asked for a pair of road shoes for Boston. If not I'll wear the ones I have—they'll be ok. I filled out a liberty chit for the Boston Marathon. If it is signed I hope the Chief will take us up to Hopkinton, I'll be here until after the marathon. I'll go see the Roller Skating Varieties at the Boston Garden if I can walk after the race. I'll see how I feel after 10 miles, if I feel good I'll go out to try and win if not just try to finish and place. I'll take a workout tonight in the gym."

April 18- (Boston) "My entry is in for tomorrow (Boston Marathon), and I have a special liberty from 7 am tomorrow to 8 am Thursday. Most of the runners are getting a train out to where the race begins at 8 am tomorrow. So they had the interclass track meet yesterday, or did it rain? That's all if I win tomorrow...?"

**The 906, Browning's LST that was decommissioned
due to damage during World War II.**

April 19- "I ran in the Boston Marathon, finished 22nd in the race. Saw Jock Semple and Ted Vogel at the race. Went to sick bay for treatment for a bad case of blisters, sore legs and a cold."

(Note: The BAA's official records and most subsequent books on the history of the Boston Marathon missed Browning's finish. His Chief had entered him as Harrison (his real first name) Ross of Boston, MA (his duty station) and not Browning Ross of Woodbury, NJ.)

May 9- "I returned home on leave. I practiced Pole Vault at Woodbury's track with Babe."

June 3- "Underway, destination North Africa. Censors restrict me telling you exactly where. Off the coast of Tunisia, our LST had a collision with the US Liberty's bow guns in the fog." (This is one of two collisions Browning's LST's would be involved in during the war; luckily, he was unharmed in both.)

June 19- "Took a track workout every night in Palermo getting ready for the Naples meet. We are getting ready to go to Oran Algeria."

July 3- "I bought a ring for 15 cents. You see a lot of beggars and bombed out areas in Italy."

July 9- "I'm entered in the Allied track championships in Mussolini Stadium in Padua Italy."

July 14- " I finished 8th in the 5000. I ran lousy. A 41-year-old Arab from France won the race in 15:45. Just read where Anderson ran a 4:01 mile and Haag a 4:02. We had Invasion practice for August and saw a huge fire in a hill in Naples. Sailed to Corsica to let off Moroccan troops and to Southern France to take on German prisoners. Avoiding German anti-aircraft guns, German ships and sea mines around Corsica. Pulled a muscle in my upper right leg sprinting on the deck."

Browning's diary resumes with news of damage to his LST a second time, this time more serious.

Oct 18- "We ran into a storm underway which pushed us into the rocks, we lost a small boat. Serious damage to the bottom of the ship, all of our clothes soaked from sea water. Twice the engine room was completely flooded. We are stranded awaiting help."

Oct 19- "Ship still aground. It's a clear day but still rough sea water coming over the port side. Half the men left the ship, fully packed via rope pulley to shore. I had to stay on board; there is no water to drink on the ship except for one canteen a day. We are low on food too.

There is a Board of Inquiry onboard ship investigating the shipwreck. We are supposed to leave for Bizerte Tunisia."

Oct 30- "Finally ready to take the ship off the rocks. All the ammo was unloaded from the ship."

Nov 5- "Tugs *finally* pulled the ship off the rocks."

Nov 8- "I read where Roosevelt is leading in 32 states. In trying to free the ship they pushed it up on the rocks more.

There are more leaks and the engine room collapsed. They got all the men off the ship—14 of us and 3 officers are watching the ship from shore."

Nov 11- "Our ship is decommissioned."

Nov 14- "I got the shot for the Black Plague and we saw the Andrews Sisters perform at the Red Cross."

1945

Browning's letters home in 1945 reflect the turbulence of world events and the necessity of the Navy to constantly move troops to a variety of countries in the Mediterranean during the final months of the war.

January 3- "They reclassified us in 4 or 5 in a group and we left with 20 minutes notice, and what a rough ride. We just arrived here in _____ (censored) an hour ago. I am a little disgusted right now about when I will get back to the states. I sent you a $50 money order and bought a new dress jumper and got back and found we had 20 minutes to pack. My clothes are still at the base. We had a dance with French Waves at the Red Cross on New Year's Eve and a movie "Dr. Kildare Goes Home." As usual, it's raining. I don't know what will become of my PI transfer request now."

January 5- "The tops of the mountains are all snow covered. I just met a fellow from Penns Grove, NJ, I don't know why we stay here in the Mediterranean, but I'm not the Admiral. It doesn't pay to make friends in this outfit; they move you around so much. Keep sending me the Sunday Sports and Inquirer editorials. 2 months of base life spoiled me. I believe I like my dry land. I'd gladly change with Babe. They gave us 20 minutes to pack and go, and 3 of the boys are still in _____ (location censored)."

January 6- "Just had my inspection in dress blues and shined shoes. The food is very good—eggs, steak, and pies. Did you get the perfumes from the souvenir shop on the base? We take exercise every morning, now I'm stiff."

January 9- "Well the Camden Y Run is over for another year. It looks like I'll *never* run in it. Stillwell must be cleaning up in the trophies and medals and time prizes this year. I hope I see some of the high school track meets this spring. I weigh 155 pounds now, pretty heavy! Haven't got a letter from Babe since he's been in Alabama, tell the old boy to get on the ball and drop me a line. Saw the movie "This is the Life" with Donald O'Connor last night along with a March of Time newsreel. Can you send me a box of those salted nuts?"

January 13- "The Pharmacist thought I had Scarlet Fever last night; there was a little rash on the side of my face near my ear. I was in sick bay by myself last night and then it cleared. Something I ate I guess. Tonight's movie is the "Battle of Russia"; I saw it 3 times already. We saw the Battle of China since the Japs invaded China last night. Still, a long way to go in the Pacific war... I'll be glad to leave Europe. I've had enough of traveling and sightseeing of this continent to last me!"

January 16- "Bought 3 Silver German Stukas toys as souvenirs."

January 19- "I got a letter from Tom Canboy from Germany, 5 of them are living in the bottom floor of a building, the top floor is missing due to the bombing, and they have rain every night. Russians are moving now, captured Warsaw, at last, 15 miles from the German border in Southern Poland."

January 20- (Easing his mother's fears about her youngest son Babe going to Germany.) "Paratroopers aren't as bad off as anti-aircraftmen and signal corps are in Germany. 10, 20 days and relieved – Babe will be ok. If I had my choice again that's what I'd get in, he will get the best training in the army and by the time he has trained the war in Germany will be too advanced for paratrooper landings behind the lines anyway. When I ran in Rome last August I lived with the 5th at the rest camp and most of them wanted to try for the paratroopers. He won't get hurt jumping; they take all precautions for safety. I'll talk him into going to Temple (University) with me after the war is over, this year. I believe now that the Russians are on the move. I read in the Stars and Stripes that Dodd's isn't going to run in the indoor season; there is a big picture of him in the sports section (Gil Dodd's was a minister who broke the indoor world mile record three times starting in 1944, lowering it to 4.05.3 in 1947). The Allies will move right into Berlin. The weather is terrible in Northern Italy and Germany now with snow, rain, and mud."

Browning received word that his beloved dog Gyp had passed away and addressed a letter home "To the Ross Family minus one..."

January 23- "Here is a snapshot of the good ol' 906th Brigade gang at our worst. For liberty, I went down in the catacombs and visited a church built in 1000 AD by William the 1st way up in the mountains. We were underway last night and it was rough—I slept about 2 hours. Now to get a good chow, the last 3 chows lasted in me about 5 minutes and then the fish ate it (seasick). I guess I take after my mom on the stomach end."

January 26- Browning sent home a postcard of drawing of a sailor with an enormous butt sitting on a pier smoking a cigarette. Two puppies are in the foreground saying "Well the Navy certainly is in good shape!" Browning wrote on the back of the card, "That's not me!!"

January 27- "We Sailed to Palermo Italy." (Diary entry.)

January 28- "Somewhere in the Mediterranean... Tonight is the Inquirer Meet I guess Haag didn't make it. The Russians are going strong now, huh. Hope they don't have to slow down for supplies and heavy armor to move up. If spring ever gets here everybody will break through, I believe the Germans are reeling now. Can't think of anything else to write that the good old censorship regulations will ok-- will get some postcards of this city for my collection. Watched "Guadalcanal Diary" on the ship."

January 30- "Palermo Sicily again training with LST's (Landing Ship Tanks). Boy I hope I leave soon, we are doing exactly nothing over here except maneuvers, signal drills, practicing small boat lowering, and towing ships out in Palermo Bay, we are safe and well here, better than the Pacific. I'll go to the Pacific after a 30-day leave."

January 31- "We saw a good movie "Hollywood Canteen" and the machine didn't break down every 2 minutes like it did during Guadalcanal Diary. I've seen more movies in the service than I saw in my 19 years before. Good radio shows the last few days Bob Hope and Fred Waring, service bands long hair and jive! Remember back in the days when gasoline, tires, and bananas existed. Is Babe still going to the paratroopers? Don't worry he will probably change his mind. I guess he's with heavy weapons, that's a good division and probably not too dangerous. I learned how to determine sunrise and sunset times (by another method than looking in the papers!) I hope to spend my birthday and home and home the sea is calmer on the way home."

February 2- "It certainly is hard to write letters with this censorship business. Maybe I'll get home in spring and see a few track meets. It'll take me a year to get into running shape. I'll take Jip out for a few runs on the golf course in the mornings. I'm still reading the Woodbury Times. Boston was a good station."

February 3- "The Russians are 68 miles from Berlin. I have the 1600 to 2000 watch tonight, that's the best one. We have plenty of bakers here and get plenty of pies and cakes each day. I met Bill Bonthron today. Bonthron was the best miler around in 1936, He was one of the top milers in the 30's and beat Glenn Cunningham (in 1934) right after he set the world record in the mile (4.06.8) He's a supply officer on a base in North Africa. (A decade earlier Bonthron was the world record holder in the 1500 meters and a household name in America. (In April 2013, Roger Robinson wrote about Bill Bonthron for Running Times Magazine:

"Bill Bonthron was so beloved for lifting American spirits in the 1930s Great Depression (for his running exploits) that one popular version of Cole Porter's song "You're the Top" had the lines, "You're the top! You're a Roosevelt smile. You're the top! You're a Bonthron mile." Bonthron first topped Ironman Glenn Cunningham, Gene Venzke and the rest of that vintage era of the American mile with a world record 1500m, 3:48.8, in 1934.

Bonthron had also bettered the world mile record, with 4:08.7 in 1933, but that day he was well behind the light-footed Jack Lovelock (4:07.6), another New Zealander who impinges on this American story. Talking about the big Princeton man to the New York Times, Lovelock said, "Of all the milers I ever faced, Bonthron was the best. And also, the most unreliable. . . He was very dangerous at all times.")

Bonthron, of course, was just another American supply officer doing his duty far away during the war.

February 6- "A list is up of how much we received in 1944 $884.96. I guess I'll have $1215 saved now—I'll make sure of going to school whether I get a scholarship offer or not, and the GI Bill will set me up too. Well, the Americans have Manila now. The Germans are going to be harder to beat than Japan. They are plenty smart and have plenty of divisions to defend their fortresses. I read they are going to build a new West End school on Green Street in Woodbury, that's a swell place for a school."

February 8- "I just received a package with dungarees and 6 pairs of sweat socks and Woodbury Times with coverage of football from Cap Paine. This is the first winter I've ever seen without snow. People here are bad off, food is hard to get and everything is wrecked, it will take time to get their countries back on their feet. The Navy has opened public baths and a soup kitchen and they are employing some workers in ship repair. Prices are sky high; everything good is on the black market."

February 13- "I have the 12 to 4 am watch tonight. Ow! The 265th could get another star on the Russian campaign for the invasion of Elba last June; I guess we just missed that."

February 15- "Saw Scammell and the boys, Scammell said he last had a shower in November! Censorship allows us to tell where we've *been* so I'll have something to write. Best city I've seen since I've been over here by far is Rome. I've been to Marseille, Tunis, Algiers, Palermo, LaTania, Mt Vesuvius and Mt Etna the 2 largest active volcanoes, catacombs of Palermo, Corsica, Sardinia and the Rock of Gibraltar too."

February 20- "We are in the Mediterranean area. Went to the Navy boxing matches, and we saw a good movie- "To Have and Have Not." Babe should be home this month. Plenty of oranges and tangerines here, I usually get a half dozen each day and bring a basket full back for liberty. Just sent you a record I made in town. I said about 3 words and then screech! Bang! $1.25 please, finito! Bob Anthony had a big one made but I didn't think I could talk for six minutes. Personnel here live in a hotel that used to be a European resort that overlooks the sea- some place. I see where Roosevelt, Stalin, and Churchill are meeting in the Black Sea area now. I hope the war ends soon; time sure goes slowly over here anymore."

February 28- "I just finished reading the 30 letters I got last weekend. Shock, the fellow here from Penns Grove was showing me a DuPont Plant paper article about heroes, and George Benjamin's picture was on the front page-- killed in Leyte! Cap just said he received a Christmas card from him from Leyte Island."

March 1- "I got this letter from the Drake coach; their cross-country team won the National Championships this year. I don't think I'd like to go all the way out to Des Moines to go to school if I can go closer to home. Show the track letters from Drake to Cap. Track and sports, in general, are going to have some boom after the war."

March 3- "No night watch tonight so I have the pep to write a letter. Heard where they landed on Iwo Jima and Corregidor. I'll bet Harold is in Manila Bay now. The radio said PI boats were in the harbor. Can you write to Scammell's mom and tell her that her other son is safe. He joined the Navy when Babe was drafted. I put in for a transfer to PI not interested in Signalman rate stuff! If I could get PI, I'd get back in condition in no time.

I'd like to see Scotland, England, and Ireland. Gunter Haag ran last in IC4A in 4:31. I bet I could have run around 4:20 or 4:16 this year indoors. Still, listen to the war news every hour. This spring Germany will really be hit hard. Did Phil Stilwell join the Army? He's doing some great running. I'll write Dave Williams as soon as I have time. Ski troopers will keep him in good condition. I have $50 to send you as soon as I get to a fleet hospital."

March 6- I received another letter from the Drake Coach; he has a lot of prospects. I've stood a lot of watches and could use some sleep!

March 9- I haven't had time to write, we have been plenty busy the last few weeks. I got 17 letters and your card with Dentine gum, 2 letters from the Drake track coach and 2 Vmails from Cap. Cap got a card from George Benjamin. Saw "Human Comedy" with Mickey Rooney."

March 13- "Only 4-5 hours a sleep at night really wears you down. They crossed the Rhine yesterday, wait until the big push starts this spring than the Germans will wish they never started a war. I'm willing to bet that Russia will fight against Japan after Germany is beaten. Babe will probably come to this theater instead of the Pacific. Brazilian troops come over for replacements for the 8th Army in Italy. What a front that is, nearly every nationality possible. Italian troops on our side there and Italian troops against us in Northern Italy. It's beginning to look like I will be over here for the duration anymore."

March 17- "I read Phil Stillwell ran very good in getting second in the 3 mile National Championships. He's much better at 2 or 3 miles than the mile. Most have been a cold winter in the states; I never saw snow here except in the mountain tops. Saw Port Ferro in Elba, Italy where Napoleon was imprisoned. He is still quite a legend on the island as they sell copper statuettes of Napoleon. Food is hard to get on the island, only so many grams of flour for bread and what they get from fishing. Saw good pictures of finishes of the Millrose Games in Yank magazine."

March 23- "Your packages of nuts came fast! Florence is a beautiful city; the Arno River is like Rome on the Tiber. Got a letter from Tom Canboy in Germany, he said Dave Williams is in Italy. He met Dave's brother Nick in Germany. I'll write Dave a letter, now I may get to see him. I'll save my money for school and clothes after the war."

March 29- "First thing I will do when I hit the states is buy a quart of milk!! If I remember what it looks like. Army track meet here in April, I signed up for the 880 and pole vault. 20 to 1 that we won't be in that city on April 7. Just read in the Woodbury Times that Bill Beck was killed in action. He ran the hurdles when Walt Chew was captain. Ha, Babe had a rough trip across to England, France, and Italy—in Feb and March the ocean wouldn't be any too calm. The allies are crossing the Rhine. The army is holding a sports school in Rome for officers and enlisted men to serve as coaches and instructors in a post-war sports program after the war in Europe. Glenn Cunningham's track coach at the University of Kansas is an instructor. I'd join if I was in the army."

April 4- "Yanks only 150 miles from Berlin now. I got 2 $100 money orders and now I'm busted until payday. We went to the British Athletic Stadium and took a workout. I ran a half in 2:25, did exercises, sprints and jogged a mile in 6:05! Not bad after the long layoff I had. Going to work out from now on as often as I can and take exercises even underway when it's calm. Hoping to run a track meet this Saturday, doubt I'll be there though. Saw "Objective

Burma" with Errol Flynn, Babes in Burma. Cap said Leslie gave him $25 for a perpetual George Benjamin Memorial trophy for the weight men. Can you send me the sports section for the Camden Meet?"

April 6- "Last Easter I was home and now I'm underway in the Mediterranean Sea some place. Save clipping for my book about Alexander. Ask Mr. Williams if he saw this clipping about Dave, he had a big write up in the Stars and Stripes for finishing 3rd in a 5-mile run and being congratulated by General Truscott the 5th Army General. The 10th Mountain Division is a busy outfit. Every time you read about the war in Italy it mentions the 10th Mountain Division up in the mountains. I just heard on the radio that the Allies landed about 350 miles from Japan; I guess the Germans will put up one more stand and then they are through- I hope. Hard to write a long letter with these censors. Saw the movies National Velvet and Dark Waters. I saw Paul Isenberg the Moorestown Track Coach at the Red Cross. They went into his office and told him I was from Woodbury, he's a good friend of Cap. When I told him my name he asked me if I was the miler. He was the coach when we ran at Moorestown Junior year. He asked where my brother was now. I also saw Frank Gattuso who I wrestled against from Paulsboro. He won the state 128 lb. wrestling title. I wrote to Dave Williams a few days ago maybe I can get in touch with him later on. Allies are across the Rhine mopping up—this spring the Germans are disorganized."

April 10- "So Babe's in Northern France and Belgium. I'm studying the 1st Armies every move now that Babe's in on a gigantic map they have here. It shows the progress of each Army and the Russians in Germany. Today's map had "Vienna occupied" written on it. The sidewalk is crowded with people studying the map. It will be a great day in Europe when Germany is defeated. Get Gip in condition to run around the golf course with me in a few months. I'm still hoping to be home by the end of track season. I hoped to see the Penn Relays but have to stand watch. Just saw the movie "Lassie Come Home"-- it sure was good."

April 14- "I got birthday cards and a letter and results from the Drake Track Coach and a letter from Dave Williams. Dave met Evans who an 880 from Woodbury when he ran in Florence. There is a track meet in late April or May; Dave's going to let me know about it. He's been up on the front for a couple of months now. Kirby leads a dangerous life, there was a write up about the 906th (involved in the battle for Peleliu) I'll have to bring home because of censorship. Heard the news about Roosevelt (passing away) when I woke up yesterday, all the flags are at half mass. Well, it's time to eat breakfast."

April 17- (Mediterranean Area) " I got a letter from Iwo Jima; John Residence's luck was with him in battle. His fondest desires are a pint of milk from Grossman's and a quart of Tomkins Ice Cream. They had memorial services for President Roosevelt yesterday. The whole issue of the Stars and Stripes was devoted to him. It seems funny to say "President Truman". About all I remember of Presidents is Roosevelt. We had calisthenics at 6:15 am, my aching back! Heard the Americans are only 35 miles from the outskirts of Berlin, expect Babes within 100 miles. Had another letter from the Drake Coach with results of their indoor meets, they were undefeated."

April 22- "Won't be long now and I'll be of voting age. I got the Inquirer sports section with coverage of the Camden Indoor meet from Cap and I'll send it to Dave Williams or Babe. With the Arabs, French and Italians here, I can speak a little of nearly every language in the book now with a little arm waving and sign language mixed in."

April 24- Postcard from the Red Cross in France, "Bless you mom a prayer from my pen always for your welfare," loving you-- Brownie." "Well, Russians are fighting in Berlin now at last. I'll be glad when Americans are linked up with them. I guess Dave is above Bologna now. I thought they would never take Bologna. Babe will be getting to see some of the big German cities and Berlin soon, maybe he already has seen Leipzig and maybe Berlin will fall on my birthday Thursday. I guess track season is well underway again. Woe is me; this is my favorite month of the year with the Penn Relays and all. Here I sit 4000 miles from home. One day the rumors are thick about seeing the USA this spring and the next not so good. I eat a half dozen blood oranges a day. Nuts, grapes, lemons, and tangerines seem to be in season all year long."

April 26- "Well here it is my birthday. What a place to spend it on and LST in the Mediterranean with no liberty today even. If this war ever finishes I'll go to school at Temple or a school around home. I've had enough traveling to last me a while. The only thing that will bring me back to Europe is an Olympics which I hope to see whenever they hold it. Read in the Stars and Stripes that Johnny Kelley won the Boston Marathon. I wonder if Semple took up a team from Sampson this year. The Woodbury track team looks pretty good. Boy, I hope they keep it up and go undefeated this year."

April 27- Happy Mother's Day Card sent from Italy.

April 28- "I got to vote yesterday, right on my birthday—the primary election ballot for Woodbury. It sure did reach me at the right time. Today and tomorrow are the Penn Relays; I wish I could see it. That's the best track carnival in the USA. I like to see the relay races more than the individual races except for the milers. I read Haag is going to run in the Relays in a special mile run. Could you send over a pair of running shoes or low sneakers if there are any around and running shorts? When I get a chance to take a workout, which is very seldom now, I have to wear dungarees and the high army shoes that I wear every day when I run. I guess I'll be over here this spring. I thought I'd be home last Christmas but I'm still here. If I'm here this summer I can run in the track trials. I'll have a month or so of practice and maybe can do a little better than last year when I only had a week of practice.

I saw a good pair of brown track shoes in a sporting goods store in _____ (city and country censored) a while back—no ration ticket, everything in stores here seems to be rationed."

May 2- "I made a rating, took a final test of 80 questions. Relief not to be an S6 anymore. I'll be making $96 dollars every month overseas base pay. We'll they got old Benito Mussolini at last and civilians seem plenty glad of it. That drive in Italy was a surprise, there went through Po Valley like wild-fire. Read Phil Stillwell ran 2nd in the mile at Penn and Haag ran 4th but his time was good. Must have been poor handicapping to run 4:12 and finish 4th! Joe Sullivan's pet argument is about McGinley's (poor) handicapping. Maybe Babe's learning Russian now."

May 4- "Babe said he is still fighting against the German troops. Things have happened so fast in the war up here. Latest we heard Hitler and Goebbels committed suicide and Berlin fell in a weeks' time—that's fast! Berlin is bigger than NYC. Biggest excitement is the Germans surrendering in Northern

Italy after the stalemate in fighting so long (2 years) below Bologna. Don't send my track shoes over. I'll be home soon before school starts again."

May 5- "Saw the USO play "Ten Little Indians" sure was good. It's the first stage play I've seen besides high school plays. Germans surrendered in Northern Germany, Netherlands and Denmark this morning. The news looks great, huh? Navy personnel are now living in a 100-room Hotel Villa overlooking the Mediterranean up on a hill. It used to be a resort for Europe's kings and queens. Liberty announced- hot dogs! I'll call you; food is good, steak for lunch. I can see people on the beach with the long glass. Dear Mother, Love and kisses Brownie."

May 15- "Went swimming in the Adriatic. I went surfboarding on the back of a small boat, and I being a veteran surfboarder took a fast turn on the board and I went up and down and I came out with a cut on my right leg and shin bone and bruised my knee. Spent the day underway listening to President Truman and Churchill and the European Allied leaders giving speeches. I went up in a B-25 that had 109 missions painted on the sides. What a relief it is to know that war is over here. These countries are really leveled off from air attacks and war. They have had <u>enough,</u> believe me. Passed a POW camp, they come in faster than they can get rid of them. Had VE Thanksgiving services this morning with Turkey, stuffing and cranberry sauce."

May 20- "First part of letter censored... Friction between Tito partisans and Allies. It sure will be good to get back to the states and see towns that aren't wrecked by bombs. Perfect weather, it never does rain here in summer."

May 29- "I went sightseeing in the hills behind Trieste Mountain up to Yugoslavia. Tito's picture is on every building and wall in the city, same as Zara. Even the Yugoslav women carry machine guns and grenades. We each picked up a German helmet in the hills as Germans left them behind as partisans moved in. We were the first Americans up there as German equipment was scattered all over the area and no American armies are in the area. The civilians all liked us when we told them we were Americans; everything was free—rides on the trains, even bags of cherries and strawberries at the markets. Yugoslav troops and Allied New Zealand and British troops all carry arms and parade around the city in formation but seem friendly."

June 1- "John Residence is in the rest camp, very lucky on the two slight wounds on his hand and his helmet dented, he was scared to death. Buzz traveled 1600 miles the last few months and met his brother in Guadalcanal. Bill Forsheim was killed in the Pacific in Iwo Jima, tough break. Marseille and Trieste the best places I've been. When I come home I'm going to work out at school in the afternoon and run on the golf course in the mornings. Our strength in the Pacific will be 7 million men, it won't take long to beat Japan, and I believe 6 or 7 months- a year at the most. I think I'll be able to enter Temple on some Physical Education studies soon easy enough without taking another year of foreign language and Algebra. I'll get $50 a month while I'm in school, that's alright. Save me a shoe stamp so I can buy a good pair of Flagg shoes when I get home."

June 9- Sicily- "Boy that letter of mine was really censored! Had a vmail from Babe in Southern Germany and it didn't even have a censor stamp, boy this censorship business! Saw the Woodbury Times with Babe's picture on the front page. Read in the Stars and Stripes where they picked up Axis Sally in Turin. She's a propagandist known to every soldier and sailor in the Med. theater. I guess we used to listen to her quite often mostly for the music. Pretty good movie last night-- Together Again. Dell sent a clipping about Woodbury and other Group III teams forming their own league called the Colonial League, it's called the Colonial because all the cities in the conference can trace their histories back to the Colonial days, making the remaining Camden Suburban League Group IV schools. Cap was elected the first President of the Colonial Conference. Pay day is this afternoon, hot dogs! All the tension of the war has lifted and the people are starting to work again building up the ruins. Saw Bari, Ancona, Brindisi, Taranto, and Trieste."

Note: After the war ended in Europe, the military formed numerous athletic teams to occupy the troops overseas. Roscoe Lee Browne was one of the non-commissioned officers tasked with recruiting Americans for the Allied track meet. In a video interview with the Visionary Project, he recalled driving around in a jeep to one of his stops to visit the 92nd Infantry Division where he told a group of soldiers "Just signup, you don't have to be any good to participate." One of the soldiers he spoke to turned out to be eventual four-time Olympic Gold medalist Harrison Dillard. After Dillard won 4 events in the GI Olympics, General Patton told the Stars and Stripes newspaper that Dillard was "the best god-damned athlete I've ever seen."

June 12- "I entered a Track meet June 24 at _____ Stadium; I hope I am still here to run in it. I may be on the way back to the US. I entered the 800 and 1500 instead of the 5000 like last summer. Saw "A Tree Grows in Brooklyn" last night. Boy, that was a good movie. We see a movie every night unless I have signal watch. The souvenir shops in town have good leather gifts from Cairo, Egypt in stock—wallets, pocketbooks, boots, and perfume but you have to wait for 2 or 3 hours in line. Allies are opening a lot of rest camps in France and Northern Italy. We contribute a $1 for kids camps for the summer-— 50 cents per kid, it's a good idea. They are starting tournaments now that war is over in track, tennis, and baseball. Received Pops letter and the Woodbury Times up to May 9th-- about the War's end."

June 16- We saw "Sunday Dinner for a Soldier". Roscoe Browne was second in the 1500 and Pin Davis also from Woodbury was 2nd in the 800. Picture of Dave Williams in the paper, he's favored to win the 1500. I've run a mile or so every day lately for the track championships June 24 in Naples. I'm pretty sure to be home before the finals in Rome."

June 20- "Entered in the zone meet in Naples, worked out with the base track team for the first time. I had been running by myself every day. We are going to work out each evening at the local stadium track, it seats 35,000. I ran a time trial for the mile last night, ran 5:14 not too bad for a beginner in tennis sneakers. I ran sprints with the dash men. If I place in Naples, I'll get to the Mediterranean Finals in Rome or Milan. In the 5th Army Meet Don Evans ran 800 meters in 2:08.8, Roscoe Browne ran a 53 second 400 to reach the finals. Dave Williams 1500 is a final. I hope he wins along with Evans and Browne, and then if I win I'll get to see them in Med Finals. Phil Stilwell lost in the state meet in the Penn Invitational in 4:29.3; high school milers this year must be lightning! I'm not stiff with 2 weeks practice; I can do 4:45 or maybe lower for the mile I believe. Got writing paper from New Zealand soldiers in Trieste."

June 22- "Dear Mother and Pop and Gyp, no track meet for me. Some athletic office canceled our team because we didn't have a full team. We had an Italian coach and 5 Italians on the team. I won the 100 in 10.6, the lay-off and the added weight helped me. Roscoe Brown was second and Dave Williams won the 1500 finals in the 5th Army finals. The movie is Janie tonight. Think we will be hitting the states in the near future."

June 24- "Won't be long now and I will be seeing good old NY soon. We recently heard a lot of good dope. I ran 4:40 for the 1500 the other night. Working out with the Italian track team every night. Kismet is the movie. Okinawa battle is over now that will make for some good bases. It never rains here, not sure how they grow crops. Some cactus as high as a foot high here and it's used as food. There are also lemon and orange groves everywhere and grapes and nuts of all kinds."

June 30- "Nightly workout at the track and I brought my 1500 time down to 4:26. I won't be out of shape when I get home in August or earlier. I'm going to run in as many AAU meets as I can. I'll take Drip, Drop and Droop to see the A's play some afternoon at Shibe Park."

July 1- "Dear Mother Happy Birthday! I'll call you and Aunt Anna when I get into NY. Dave (Williams) won the 5th Amy finals. Bill Seides and Jim Baptiste were killed in action."

July 7- "Had 4 shots, typhoid, tetanus and 2 shots for the plagues. I just talked to Scammell via blinker signal. (Browning and other naval personnel were told they would be sent to the Pacific to fight Japan.)"

July 9- "We passed the Rock of Gibraltar; we are the last LST to leave the Mediterranean underway for the United States."

August 5- (Browning arrives at Portsmouth, VA) - "Maybe I'll report to Philadelphia Navy Yard from here. It takes 10 hours to get to Philadelphia from here. I feel that I got a good break; I'll be home when school is on and can work out with the cross-country team and see a few football games. We can get milk by the pints here in the Yard. Try to sleep with the rivets drilling night and day on the steel decks. When I'm home on leave the war may be finito! (That's Italian!)"

August 10- Postcard- "Just heard that Russia joined up, Boy! It won't be too long now with the new atomic bomb and Russia invading

Manchukuo." Letter- "We heard the Japs surrendered on the radio today. Maybe I'll get out of this outfit by Christmas. I won't go have to go to the Pacific now. Going to hear Gil Dodd's talk. Working for HR Liberty and sea pay on the ship in the Portsmouth Yard. I'm spraying ships with green Pacific camouflage."

August 13- "Still waiting for the Japanese reply, doesn't look like they will send a reply today. We get milk every meal now and steaks, chicken, ice cream every day. Maybe the war will be over when you get this."

August 16- "War should end today at the latest. Got quarter sleeves and shorts, Pop can have the shorts. 6-12 watch saw "The Clock" with Judy Garland, pretty good picture."

August 17- "Happy Days, war is over at last!! I guess you read about the Navy discharge system, that gives me a big 23 points (half enough, what a system). Big celebrations here in Norfolk."

August 23- (Last letter home.) - "Here are pictures of the ceremony to present Mrs. Benjamin with the Congressional Medal of Honor, show it to Cap and save it for my book. The kid from Penns Grove gave it to me. Tough break that Benjamin was killed, boy I'm glad this war is over with. I wish I could get discharged before February than I could start in at school then. Babe ran ok; I hope he places in the 3rd Army Final Meet. Saw the movies "I'll be Seeing You" and "A Medal for Benny"."

Browning remained in the Navy nine months after the war was over. While preparing for discharge, he ran for the Navy track team and started training again. In an interview for the Catholic Star Herald, he said "We (Navy team) went to Madison Square Garden for the Knights of Columbus track meet. There I won a two-mile handicap race and I met up with Villanova coach Jumbo Elliott again. We had met overseas in North Africa and became friends (while Browning was scraping the rust off a ship) After the Meet at the Garden, Elliott offered Browning a scholarship to Villanova, and a chance to run with George Guida from Philadelphia, who Browning had befriended during the war. Guida had also put a word in with Jumbo about Browning when he returned to Villanova after the war. Despite being heavily recruited by Drake during the war, Browning decided to stay closer to home and attend Villanova. Browning and Guida would become Villanova's second and third Olympians.

Villanova teammates George Guida and Browning Ross get the workout from a recuperating Coach Jumbo Elliott at his home.

Jumbo and Villanova

WHEN BROWNING ARRIVED AT VILLANOVA, the small Catholic College 18 miles from Philadelphia in 1946, there were already three institutions at the college.

The first institution was Coach Jim "Jumbo" Elliott who started coaching track after his graduation from Villanova in 1935. The second was Jake Nevin the diminutive trainer who had arrived in 1935 with Jumbo. The third was "Count Villan" a real wildcat who served as the school's mascot. Count Villan was housed in a cage in the Villanova Fieldhouse when not traveling as a good luck charm with a Villanova team.

The irrepressible Nevin gave each new Villanova runner his "business card" which read, "John "Jack" Nevin, No Address, No Phone, No Business, No Money."

Philadelphia native George Guida had received a scholarship to Villanova in 1942 and then put his college career on hold to enlist in the Navy. Jumbo Elliott also put his coaching career on hold to enlist in the Navy. All 3 would cross paths during the war.

Browning continued to compete for the Navy team for his final year of service before his discharge, while Elliott and Guida returned to Villanova. Elliott was in attendance when Ross won indoor Knights of Columbus two mile for the Navy, in Madison Square Garden and offered him a scholarship to Villanova immediately after the race. Browning recalled, "Jumbo and I first met in North Africa during the war when I was scraping the rust off a ship. I was getting ready to apply to Temple when I got the scholarship offer."

Jim "Jumbo" Elliott was a 160-pound gangly sprinter, quarter miler and captain of the golf team when he attended Villanova. He acquired his nickname from Jumbo Elliott a large pitcher who pitched for the Phillies during the 1930's. Jumbo earned only a few thousand dollars as Villanova Track and Cross-Country Coach but became a millionaire selling heavy equipment to contractors as president of Elliott and Franz in Haverford, Pa., a few miles away from Villanova.

Jumbo quickly sold Ross on Villanova. Elliott's philosophy was summed up in a March 1980 profile in Sports Illustrated: "Early in life Jumbo found his salvation in sales. "No matter what you do, life is selling, "he says. "Selling yourself, selling a program, selling this, selling that."

When Browning, a Methodist, arrived on campus at the Catholic College, he quickly renewed acquaintance with George Guida, a sprinter from South Philadelphia who he had grown friendly with at various high school championship track meets in Philadelphia and again in the Navy during the war. Browning developed an interest in Physical Education Instruction in the Navy and decided to pursue a teaching degree at Villanova.

Browning recalled Jumbo getting him and his Villanova cross-country teammates jobs delivering phone books to Main Line mansions his first semester. "The houses were huge and they all had equally large accompanying buildings that used to be servant's quarters. It was tough at first to determine which one was the primary residence when we delivered those phone books."

"Jumbo assigned George Thompson as my roommate for most of my years at Villanova, and we became close friends," Browning said. Later, in the 1960's, Thompson would write to Browning "keep your eye on my niece who is a pretty good tennis player in Florida, Chris Evert."

Browning was undefeated in dual meets in his first year of college cross-country despite a tough academic and meet schedule.

Villanova's dual meet opponents included Army, Navy and a Fort Dix, NJ team stocked with active duty soldiers. The Fort Dix team included Jack St. Clair who would go on to coach Temple and the Penn Athletic Club. The Philadelphia Bulletin called the Fort Dix team "one of the best teams in the eastern part of the country". Browning finished his last dual meet against Fort Dix with a win running the 3.5- mile course in 16:59.

At the end of the cross-country season, Browning lost a race for the first time in his high school and college career. In a November 1946 write up in the Villanovan, the Villanova school newspaper, "Browning suffered his first loss in the IC4A meet in Van Cortland Park in New York, halfway through the race he was in third place in the big field when someone stepped on his heel and his shoe came off. Several men tripped and fell over him, and by the time he was up and had his shoe on, the rest of the field was out of sight. He did, however —and it is a tribute to his greatness, recover and finish as the first Villanova finisher."

The Villanova also ran this article on the front page next to news of the Villanova cross-country team's victories, "The Student Council has voted to accept the offer of Phillip Morris Company to give the Villanova student body an Admiral Television if collectively they can accumulate 60,000 Phillip Morris (cigarette) wrappers.

Though 60,000 seems to be a large number of wrappers to accumulate for a student body the size of Villanova's there is no doubt that the goal can be obtained if there is complete cooperation by everyone.

A Depository for the wrappers is situated in the Pie Shop where a thermometer will be located to indicate progress."

In the 1947 winter track season, Jumbo was suffering from Rheumatic fever and unable to coach. Confined to home and bed rest for two months, Browning, George Guida and other members of the track team would meet Jumbo at his apartment not far from Villanova to get their daily workouts. They would then run their workouts on wooden boards set up outside to get the feel of indoor tracks, and then return to Jumbo's apartments to report on their progress.

During the season Browning was reunited with another friend, Dave Williams who enrolled at Villanova with Browning's encouragement. Williams still had eligibility after giving up a running scholarship to Georgetown after competing for two years to enlist in the Army serving with the Tenth Mountain Division in Italy.

Williams lived only four miles from Browning's hometown of Woodbury, NJ in nearby Gloucester City, NJ. The two friends teamed up for many Villanova relay victories. The Villanovan described one such race: "The Millrose Games saw the formation of a Blue and White two-mile relay team composed of Roy Cameron, George Thompson, Dave Williams, and Browning Ross. This foursome with Ross turning in a superb anchor leg "out-footed" the New York Pioneer Club and Columbia to win in 7:57, a time that has been excelled only by Fordham in the East this year."

Browning accepted an invitation to run in the Sugar Bowl Invitational Track meet on December 28 in New Orleans where he finished third in the Steeplechase in his first attempt at the event.

Jumbo Elliott recalled a cross-country race against Navy in which Browning and George Thompson were running one-two and Browning started to pull away, "Thompson, had bad eyesight and got lost running around a building in Annapolis. "Brownie, where are you?" he yelled. "Wait up, Brownie, here I come!" Browning waited for Thompson to catch up and they finished first and second."

Ross opened his 1948 indoor season with a stopover at the Washington Star Games en route home from the Sugar Bowl track meet in New Orleans.

According to the Philadelphia Inquirer, "On the flat boards of the National Guard Armory in the Capital, Browning rolled to a startling upset in the mile. With a 4:13.7 performance, Ross beat not only Tom Milne, North Carolina's National Cross-Country Champion of the previous year, but also the New York AC's Bill Hulse, whose 4:08 in a second-place finish to Sweden's Gunder Hagg in 1943 was still the fastest mile ever clocked by an American on a cinder track in 1948.

That victory established Ross as a miler. In the evening, a few hours later Browning collaborated with Billy Curran, Pete Simigan and George Thompson to lead the Villanova blue and white to victory in the intercollegiate two-mile relay championship."

In the book "Jumbo Elliott, Maker of Milers, Maker of Men" Author Ted Berry wrote, "Browning often recalled the time Jumbo made one of his frequent last-minute relay substitutions, this time inserting Browning as the last- minute anchor leg of the 2-mile relay in the Penn Relays.

Browning said, "Jumbo guessed wrong that day. I had a 15-yard lead but got passed in the home stretch by Joe Deady (a top half-miler from Georgetown)." Dejected, Browning walked to the southwest corner of Penn's Franklin Field to where Jumbo always sat, thinking over what he would say to Jumbo. "I saw Jumbo watching me walk up the steps and he didn't look too happy.

He stood up and the only thing I could sputter to him was an apologetic "Jesus Christ, Jumbo!" it was the only thing I could get out. Jumbo, who stuttered, stuck a bony finger in the middle of my aching chest and said: "Thhat's who I'm gonna have run the anchor for us nnnnext year!"

Browning recalled purchasing a rare pair of white racing flats and wearing them to practice. "Most of the running shoes were black in those days and Jumbo took one look at them and let out a "wolf whistle". He kept up whistling at my shoes for a couple of days."

Browning also remembered an April meeting with Jumbo and the track team in a classroom before the Penn Relays to talk about who would run each relay leg. "No one was paying attention to him and there were a few minutes of talking before everyone noticed Jumbo was staring at us, not speaking. Then there was an uncomfortable silence as he continued to just stare before finally saying, "You wasted 5 minutes of my time, now I just wasted 5 minutes of yours. Jumbo's favorite saying was 'runners make runners'."

Browning Ross signing autographs for London youth before the 1948 Olympics.

1948 Olympics

IN THE SPRING OF 1948, Browning looked forward to trying to make the US Olympic team in London. He was in the enviable position of trying to decide which of three distance races gave him the best chance to qualify for the team.

Although he had frequently run the 800 for Villanova in relays and had won the 1946 and 1947 Berwick 9 mile "Marathons" he thought his best chance of qualifying for the team was in the middle distances, the 1500 meter, and 5,000-meter distances instead of the 10,000 meters.

He finally settled on the 3000-meter Steeplechase as his best opportunity, figuring the balance of speed and strength needed for the Steeplechase might give him an advantage in making the team.

Browning had honed his speed running so many relay legs for Villanova. He had also developed strength and the ability to recover quickly from his frequent racing during his first 3 seasons at Villanova, and from frequent racing on his own on weekends in the off seasons. He felt all of the racing gave him a strong aerobic base and hopefully a competitive advantage over the other American hopefuls in the grueling US Olympic team qualifying process.

Browning remembered, "Jumbo took me over the University of Pennsylvania and set up the hurdles in zig-zag position, and I ran them hour after hour. In about two weeks I had the event down pretty good."

To make the team, Browning had to first qualify for the 1948 Olympic trials by winning the NCAA Steeplechase Championship for Villanova in June at the University of Minnesota. He finished first in 9:25.7 This National Championship earned him an invitation to the run the AAU Championships at Marquette University three weeks later. In the AAU meet the top six moved on to the Olympic Trials and Browning qualified for the Olympic trials by finishing third in the AAU Steeplechase.

A week later he had to race again at Northwestern University in Evanston Illinois and he finished second to make his first Olympic team as a Villanova Sophomore.

Great Britain had been awarded the 1944 Olympic Games in June of 1939 but those Games were canceled because of the World War II. The 1948 Olympic Games were again awarded to Britain and were known as the "Austerity Games," because food, gasoline, and housing were still rationed. Male athletes were housed in the Royal Air Force camps and female athletes in London College dorms.

Browning said, "I was surprised at how much evidence there remained of the devastation of the war in London during the Olympics." In fact, tanks, and military vehicles were seen near most of the events and battleships can be seen anchored off shore during the rowing events in videos of the 1948 Games.

In London Browning roomed with 40-year-old marathoner Johnny Kelley. Kelley had run the previous Olympic Marathon in Berlin in 1936 and would go on to even greater fame by running 61 Boston Marathons. When I spoke to Kelley in 1990 about rooming with Browning, he said, "Besides being a great runner Brownie had a great sense of humor, and was a true gentleman, it was a pleasure to room with him."

Browning was the only American to qualify for the Olympic Steeplechase final finishing fourth in the Second Heat in 9:30.4 He led the race into the sixth lap before finishing seventh in the Olympic final in 9:24.1 as Sweden swept all three medals.

Browning's Villanova teammate Guida was sixth in the 400 meters.

Browning also renewed a friendship with another US Olympic marathoner, Ted Vogel who he had first met in the 1944 Boston Marathon while in the Navy.

During the marathon, the final event in the 1948 Games, Browning borrowed a bicycle from a spectator and covered most of the distance alongside Vogle up to the Olympic Stadium. Then he returned the bicycle. Years later Browning laughed and said "Can you imagine trying that in the Olympics today? There were a lot of people running and riding bikes alongside the runners in that race."

Browning was given a welcome home parade through Woodbury after the 1948 Olympics. It made him uncomfortable and he often said he thought Woodbury's returning World War II vets should have been a parade instead of the returning athletes.

Browning had started dating Sis Kelly of Gloucester City, NJ. Sis worked as a secretary for RCA in Camden, NJ.

Browning was averaging about 25 miles of running a week at Villanova, much of it speed work.

Sis Ross recalled, "Before they built the Schuylkill Expressway (a highway linking Philadelphia to Villanova) Browning would occasionally run the 26 miles to or from Villanova to Woodbury if he didn't have a ride."

Browning liked to talk about Jumbo's legendary temper, "About the maddest I ever saw Jumbo was when he found out that during Easter break that four of us drove down to Florida to run the Florida Relays without his permission. He probably never would have known except we won a couple of the relays, the results made the papers, and we all came back with bad colds!

Browning's brother Babe, then an outstanding runner for Tennessee, also ran at the Relays. Babe told me years later, "I was shocked to see Brownie and his Villanova teammates show up in Florida. I never expected them to be there. They ran their races and won beating some good teams, and then took off for the drive home for Villanova right after the race."

Browning, "When Jumbo would find out I ran a road race on the weekend he would get angry and say 'Thhat's it! Go back to the dorm and pack your bags! Go back to the Jersey tomato farms!!'

Then Jumbo would cool off and forget the whole thing by the next day's practice."

Browning returned to Europe in the summer of 1949 for an AAU sponsored track tour of Scandinavia consisting meets against a combined Scandinavian team consisting of athletes from Finland, Sweden, Denmark, Iceland, and Norway. Browning wrote this about the trip, "Two characteristics distinguish the good athlete the world over. First, he wants to win; second, if he cannot win, he wants to study the man who can and equal or improve upon his technique. We watched the Scandinavian distance runners most carefully.

In training, we ran with our fine companions and competitors over pine roads and along the woods and trails along the quiet lakes. After the competition, we eased our tired muscles in a Finnish Sauna Bath at an athletic clubhouse in the forest; we brushed ourselves with birch branches in the steam and finally took a quick swim in the cold fjord. We completed in at least a dozen meets, and made a loop of Norway."

The US team consisted of just five athletes, Browning, 1948 Olympic 800-meter gold medalist Mal Whitfield, Bob Matthias the 17-year-old Olympic gold medalist in the pole vault, Frank Fox a versatile 400/800-meter runner, and Victor Frank a discus thrower.

In one of the meets in Tonsberg Norway, Matthias won the pole vault, discus and finished third in the long jump. Browning won the 3000 meters and finished second to Fox in the 400 meters.

Browning's first place prize was a whale's tooth. After additional races in Norway, Finland Sweden, and Ireland Browning returned home for his senior year at Villanova.

Upon his return, Browning wrote about the meet in an article titled "Norwegian Notes," published in the Lynx, the Villanova student quarterly publication."

Ed Phetteplace wrote of the tour, "Jumping from plane to plane the tour consisted of 16 meets in 22 days with Browning running the 1500 meters, 3000-meter steeplechase, and cross-country races."

With Olympic and international experience under his belt, Browning continued to win cross country, indoor track and outdoor track races in his final year at Villanova.

In the 1949 cross-country season Browning finished second in the IC4A Cross Country Meet to a future Medal of Honor (Korean War) recipient Richard Shea of Army.

In indoor track, Browning won the Washington Evening Star Indoor mile in 4:13.7, outkicking National cross-country champion Jack Milne by two steps.

In outdoor track, Browning set stadium records at West Point, NY in the 880 and mile runs in 1949 and 1950.

The 6th Annual Philadelphia Inquirer Invitation Indoor Track Meet Program on January 20, 1950, offers a snapshot of Philadelphia and the USA at the time. A full-page picture ad on the inside cover features Bing Crosby urging readers and runners to "Smoke My Cigarette- Milder Chesterfield. ABC- Always Buy Chesterfield. The Best Cigarette for You to Smoke." The ad also mentions Bings' radio show sponsored by Chesterfield "every Wednesday at 9:30 on the CBS radio network" along with Bings latest "picture" with Frank Capra- "Riding High".

The indoor meet was held at Philadelphia's Convention Hall home of the Philadelphia Warriors and later the 76ers. Both NBA teams played their home games in front of the 12,000-capacity present for the meet. Many of those in attendance smoked cigarettes or cigars.

In the 1950's daily newspapers were flush with cash and the Inquirer hosted the meet as part of its Inquirer Charities contribution to the city.

The feature race was the Philadelphia Inquirer Mile which featured national champion runners Gerald Karver, Fred Wilt, and Browning as well as Olympian

John Joe Barry from Ireland, soon to be Villanova. Browning represented Villanova and was also entered in the 26ᵗʰ and final event, the Two-Mile College Relay. Dave Williams, also soon to continue his education at Villanova ran the 1,000 with Woodbury's own Roscoe Lee Browne. Dave Williams' father George, a pioneer of South Jersey Running was one of the head officials.

The meet program, published by the Inquirer, and the Inquirers' radio stations also featured a profile of Villanova Coach Jumbo Elliott. In the article, Elliott ponders his "all-time team" from the start of his Villanova coaching career in 1936 until 1950. Jumbo naturally names Browning as one of his all-time best. "Browning Ross, Olympic steeplechaser who has broken .49 seconds for the quarter, covered a half in 1:45.1 and mile in 4:12 and longer distances incommensurate time, even up to the exhausting Berwick Marathon while still in college. Jumbo adds, "Even *one* good man can bring a school recognition in track." The program also has a profile of FBI agent Fred Wilt who had lost to only one American in the past year (Curt Stone in a two mile) in a variety distances from the mile to 10,000 meters to the AAU Cross Country Championship.

The most interesting profile in the program was a feature on Ben Ogden Track and Field's "Father of Invention." Ogden, the Temple track coach invented a starting gate for sprinters similar to the starting gate at horse races that prevented false starts. It was used in the 1949 Penn Relays and was discussed as "being used in the next (1952) Olympiad. Ogden also discussed eliminating cinder tracks in favor of a 220-yard banked board track that would enable more schools to have tracks and a "catcher" for pole vaults that would use netting to prevent pole vault injuries.

Fred Wilt won the mile in 4:11.8 in an exciting race with John Joe Barry and Browning 8 yards behind. Roscoe Browne won 1000 in a meet record and Curt Stone won the 2-mile in 9:07. Roscoe was the AAU National Indoor Champ at 1,000 yards at Madison Square Garden a week later running 2:15.6. He would also run the fastest time in the world for 800 meters the following year-- 1:49.3.

Browning won both the indoor Mile and Two-Mile AAU championships in 1950. He also continued to win races almost every weekend in the offseason, including his third and fourth AAU 10k Cross-Country Championships in 1949 and 1950 (Barry was runner-up). Browning continued his streak of winning and setting records in major off-season road races at a variety of distances such as the Camden, NJ 4.7 mile YMCA run and the Berwick, PA 9 mile run.

As Browning's Villanova career came to a close Jumbo Elliott reminisced about his career in an interview with the Philadelphia Inquirer:

"Browning is one of the most versatile runners I've ever coached. He's bettered 49 seconds for the quarter, and he's done the half in 1:54.1. So, he has speed as well as durability.

The only trouble I ever had with him was in trying to get him to ease up in his training. He wanted to run all day—and at all distances. Whenever I didn't see him, all I had to do was pick up a paper to read where he'd won some street run. He must have more trophies than anyone in the country.

He never rested, even during the summer. Don't forget, he competed in Europe following the Olympics, and the following summer he went abroad again.

But I think he's all over that now. He laid off competition four months last summer, and the rest did him good. If you don't think he's a better runner for it just look at his records."

When Browning graduated Villanova in 1950, it was an era when most college athletes stopped competing upon graduation and focused their energy instead on their working careers.

For Browning Ross, college graduation was just the beginning to a lifetime of significant running accomplishments and contributions to American distance running.

Irish Runners and Villanova teammates John Joe Barry and Jim Reardon rush to catch a train on the way to a meet at Madison Square Garden in New York City.

The Ballincurry Hare

JOHN JOE BARRY WAS POSSIBLY one of the most interesting characters, biggest talents and saddest stories of all Villanova runners.

Barry arrived at Villanova in February of 1950 after running on the American indoor track circuit for two months. Before his arrival, he was picked by many to be the first sub-four minute miler. In his autobiography "The Ballincurry Hare" Barry said one of the reasons he picked Villanova was its proximity to fly to Dublin's Shannon Airport, but he did not return to Ireland for 17 years.

During Barry's first year at Villanova, he clashed with Jumbo over race appearance fees that Barry had been accepting for running indoor races.

Jumbo and Father McKee, the Villanova Chaplain sat Barry down and told him it was illegal to accept the race appearance money he had been collecting and ordered him to send all of his race winnings to his mother in Ireland so he and Villanova would not be ruled ineligible. Barry complied but had further run-ins with Elliott. Barry remarked that Elliott reminded him of General Eisenhower.

Browning said, "John Joe really had a swagger and was extremely confident. When he and I would train together, he would say in a thick Irish brogue, "Now Ross you run all out and I'll run as slow as I can and you try to stay with me!" It was a line Browning enjoyed and would later repeat to the runners he coached.

Browning also remembered, "Barry was always complaining about Jumbo's workouts, constantly asking why we were doing a workout out of earshot of Jumbo. But Jumbo found out and confronted John Joe, he said, "John Joe I heard you were saying behind my back that I was the worst coach you ever saw."

Barry said, "Now Jumbo, I didn't say you were the worst coach I ever saw, I just said I've seen better." Boy that really made Jumbo hit the roof, he got even madder and said you SOB, get out of here!"

For his part, Barry wrote about being "a rebel" and giving only "70% effort and 30% excuses." He remembered traveling to indoor meets with Villanova at Madison Square Garden and Jumbo giving instructions to the telephone switchboard girls in the hotel to cut off all communications for his athletes with the outside world while they were at the hotel.

Browning also recalled an example of Jumbo's vigilance in protecting his runners, "We were just settling into the Paramount Hotel before a meet at Madison Square Garden, and we heard a knock at the door. I opened the door and there were two young girls in their early 20's standing in the hallway. Before we could ask what they wanted, we heard Jumbo's thundering voice, "Get the hell away from here!" They quickly scattered. Jumbo thought he had to be on guard in the city and anyone hanging around was probably up to no good. He must have stayed up all night looking out for us."

Art Morrow of the Philadelphia Inquirer wrote about Barry during his Villanova peak in peak January of 1951. Here is an excerpt from an article titled "Barry Heads Villanovans in Inquirer Track Meet."

"Although the one sold insurance in Dublin and the other clothing to Scotchmen in Glasgow, James Patrick Reardon and Johnny Joe Barry both regard themselves as Tipperary men, and at the slightest sign of provocation, even Comin Clancy joins them in singing the song the late John McCormick made famous about the Valley of Slieb na Man, or the Valley of Beautiful Women.

Reardon and Barry grew up as runners. They were raised on farms, and the chief product of their Tipperary country is horses— Irish jumpers. "Beautiful animals," Reardon expounds. "With enormous fetlocks. After the Second Crusade, they brought Arabians back to Ireland, and ten crossed them with Irish draft horses. We call our jumpers "Orabs".

So, Reardon and Barry have learned to run by chasing Irish jumpers and herding them into barnyards and fields. It must have been good training, although the constant running on turf and grass left them with little experience on cinders and absolutely none on boards until they came to the U.S.

But by way of preparation for his second voyage across the Atlantic—he was four when his parents moved back to Ballincurry from Joliet, Ill—Barry blazed his name around the foot racing world in the summer of 1949.

In June, he ran the third fastest mile recorded that year 4:08.6 and a month later at Dublin, he defeated U.S. Champion, John Twomey. Later he was clocked in 3:51.4 for 1500 meters, 8:17 for 3000 a 13:56.2 for three miles—which made him the Irish champion and record holder at virtually every distance from 440 yards upwards.

In the National Guard Armory in Washington D.C., he roared from behind to beat Penn A.C.'s Horace Ashenfelter in the two-mile run. Six days later in his first taste of banked board completion, he chased Wilt to a new district record of 4:11.8 running a 4:12.9 mile.

But Johnny Joe had his troubles—constant toothaches. Even the night he beat Ashenfelter by five yards in 4:11.5 for the National AAU championship last February his gums bled and he'd had no solid food in three weeks. By March, however, the infected teeth had been removed and early in that month, he performed a feat with few if any precedents.

First, he roared to victory in 8:57.9 in a special two-mile feature at the Heptagonal Games in Boston beating Wilt by in a race that saw the first four men break nine minutes with Ashenfelter third in 8:59 and Twomey third in 8:59.1. The next night Barry beat Twomey, Kirwan, and Wilt in 4:11.6 at the New York K of C meet. Shortly after winning the Canadian Legion Mile at Montreal two nights later—his third triumph in four days—Barry came down with a cold and had to curtail his campaign because his mother fell ill and he had to fly back home to Ireland."

Alex Breckenridge, another Villanova Olympian was born in Buffalo New York, but moved back to Scotland. Raised in Scotland he had the Scottish Junior National cross-country championship and broken the Scottish national record for the Mile. "I was fortunate to compete against John Joe and Fred Dwyer in separate track meets in Glasgow, Scotland in summer of 1953. I believe they put in a recommendation for me with Jumbo. I came to the U.S. not knowing if I had a scholarship or not. I stayed with John Joe and met Jumbo or the first time in early September.

Jumbo put his arm around me and said, "I won't give you any bum steers." I doubt if I knew what it meant at the time but as busy as he was, he was a caring coach, and after "Ronnie" Delany joined us in September of '54 I had the best training partner I could have wished for. Jim Tuppeny was Jumbo's assistant while I was at Villanova. He had been Don Bragg's coach at Penns Grove and must be given much credit for Don's progress. Don and I met again in the 1960 Rome Olympics where he won the gold in the Pole Vault and I finished 30th in the marathon, won by Abebe Bikila running barefoot. John Joe introduced me to Brownie at a cross-country run in Fairmount Park in Philly.

Barry had some great races but never reached his potential. He said the low point of his running career tenure was being stranded at Villanova with

Cummin Clancy in 1952 because Ireland would not pay to fly him to the Olympics in Helsinki. Barry wrote that decision took the wind out of his sails for running. He graduated Villanova in 1954 with an Economics degree. Barry became close to Browning and Sis Ross.

They introduced him to a Woodbury girl that he soon married, helped him find a job and an apartment in Woodbury. The Barry's settled nearby in an apartment in Woodbury close enough for John Joe and Browning to train together. But John Joe was getting restless and tired of the expectations of being a great runner.

Describing himself as feeling "ground up," Barry brought his running career to a halt on July 4th after running a half-mile race in Woodbury, NJ he stopped his car on a bridge over Woodbury Lake, "I tied everything into a real nice floating bundle, using my running shoes to complete the last act, got out of the car and with one big heave said to myself: 'Here goes Jumbo, Ireland, the USA, track and everything else that goes with my last 12 years in the bloody game."

Even though I had graduated two years previously I still had him (Jumbo) on my mind. I leaned over a small bridge and watched them float slowly away. I felt a great moment of relief."

Barry may have felt momentary relief but without the anchor of running in his life he would soon also leave his wife and job and drift into a life of heavy drinking and gambling. Barry would later write that he thought he could have fulfilled his potential if he had returned to Ireland and continued the training and simple healthy lifestyle that had made him a world class runner in Ireland.

Irish Pipeline

AFTER THE 1948 OLYMPICS, BROWNING won races in Paris and then traveled to Ireland where he finished second in a mile to Irish mile champion and Olympian John Joe Barry.

Next Browning and George Guida traveled to Dublin for a meet. In Dublin Guida reunited with his friend Irish 400 meter Olympian Jim Reardon in a Dublin hotel. Reardon asked questions about the States and Villanova. Ted Berry wrote about the meeting in his biography of Jumbo Elliott: "What's it (The United States) like?" Reardon asked, "What's that coach of yours like?"

"It's beautiful in the States," they answered. "And the best part is Villanova. Jumbo is an Irishman-- just like you; you'll be fine with Jumbo."

When Browning and George returned to school and told Jumbo of the meeting he followed up and offered Reardon a scholarship.

Reardon would soon be the best man at Browning and Sis's wedding. Browning remembered Reardon's arrival at Villanova as a surprise for Jumbo: "Reardon arrived bright and shiny, with orange shoes and a big tweed suit and his hair parted right down the middle. He also arrived with a wife-- an Irish beauty queen he had married before coming to the states."

Mr. and Mrs. Reardon were quickly accepted by Jumbo. Reardon was unaware of one of Jumbo's precepts that his teammates had heard so often they knew by heart, "There are only three things you can do at school. There's the studies, the social life with girls, and the athletics. You can only do two of them, no more. You can't do all three of them and expect to do them well.

It can't be done, besides there's plenty of time for all that (romance) business after graduation."

Two months after Reardon enrolled at Villanova, Irish Olympic miler John Joe Barry arrived at Villanova. He was followed six months later by fellow Irish Olympian hammer thrower Cummin Clancy.

The "Irish Pipeline" was formed. A term that would describe a steady supply of great Irish runners to Villanova, including Olympians Ron Delaney, Eammon Coghlan, Sonia O'Sullivan, John Hartnett, Gerry O'Reilly, and Marcus O'Sullivan.

O'Sullivan would later run over 100 sub-four minute miles and also become Villanova's first Irish-born Track and Cross-Country Coach.

When asked about the Irish Pipeline, 1956 Melbourne 1500-meter gold medal winner Delaney told me, "George Guida was definitely the one most responsible for persuading Reardon to come over (to Villanova) and starting the Pipeline. I think Browning may have had a little more to do with John Joe Barry coming to Villanova.

The "pipeline" continued into 2017 as Dublin-born Siofra Cleirigh Buttner was named the most valuable runner at the Penn Relays in 2017 for leading the Wildcats to a rare sweep of the Championship of America distance relays. Cleirigh ran the 800-meter leg of the distance medley relay on the first day of competition at the Penn Relays, then anchored victories in the 4x1500 meter relay and the 4x800 meter relay over the next two days of the Relays.

Almost 70 years after Browning and George Guida's meeting in a Dublin hotel the Villanova Irish pipeline is still flowing.

Villanova teammates Browning Ross and Dave Williams at the Penn Relays.

Bella Gambas Dave Williams!

ONE OF BROWNING'S LIFE-LONG FRIENDS, Dave Williams was born and raised in Gloucester City, New Jersey. A Gloucester Catholic High School graduate, Gloucester Catholic did not have a cross country or track team when Dave Williams graduated in 1937 so Dave started running as a boy with his father George, an accomplished runner in the 1920's and his uncles Harry, Thomas, and William through the streets of Gloucester.

In November 1935, the AAU Senior Cross-Country meet was held in Dave's hometown of Gloucester City. It attracted a field of over 100 runners, a huge turnout for the time. It was one of Dave's first races. The race started at the old Gloucester High School and ran through Gloucester on a cold wind-swept fall day. The race was won by former Michigan State track star

Tom Ottey who had also won the AAU Mid-Atlantic Senior Cross Country Championship races in 1929, 1930 and 1931.

Williams, a junior at Gloucester Catholic finished only 13 seconds behind his father who won the Gloucester City title. He was from then on "hooked on running and racing."

Williams soon became, according to the Philadelphia newspapers of the 1940's, "one of the best runners in the country". Some Gloucester contemporaries remember: "If you saw someone running back then in Gloucester (in the 1930's-40's) you knew it was one of the Williams family, they were great runners." In the next four years, Dave Williams became the top runner in the Philadelphia/New Jersey area winning a number of championship distance races for well over a decade.

Williams went to Georgetown in 1942 on an athletic scholarship and quickly made a name for himself becoming the Hoyas top miler and Cross -Country runner.

The New York Times of May 23, 1943, noted that Frosh Williams won the mile in the first race held on the brand- new Georgetown track: "**Dave Williams beat a heavily favored Fordham runner in 4:24. Gate receipts for the meet were turned over to the Army relief fund.**" Williams won a series of races that year for Georgetown including an indoor Melrose Games mile in 4:19.

As a sophomore Williams continued to run for Georgetown and for Shanahan Catholic Club of Philadelphia in open races.

The Philadelphia newspapers note that he was unbeaten for two years, before finishing third in the national 10,000-meter championships in Newark New Jersey. The Courier-Post on December 5, 1943, reported: "**Dave Williams is <u>the</u> outstanding runner in the East if not in the country.**" Williams remained one of the best runners in the country winning most of the major AAU races through the 1940's, a survey of some of his major wins:

* On December 1941 while a freshman at Georgetown, Williams won the Hail America 6- mile championship at the Penn AC boathouse in 31:09, pulling away from the field at the halfway mark of the race.

- On December 6, 1942, Williams won the Camden YMCA 4.7- Mile Street Run, the biggest race in the Philadelphia area at the time in 23:04. Williams did what had never been done before in the race-- he won the time prize and was the first to finish. That is, he started 5 minutes behind the field and still won. (Until 1957 most races were started with handicapped starts). The Courier Post, "The second- place finisher was Browning Ross who was the New Jersey state mile and cross-country champion at Woodbury and was running for Shanahan Catholic Club managed by future Villanova coaching great Jack Pyrah."

  On Thanksgiving Day 1942, Williams won the Mid-Atlantic AAU Championships at 10,000 meters. In a Philadelphia Bulletin Headline, Dec 13, 1942: "Williams overcomes 5 minutes 30-second handicap to win Nativity CC Run."

  On February 28 Williams "lapped a star-studded field to win the AAU two-mile championship at Penn in 9:40." Described in the Philadelphia papers as "an exceptionally good time despite cold and high winds".

- In March 1943 Williams ran 24:31 for a 4.5-mile race put on by the Camden County Parks Commission at Cooper River beating Browning Ross by 58 seconds. Ross had recently won the AAU indoor mile championship while a student at Woodbury.

- On November 29, 1943, Williams won the Mid-Atlantic AAU 10k championship for the second year in a row at Fairmont Park in 32:21. Philadelphia Bulletin, "Williams came from behind to out kick Tom Crane of Catholic University." Dave Williams's time over 70 years ago might still win most 10k races held today.

The Philadelphia Inquirer describes an April 3rd, 1943 AAU 4 ½-mile street run sponsored by the Ontario Athletic Club-- after the first two runners with a handicapped start (1 min 50 seconds advantage) had just finished: "The battle for third was one of the best features of the race as it involved the two best in the field-- Williams Georgetown ace and AAU

10,000 meter champion had the best actual time 23:27, Ross New Jersey Interscholastic champion the second best time 23:55. Ross who started 30 seconds behind Williams held the lead until the last mile, then Williams the only scratch man in the field drew abreast. Entering the last quarter mile, Williams drew ahead and stayed there until 50 yards from home. Here Ross opened a driving finish and beat him to the line by five yards."

In 1944, Dave Williams put his running career on hold and joined the Army a decision that most likely cost him a berth on the US 1948 (London) Olympic team. He transferred out of his original regiment and into the 10th Mountain Infantry Regiment of the Army (an equivalent of our Special Forces today) to fight in World War II.

The move may have saved his life, as his original regiment suffered heavy causalities. The 10th Mountain Regiment also faced fierce fighting in Italy. Williams was trained to ride horses and to ski as part of his special combat training. Noticing his exceptional running ability, Williams was pulled from the foxholes and front lines in Italy and given the opportunity to "visit Venice or run a race in Florence". His daughter Alex Williams: "Being the true runner he was, he chose the race of course."

Despite little training, Williams won the Fifth Corps Mile Championship by a large margin in Florence. Williams then represented the Armed Forces in track meets throughout Europe. Alex Williams: "There was a great article about a "fouling duel" he had with an Italian runner in a race—they say the dual arose because of "cultural misunderstandings" in the article. But the feisty Gloucester boy that he was, he said it was a result of the other runner trying to push him out of his lane! He realized that the vehement whistling after the incident was the actually the fans booing—but he pretended to think otherwise and ran in gesturing as if accepting the crowd's approval!"

Williams continued his running while housed with an Italian family. A teenage girl in the host family's house watched him return from a training run and cheered him on: "Bella gambas, David, Bella gambas!" (Nice legs David, Nice legs!)

Browning and Dave continued their friendship through regular correspondence during the war.

After the war in Europe ended, Williams was told to prepare to be part of the invasion of Japan but then got the news that the invasion was off when the atomic bomb was dropped on Japan. Upon his return to the States, Williams finished his service in the Army and soon resumed his running career as one of the top runners in the Philadelphia/ South Jersey area.

* In 1946, Williams won the 10k Street Run from Camden (N.J.) To Maple Shade (N.J.) in 33:47.
* In 1947, he won the Breen McCracken VFW 3-mile run in Philadelphia winning the best time prize with a time of 15:35.
* In 1949 Williams ran 23:47 in the 4.7-mile Camden Y run as one of the fastest "scratch runners".

After Williams returned from the war he married Marcella Manion, his sweetheart from Gloucester City. Their first child, daughter Marcella was born and he resumed his education at the University of Michigan. Moving his wife and daughter to Michigan to stay with the Michigan coach. Williams ran well but soon became homesick. Before he entered the service, Browning had been one of Williams toughest competitors as well as a young runner he had helped mentor.

Browning supplanted Williams as the top runner in Philadelphia after the war. Williams transferred to Villanova in 1947 where he completed his college eligibility running for legendary Jumbo Elliott (whose curmudgeonly personality he did not care for) and combined with Browning on some record setting Villanova Distance Medley relay teams.

On his return to Villanova Dave and Marcella Williams worked part-time jobs as a cook and butler for a wealthy family at Villanova when second daughter Alexandra (Alex) was born in 1947. Alex recalls: "I know my dad wasn't much of a butler, but fortunately my mom was an excellent cook!" The Williams family moved back to Gloucester.

In the late 1940's, Dave and Browning frequently met in Gloucester to train together. Joe Murphy, a neighbor of the Williams family remembers, "I was about 9 years old and Dave and Browning would come to my house early in the morning and bang on the door wake me up to go running with them. They were obviously two of the best runners in the country so I was honored that they would do that. I would try to keep up with them as long as I could. They ran through Gloucester and nearby Brooklawn and back. At some point, I would fall off the pace and have to run back by myself but it was a thrill and honor to run with them." Murphy went on to a great athletic career at Gloucester Catholic and made a number of South Jersey Hall of Fames as an athlete and coach.

In 1948 Browning and Dave met newly arrived Father Lucitt of St Mary's Church in Gloucester and the three formed the St. Mary's track guild as part of St Mary's Guild activities. The St. Mary's Guild was started in the Depression as a way to provide recreational opportunities, apprenticeship, and craft training for St Mary's grade school students.

The St Mary's Guild track team started the first running team for grade school students in Gloucester and led to the first track teams for St Mary's grammar school and Gloucester Catholic. Murphy would return to Gloucester Catholic to coach one of the early Gloucester Catholic track teams and the Gloucester Catholic baseball team in the same season—running from field to field.

The Williams family would grow to five children as David Jr., Celeste and Lisa followed. The family moved to New Castle, Delaware in 1954. Dave continued to run well; in 1956 Dave Williams ran 24:37 in the Camden Y run to again place among the top finishers.

Williams continued his career as an English teacher and cross-country and track coach in Delaware; passing on his knowledge and love of running to his own children as well as to the Delaware runners he coached at DeLaWarr, Conrad, and William Penn High Schools. His cross-country team at DeLaWarr High in Delaware won a state cross-country championship.

The popular coach would often be joined at home by visits from his teams at Christmas or for group swims in his swimming pool after long runs down Delaware's dusty Route 9.

Williams continued his own running in Delaware races. He won the Delaware State two-mile championship at the age of 39 out kicking some premier college runners in the field to win with two of his daughters in attendance.

Williams survived colon cancer in his 40's and continued to run with half a colon (using some classic English teacher humor he referred to it as his "semi-colon") for more than 30 years.

He also ran and placed well in the Caesar Rodney half marathons in the 60's (The inaugural 1964 race was won by his friend Browning Ross in 1:07:24). While Williams continued to win his age group and finish near the front of the pack in Delaware races at a variety of distances, he even returned to his hometown of Gloucester New Jersey, in 1980 with one of his daughters to run in the Gloucester Sportsman AC 4-mile race. The race is now legendary race for a train that stopped everyone except winner Larry Schemelia-- who had a large lead. Once the train passed, the entire field made a mad sprint for the last half-mile of the race. Ironically, Schemelia a high school state champion in 1969 from Gloucester High and a junior college National Champion was the best runner from Gloucester since Dave Williams but the two never met at the race.

Daughter Alex remembers her father's racing advice: "Dad would always say if a runner has enough left at the end of the race to sprint, they didn't run as hard as they could have during the race." Running was obviously in the Williams genes. Dave's sister Veronica (Hermanson) was also a fine runner-- unfortunately in an era where there were far fewer opportunities for women runners. (Dave's daughters are still active runners and have run 3 marathons including London.)

Dave Williams had another talent besides being a champion runner and coach-- he was also a fine singer. His sister Sarah Murphy recalls her brother dressing all in green and visiting the senior homes to serenade the residents with Irish songs on St. Patrick's Day with his fine tenor. He also sang the National Anthem before the Cape May Footrace each year.

Dave Williams continued to enjoy his daily runs into his 70's, and still won an age group prize at age 70. He was fit enough to easily run up to seven miles at night. His son David Jr. received an insight into what had made his father a champion runner. "I would play golf with my dad after his retirement and he was still fiercely competitive. He never played much golf but he could "will" a putt to go in from 30 yards through force of his will and his competitive fire. He would end up making friends and knowing everything about strangers we had just met on the golf course. He was always interested in others." "He could also look at two runners and say this one has more talent but the other runner has more heart and will be tougher to beat." Alex Williams: "My mother always said my dad was 90% heart, my dad would always say when he talked to an audience of runners that running was the one sport that you could participate in and succeed on the basis of heart and not natural talent alone."

**Browning on the cover of Amateur Athlete magazine for
his 1952 National AAU 30k Championship.**

Sis and Browning Ross after one of Browning's victories.

Browning, Sis and the Duke

WILLIAM (BILLY) THOMPSON, THE "DUKE of Gloucester" looms large in the history of Gloucester City, NJ. Thompson was born in Ireland and moved to Gloucester in 1870 at the age of 22.

He worked at a hotel near the Delaware River, and when the owner would not sell the hotel to him he built and opened his own hotel. Thompson next bought the Hugg Fisheries which gave him rights to the waterfront and enabled him to serve Gloucester City's renowned Shad dinners.

Thompson soon owned 3 and a half miles of Delaware River waterfront property stretching from Westville, NJ to Gloucester. He constructed a 900-acre amusement waterfront "Beachfront" entertainment complex and a hotel and cafe said to seat 5000 diners in Washington Park in Westville.

Thompson also built a railroad connecting Camden and other parts of South Jersey to his complex, and a ferry to carry Philadelphians back and forth across the River.

Accounts of the day said the Duke's amusements were so popular "workers carried dollars by the wheelbarrow full" from the various attractions to Thompson.

Because of Philadelphia's blue laws, the Philadelphia Phillies and A's practiced Sunday on his fields, and the A's occasionally played games in Gloucester Point during this time.

Thompson also hosted boxing matches with visitors taking on the Gloucester Champion. Gloucester had 98 bars, casinos and a number of other attractions including "mermaids" and fortune tellers.

The biggest attraction that Thompson built was a horse racing track on Charles Street. It quickly drew immense crowds and national attention as well as the scrutiny of state officials.

Thompson had also gotten involved in politics and as his political fortunes crumbled his business empire did as well. A fire burned down his amusement park and an anti-gambling faction in the state shut down his race track after 3 years. Thompson soon became bankrupt and needed donations from friends to return to visit Ireland. The Duke died in Ireland, but his wife had his body returned to Gloucester's St Mary's cemetery for burial.

The Duke left behind ten children and a smattering of buildings from his empire including the Thompson Mansion which became an immigration station and later a coast guard base. There was also a swimming pool and pool building built where the Huggs tavern one stood. The Huggs Tavern was where Elizabeth "Betsy" Griscom, a Quaker, married Anglican John Ross to become Betsy Ross. Browning was often asked if he was related to Betsy Ross. He would usually nod yes, and smile. Years later singer Cyndi Lauper would nod to her friend and Browning's daughter Bonnie Ross being related to Betsy Ross in her autobiography.

The pool building held pool equipment, swim lockers, concession stand and popular "Park Dances on its second floor.

Browning came back to the "Park" dances in Gloucester City, NJ during his leave from the Navy. The dances featured large French doors that looked over the Delaware River and captured cool river breezes on hot muggy summer days.

Browning met an attractive girl named Rosemary "Sis" Kelly at one of the Park Dances. Sis was one of ten children of the Kelly family, a Roman Catholic family who attended St. Mary's church and lived less than a mile away from the Park in Gloucester.

The Gloucester Kelly's were said to be distantly related to Philadelphia's renowned Kelly family which included Olympian Jack Kelly and Actress and Princess Grace Kelly. Browning had met and befriended Olympic rower Jack Kelly at the 1948 Olympics.

Pat, the youngest of the 9 Kelly sisters remembers Sis having a lot of boyfriends before she met Browning. "Sometimes Sis would have one boyfriend leaving the back door and another coming to the front. One time I asked her if I should go to the movies with a boy that asked me out that I wasn't sure I liked. She said, "Sure, go to the movies with him, it's just a date, you don't have to marry him!"

"Once Sis started seeing Browning that was the end of her other boyfriends, Browning was humble and very funny, and she became serious about him. He was also quiet. When my parents would have a party at the house Browning would usually stay upstairs and read the paper. He wouldn't be downstairs partying.

He never talked about his running accomplishments, but after I got married, my husband Jack, and Brownie ran from Cape May Beach to Sea Isle City. When they got there, Brownie said to Jack, "Let's run some more miles down the Garden State Parkway." Jack was 18 at the time, on the football team and in great shape, but he couldn't go any further. But Brownie did run down the Parkway and then back to Cape May."

Browning was still attending Villanova while he and Sis were dating, and Sis later remembered, "Before they built the Schuylkill Expressway (the major highway from King of Prussia/Valley Forge to Philadelphia) Browning would occasionally run to or back from Gloucester to Villanova, it's almost a marathon distance!"

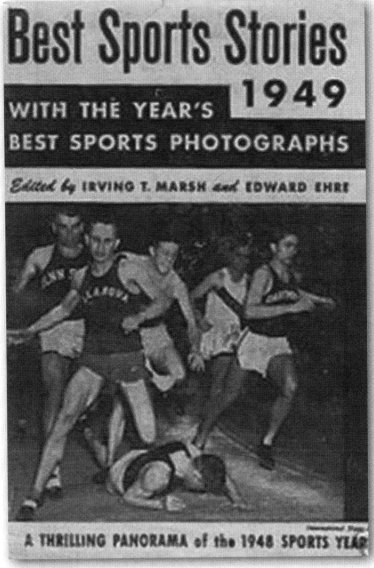

Browning Ross on the cover of Best Sports Stories of 1949.

After Browning graduated Villanova in 1950, he and Sis became engaged. They were married June 10 1950. Because Browning was not Catholic they were married in the rectory of St. Mary's in Gloucester and not in the church. Browning and Sis settled into an apartment in Gloucester City.

St. Joseph's University Cross Country Coach Browning Ross wearing a Villanova singlet (on left) with the team following a barefoot workout.

In 1951 Browning took over as Saint Joseph's College track coach for one year. A write up in "The Hawk," St. Josephs' newspaper contained a great summary of Browning's career to that point.

"Browning Ross succeeds Mr. George Bertlesman as the new track and cross-country mentor. His athletic endeavors I high school and college earned him not only regional and national prominence but have also crowned him a champion in almost every civilized country in the World. Browning's stellar feats began when he was at

Woodbury High. In 1943 Browning was the New Jersey State cross country champ, the New Jersey State mile title holder, and was victorious in the National Interscholastic mile race at Franklin Field."

"In July of the same year, our new coach joined Uncle Sam's forces in the U.S.S Navy. Serving in Europe for eighteen months of his tour of duty, Browning had little time to participate in any track meets and it was feared that a fine track career might be ended. Bur prior to his discharge from the Navy in March of 1946, he won the K of C Indoor Two-Mile Championship in New York City. One of the most talked of freshmen ever to enter Villanova; our very personable coach began his collegiate career in September of 1946. As a yearling, he finished second in both the National AAU 10,000 meters and the IC4A mile run.

As a sophomore, possibly his greatest single season, Browning won, among many other events, the Washington State Indoor mile title in the very fine time of 4:13.7, the NCAA 3000-meter steeplechase event. Later in the season, he was named to the All-America track team. It was also during 1948 that Browning made the U.S. Olympic Team that traveled to London. During his stay in Europe, he raced in England, Ireland, France and Norway. It was in the latter country that he acquired new Scandinavian methods of training runners which he hopes to apply in his teaching Hawk cinder-men."

"During his junior and senior years at Villanova, he finished second and third respectively in the IC4A and NCAA Cross Country meets. He holds the very unusual distinction of never being beaten in either the mile or the two-mile races while at Woodbury and Villanova and is seven times Middle Atlantic and AAU mile champ. His best time for the mile is 4:13.2, and 9:09.7 is his best for the two mile. He holds the Middle Atlantic Cross-Country record as he traveled the 10,000-meter distance in 30:33.

In February of 1951, Browning graduated with a B.S. in Education and then immediately returned to the cinders. In the next three months, he traveled to four different continents and visited over twenty world republics, racing against the finest competition in the world. Browning looks upon his initial venture at coaching as a challenge and hopes to field a properly balanced group of seasoned veterans and promising freshmen that will lead to an unbeaten season."

The St. Joseph's track team finished 8 and 1 under Browning. Their only loss was to a powerful LaSalle College team... Browning left St Josephs to run in the Pan Am Games and to resume training for the 1952 Helsinki Games, and Bertlesman returned as Coach.

In June 1951, Browning and Sis's first child, a daughter, Bonnie was born. After graduating from Villanova, Browning took the mail carrier test and was hired as a Woodbury postman. This article appeared in the Woodbury Times weekly news section the same month:

"Thoughtful- As one of the United States top distance runners Browning Ross has frequently heard the plaudits of the crowd, but he remains the same "Brownie" who thrilled schoolboy sports followers with his cinder path deeds while at Woodbury High School. He was always unassuming and thoughtful of others. Ross has been carrying mail in Woodbury this summer and this incident shows he still has those traits. One of the homes on his route had been waiting anxiously for weeks for a letter from their soldier son in Korea. Browning had completed his day's delivery and upon his return to the post office that afternoon he saw a letter from the soldier, which had arrived after the morning mail, had been sorted. Knowing the anxiety of the family, Browning didn't wait until his regular delivery the next morning. Instead, he made an extra trip that afternoon to deliver the long-awaited letter. It was his thoughtfulness that will long be remembered and appreciated by the family."

The Duke's horse racing track was eventually put to good use as a running track in a Charles Street sports complex in Gloucester. In the early 1950's Browning put on all-comers track meets at the Charles Street track in the early.

Forty years later Browning recalled: "We charged a quarter entry for each event. I had a few people in line signing up for different events and I looked up and saw Steve Van Buren, the running back for the Philadelphia Eagles in line. He told me he wanted to enter the 100-yard dash.

I told him the entry fee was a quarter. He nodded and said, "I'm Steve Van Buren." I said I know, but the entry fee is still a quarter." I felt funny saying that, but he was a down to earth guy and didn't seem to mind. Van Buren was a great sprinter in college, running 9.8 for Louisiana State. I remember him winning easily, but it was shocking to see him there in line! (Running Back Van Buren was also the Eagles first Hall of Fame inductee and was voted the greatest Eagle of all time in 2007. He led the Eagles to their first NFL Championships in 1948 and 1949).

Many remember a similar story year's later, when the Water Street track complex was long gone, cleared away for an industrial park, involving Clearview, (NJ) High School schoolboy sprinter Peanut Gaines. Gaines became a national sensation in 1967, after running 9.3 in the 100-yard dash to better Jesse Owens national high school record of 9.4 set in 1933. Gaines reported to one of Browning's all-comers meets in 1967 or 1968. Gaines was told about and paid the low meet entry— possibly 50 cents at that time to compete. Browning would continue to put on all- comers track meets by himself into the 1990's.

In the early 1950's Browning and Dave Williams were living a few streets away from each other in Gloucester, and frequently trained together early in the morning. They would sometimes stop at the home of a nearby 14-year-old Gloucester Catholic freshman Joe Murphy and ask him to run with them. Murphy would later go on to be a star multi-sport athlete and then a teacher, athletic director and South Jersey Hall of Fame coach at Gloucester Catholic.

"When two Olympic-caliber runners knock on your door and ask you to go running with them, you don't really have a choice but to accompany them. I could only stay with them for a couple of miles as they continued their training run, headed out of Gloucester but it made a big impression on me," Murphy remembered.

"A teacher and a mentor are so important in the development of a young person's life. The decisions a young person makes are heavily influenced by what a coach or a teacher might suggest. That young person is on a life path when he or she is 17 years of age, and you can't underestimate the importance of an influence like they had on me."

Browning and Dave Williams also started the Saint Mary's track guild, an offshoot of the Saint Mary's parish men's guild.

Tom Bowe, a youth at the time remembered: "Monsignor Edward (Big Ed) Lucitt was the driving force behind the St. Mary's men's Guild that was started probably by Monsignor Brick during the depression. Both priests were similar in nature, great heart, passionate and when something went wrong they took no prisoners. Big Ed was my first basketball and football coach in grammar school. The men of the Guild made fishcakes on the first floor and delivered them and other food to the citizenship of Gloucester during those awful years of the depression. During the war years, while I was in grammar school (St Mary's), all the fellows were in the service and the men's guild evolved into the junior guild. It also kept a lot of young guys out of trouble by giving them a place to hang out. Not to mention that Big Ed also kept an eye on us and the building."

Browning and Dave Williams met with the St Mary's priests Father Edward Lucitt and Brick, and proposed the track club offshoot of the guild. The St. Mary's track guild would evolve into the St. Mary's track team and then eventually the Gloucester Catholic track team. Coincidentally Joe Murphy would later start the first Gloucester Catholic cross-country team in the early 1960's, partly as a vehicle for the Gloucester Catholic basketball team to get in shape.

Browning, Sis, and Bonnie lived on Park Avenue in Gloucester City, and Browning's hundreds of trophies resided in Woodbury with his parents.

Browning Ross and Curt Stone 1951 Pan Am Games Steeplechase.

The First Pan American Games, and Sir Roger

BROWNING HAD TWO OF HIS greatest races during the Pan Am Games, in March of 1951, finishing first in the 1500 meters and second, in a virtual tie for first in the 3000-meter Steeplechase.

During the Games, Browning wrote letters to Sis describing the Games and their pomp, along with a few strange happenings including the controversial tie for first in the Steeplechase.

"Dear Sis,

We left by bus at 4 to get to the stadium on the other side of Buenos Aires and didn't arrive until 8. What a long ride! People by the thousands lined the roads all the way to the stadium. There must have been 100 busloads of athletes from all the countries.

They really take their sports seriously down here! President Peron makes everyone participate. All through the city, there are thousands of sporting clubs, swimming pools, and tennis courts and everybody plays tennis, swims, and plays basketball soccer etc.

The opening ceremony is patterned after the Olympics. Each nation marches in and they have a big fireworks display, Argentina marched in last and the whole place-- 130,000 people went mad!

They only charge 50 cents for the best seats in the house—that's why they draw so many. They should do that in the states, they would make out better.

We got back at 1 am after the opening ceremony and had supper in the mess hall here. Steaks again! Every day we have steak!

I slept until 10:30 then worked out twice today and lay in the sun in the grass the rest of the afternoon. It is always about 70-75 degrees here. They have 3 ½ hours for lunch here- Siesta time, they don't believe in rushing anything."

Browning's next letter gave a description of the Games' famous Steeplechase race. "Well Stone and I caused a little rhubarb yesterday in the Steeplechase. We had a big lead so we tied for first and the Argentines considered it an insult that we took it easy on the last two laps.

They have a rule that a runner must run to win. So, they were going to disqualify us. But after an hour of wrangling, they made Stone the winner after we explained we were taking it easy for the 1500-meter final today. Boy! When Stone and I were running in the lead you could have heard a pin drop but on the first lap when the Argentine led- what a racket! 60,000 people were there. Some race. (Note: Browning does not mention in his letter that he won the 1500 meter final).

After the race coming out of the stadium with Stone, we got cornered by about a thousand people and missed the bus. We were signing autographs for over an hour. I've never seen anything like this place. One lady wanted to give me a cow to back to the USA believe it or not! (She really meant it). So, the people here didn't seem to care who won or how. I guess it was just Games Officials from Argentina. Jim Kelly our coach said the hell with them we did the right thing.

When (Ricardo) Bralo (of Argentina) beat Jim Twomey (in the 5000) the other night the people of Buenos Aires gave him a new Buick automobile. Great place to live!

The US meets Argentina in the basketball final Thursday night in what should be some game since Argentina beat the US in Dec. in the World Amateur tournament. I hope we can get in... They have a stadium where they play that is supposed to seat over 20,000 and they pack it every night for basketball. Argentina has a player named Oscar Furlong who every pro club in the US is after. But he prefers to stay here because he makes out better as an amateur?!

I got a silver medal in the Steeplechase yesterday; you would think that they would give you better prizes for such a big meet. If we get up to Trinidad, they said we could win some silverware sets. If!! I love you more than anything.

Brownie

Curt Stone recalled the 1951 Pan Am Games sixty years later,"Browning went to the Pan American Games in 1951 and won the 1500 meters (4:00.4) and was second to me in the Steeplechase (both 9:32.0). There were only 4 American distance runners and one of them a marathoner who also ran the 10,000 meters. The other three of us tried to cover all the races. At the end of the week, we were pretty tired.

John Twomey was 2nd in the 5,000 meters, but otherwise, we were able to win the 10,000 (Stone 31:08.6), the Steeplechase and the 1500 meters. So Brownie had a Pan American championship in Argentina in the 1500 for the first Pan Am Games.

Browning and I ran into the finish together in the Steeplechase, but not holding hands as the newspaper article said and the judges made me the winner. I thought one championship (10,000 meters) was enough so I didn't press the last 150 yards and Browning refused to sprint ahead as he could have. Browning must have decided I should be the winner and refused to pass me. A sorry thing we both regretted I am sure.

The March 6, 1951, New York Times carried a major account of the 1500- meter race and its controversy:

"Browning Ross, tiny cross-country specialist from Gloucester, N.J. scored one of the victories in the 1,500-meter run, which for a while threatened to produce the first international incident of the hemisphere Olympics.

After he had staged a terrific spurt to win the metric mile, Ross and Argentina's Oscar Gauharou began arguing openly before the 10,000 fans in the vast River Plate Stadium.

However, the two were pulled apart before blows could be struck and after tempers cooled, the whole thing turned out to be a case of mistaken identity.

Ross became incensed because his teammate John Twomey had been jostled off a curve, being forced into the grass for several strides. Ross thought that Gauharou did it and challenged him. However, later members of the United States team said the jostling was done by another Argentine, Hugo Ponce.

At any rate, the officials went into a series of huddles after the incident and it was several minutes before they officially announced that Ross was the winner in 4 minutes 4/10 of a second. Chile's Aravena was second and then followed Twomey, the former Illinois star from Roseville, Ill. and then Curtis Stone of Brooklyn, already a winner of the 10,000 meters and 3,000 meters steeplechase."

The Pan Am games ended with a memorable closing for Browning and the other athletes as they shook hands with Argentine President Juan and first Lady Eva Peron before departing the Pan Am Games. Next Browning with the support of the AAU went to compete in a series of international track meets for the US.

First, to Cuba, where he won the 1500 meters and placed third in the pole vault, while fellow Woodbury schoolmate Roscoe Lee Browne won the 800 meters.

Next to Chile where Browning won the 1500 meters and the 800 meters.

From there to England for the British Games mile race against Bannister, and then a two-mile race. A London newspaper described the roar of the crowd of over 40,000 spectators for Browning's mile and 2-mile races "as loud as a Wembley Football final."

Browning also finished second in a mile race in Ireland where the prize was a "zip bag". Next, the team moved onto to run the Scandinavian track circuit for the United States in what was billed as a "mini-Olympics" against a combined Scandinavian team consisting of runners from Denmark, Norway, Finland, and Sweden. It was a trip that would have a major influence on Browning's own training philosophy.

Browning was introduced to fartlek or "speed play" training for the first time by the Scandinavian runners, and he would incorporate speed training during his runs in his own rather low mileage training with spectacular results at various distances through the 1950's.

Browning wrote to Sis every day during the trip. On his way back from Scandinavia, Browning sent a post card home, "Just arrived in Goose Bay Labrador. Decided to run against the Eskimos instead, cold up here, be here an hour, Love Brownie."

While Browning was racing in Scandinavia, Sis received a consoling letter from Browning's aunt telling her to hang in, that Browning's running and time away from home would surely be over after this trip, "The Postman's job came just in time, with young Bonnie at home and with Browning's invitations to travel to races around the world a source of worry Sis could finally relax knowing that her worries were not in vain as Browning had a steady position."

Even though her father was away from home for a few weeks on a once in a lifetime running adventure, Bonnie remembers it fondly, "Dad's prize in one of his Scandinavian races was a whale's tooth, which I brought into the show and tell in school. Not too many kids could say the same."

Browning Ross, 1951 Pan Am Games 1500 meter Gold medalist.

Boston to Helsinki

IN THE 1950's WHILE ELVIS and Frank Sinatra were dominating the American music charts, and Ted Williams and Stan Musial were gathering sports headlines for winning baseball's batting titles, Browning was garnering his own front-page sports headlines for winning more races at various distances than anyone else in the country. After graduating Villanova, he used his 48 second quarter mile speed to win a mind-boggling number of races each weekend from one to eighteen miles. He sometimes won distances at both ends of the spectrum in the same weekend.

Jumbo Elliott noted, "Browning must have won more trophies than *anyone* in the world."

In March of 1952, Browning won an invitational 12-mile White Horse run in Baltimore. In the White Horse Run Browning bucked 40 mile per hour head winds and 37-degree temperatures to run 1:07, beating some Olympians in the race. Browning had brought two of his St. Joe's distance runners, Joe Martin and John Cunningham along to the White Horse Run and they finished 8th and 9th.

Browning then went north of the border in March to win the Hamilton, Ontario around the Bay race, the oldest race in North America. Browning set a course record in running the 19 mile, 168-yard race in 1:48.25.

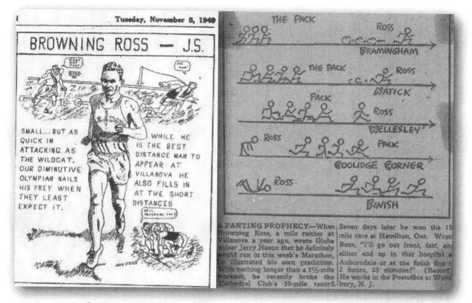

Left, Browning portrayed in a cartoon from a 1949 Villanova newspaper. Right, a few years later Browning drew this humorous self-deprecating cartoon about his projected Boston Marathon finish.

One of the races that Browning did not dominate was the 1952 Boston Marathon.

In the pre-race Boston newspaper coverage of the marathon, Browning was mentioned as one of the dark horses to win based on his victory and course record in the Cathedral 10 mile in Boston the week before. In winning the Cathedral ace, Browning cut 2 minutes 49 seconds from the Cathedral course record.

In order to enter the marathon, Browning had to find a substitute coach for his Saint Joseph's College track team who had a Meet with Temple that day. Former St. Josephs Coach Bertlesman agreed to return to St Joseph's for the day so Browning could run the marathon.

Going into the race Browning's training was subpar for the marathon distance because of work and injury. Working his full-time job as a Woodbury mail carrier, and then hurrying to St. Joseph's to coach the track team left little time for Browning to get in his usual training of 40 miles a week.

Browning had also developed a sore Achilles tendon, which bothered him on the few longer runs he was able to get in. Still, he was disappointed to finish only 19th in 3:18 in the marathon. After a strong start, he faded in the hot (88 degrees) and humid conditions. Doroteo Flores, a native Guatemalan described by the press as an "Indian laborer in a Guatemala Mill" won by 5 minutes in 2:31:53. Browning's friend Ted Corbitt finished a strong 6th.

But Boston would be one of the few races Browning would not win that year. After the Boston Marathon, Browning coined a phrase he would often repeat, "All the speed in the world won't help you when you can't run another step."

In the months prior to the US Olympic Trials in Los Angeles in July, Browning won every race he entered at a variety of distances. After Browning won the 15-mile Firestone War Veteran race in Ontario, Canada by three minutes, Ontario newspaper headlines hailed Browning with the headline the "Running Postman Rings Bell".

The following week he easily won a five-mile cross country race in Trenton in 26:41. Both races were tune-ups for the following week's invitational mile race on the Boardwalk in Atlantic City. On May 12, Browning won the Boardwalk mile in front of an estimated 40,000 spectators lining the Boardwalk from Steel Pier to Convention Hall. His winning time of 4:05 was according to the Philadelphia and Atlantic City newspapers the "fourth fastest mile timer ever run in America."

The race was loaded with Olympians and received massive pre, and post-race press coverage in the Northeast's newspapers as a serious attempt to break the four-minute mile. In a thrilling race, Browning edged 1948 Olympic 1500 meter finalist Don Gehrman, who had won 39 consecutive major mile races against top national and international competition from 1949 to 1952, and also Olympians Curt Stone and Bill and Horace Ashenfelter.

Browning followed up his mile victory by winning the AAU's Mid-Atlantic 2-mile Championship. Next, he returned to Atlantic City to win the AAU 10,000 meters in a record 31.36. A few days later he won the IC4A 5000 meters in Philadelphia in 15:26 running for the Penn Athletic Club.

Browning continued to tune up for the Olympic Trials by winning the Penn AC 3-mile race in 14:32, a record that stood for 15 years.

The cold war focused much more attention on the 1952 Olympics in Helsinki than the 48 Games in London because of the U.S. Soviet rivalry.

In June, Bob Hope and Bing Crosby hosted a 14 ½-hour telethon with over 250 performers including Dean Martin and Jerry Lewis, to raise money for the US Olympic Team.

Bob Hope started off the telethon by saying, "I guess Joe Stalin thinks he is going to show soft capitalist Americans. We've got to cut him down to size. This (telethon) is the best thing I've ever undertaken. Brother Bing and I are going to throw our best punches."

The telethon was watched by over 50 million viewers and was Bing Crosby's first television appearance. 1 million dollars were pledged; double the half-million dollar goal. Only one-third of that amount was ever collected. It was thought that some rescinded their pledges after they saw the half-million dollar goal reached. The $300,000 was enough to fund the U.S Team trip to Helsinki-- the first time the US team flew to the Olympics.

As he looked to the Olympic Trials in Los Angeles at the end of June, Browning had the enviable position of trying to decide which events he should run to try to qualify for the Olympics. He decided to run both the 10,000 meters and the 3000-meter Steeplechase. He finished fourth in the 10,000 meters behind Curt Stone, Fred Wilt, and Horace Ashenfelter in 31:03.

In the Steeple, Browning finished third behind Horace and Bill Ashenfelter in 9:08.3 to make his second Olympic team.

Browning marched in his second Olympic opening ceremonies in Helsinki. "We came into the stadium in alphabetical order and I was behind boxer Floyd Patterson. He kind of swaggered from side to side, and I kept walking on his heels. He turned around and gave me some quizzical looks!"

On his first day in Finland Browning experienced terrible stomach cramps. He was hospitalized for four days over concerns he might have appendicitis. When appendicitis was ruled out Browning was released from the hospital. With just four days of workouts remaining before his first race, Browning tried to make up for lost time. In his first workout, he stepped on a water sprinkler and sprained his ankle.

Browning recalled the atmosphere of Helsinki Games in a 1984 interview with Bob Shryock, "The Russians didn't start competing in the Olympics until 1952 in Helsinki," Ross said. "We stayed in the Olympic Village, but the Russians chose to stay outside in a different village. One day, when they came to the track, they looked at us through a fence as though we were from Mars. Life Magazine got a picture of that and ran it on its cover."

Finally getting a chance to compete, Browning finished 12th in heat 2 of the Olympic Steeplechase Qualifier in 9:44 missing a final round qualification.

Years later when I asked Browning about what had hospitalized him he said, "I guess it was just a bad stomach ache, but it sure knocked me down. When we got to Finland it was all the food you could eat for the Olympians. I remember eating a lot-- who knows; maybe I just ate too much!"

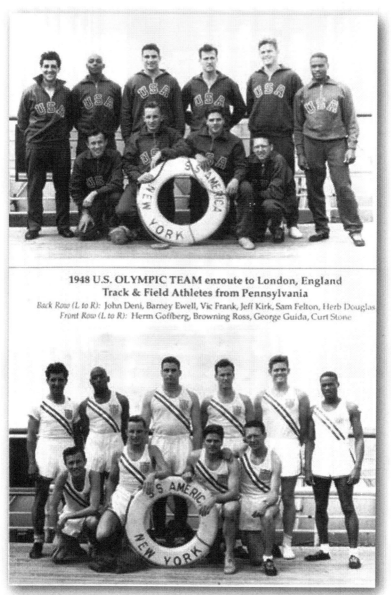

1948 U.S. OLYMPIC TEAM enroute to London, England
Track & Field Athletes from Pennsylvania
Back Row (L to R): John Deni, Barney Ewell, Vic Frank, Jeff Kirk, Sam Felton, Herb Douglas
Front Row (L to R): Herm Goffberg, Browning Ross, George Guida, Curt Stone

Browning sailing on the SS America with fellow Pennsylvania Olympians.

Memories of Two Olympics Games

Browning wrote about his experience participating in two Olympic Games for a 1976 Olympic preview that was published by the Road Runners Club in 1976.

"The 14th Olympiad at London in 1948 was significant in that the Games were being renewed after a 12-year absence due to World War II.

The British organized the Games in style; they had trained officials, they understood the principals of management, and they utilized 7 different centers to conduct the events.

Most of the competition was held at Empire Stadium, Wembley, in a northwest suburb of London. The stadium contained a newly installed 400-meter cinder track. The stadium accommodated some 83,000 spectators and was jammed for the eight days of track and field competition.

The US track team was selected only two days before our departure from New York. It was hard to realize that we had made the team even while en route to London. (One athlete managed to get leave papers from his job signed only minutes before he was to be processed for passage.)

Managers of the team were going crazy trying to get passports in order. However, we climbed aboard the S.S. America on July 14th and the US Olympic team was on its way to London town.

P.T. Barnum must have traveled with an American Olympic team since our crossing was so much like a circus. Literally everywhere on the ship, the athletes were tuning up. Hildegard, Salvador Dali, female members of the Kennedy clan (Father Joseph P Kennedy had been U.S. Ambassador to England before the war) and hundreds of other passengers took a back seat to the athletes at their shipboard training sessions. Jim Fuchs put the shot right over the net onto the promenade deck below, just missing me running by.

Bingo, horse races, movies, fantastic food, dancing and deck chairs all filled the extra hours on the "floating hotel." The climax of the trip came two nights before we docked; the athletes gave an amateur show. These athletes could draw a crowd to the theater as well as the sports arena.

While the athletes ran or lifted or swam, the newspaper reporters sulked. Even then it was all too common for the sports page back home to feature temper tantrums or rule breaking. No such stories broke as everyone bent over backward to deflect criticism. At 21 cents, a cabled word from aboard the ship, you'd want a hot story too. They were rewarded later when they could send back such stories as Olympic records by Bill Porter (100m hurdles), Ray Cochran (400m hurdles) and the fantastic feats of the immortal Emil Zatopek.

The hospitality of the English people was apparent as soon as we docked at Southampton. Passes for buses and trains in London and badges to take us inside Wembley were given to everyone. My event was the 3000-meter steeplechase. I was fortunate enough to make the finals where I led with two laps remaining and then faded to 7th in the 12-man field. Probably our best runner was Californian Bob McMillen. He was running a beautiful race in his heat of the steeplechase when he took a header into the water and had to take kidding the rest of the trip about the diving team having missed a good bet! (Pictures showed him completely submerged).

In 1952, he came back at Helsinki and finished second in the 1500 meters by inches. After the London Olympics, we competed in meets in Prague, Berlin, Norway, Swede, Holland, Paris, and Ireland before boarding the S.S. Washington on August 27th for a pleasant trip home.

The weight lifters continue to lift weights, the gymnasts continued to work on the bars, and the runners continued to run. They were simply beginning their training rot the Pan American Games in 1951 and the Olympic Games in Helsinki.

Helsinki…. a whole new ball game by then. We flew through the air with consummate ease via Pan American World Air Ways… things were better organized at the U.S. end… a spectacular nationwide telethon started by Bob Hope and Bing Crosby (13 ½ hours) raised $310,000.

Before the team left there was a rousing demonstration arranged by Mayor of New York which included a Broadway parade and an elaborate luncheon.

In Finland, there were thousands of competitors from 69 different countries and officials started thinking of fixed standards to be met by the entrants in future games. Somehow looking back, I cannot help but think the London Games brought back finer memories.

Editor's Note: Ross feels that the U.S. team felt closer on the 1948 London trip because of the time spent on the ship compared to the plane travel for Helsinki. "Since flying is the way to go now, perhaps something is missing in team spirit."

The ship that brought the American athletes to London in 1948, the SS America, had a history as eventful as any of the athletes who made the voyage onboard.

Launched in 1939 as a cruise ship in Newport News Virginia, and sponsored by first Lady Eleanor Roosevelt, the SS America was one of the few ocean liners whose interior was designed by women.

Because of a dire need for military transports in World War II, the S.S. America was pressed into military service as a troop transport ship and returned to Newport News, VA for service.

The ship was renamed the USS West Point in 1941. The USS West Point carried over 350,000 troops the most of any Navy troopship. Traveling to Italian and French ports on the European battlefront the ship also carried prisoners of war, UN officials, civilians, children, and USO entertainers. After being re-titled, the SS America she continued to make trans-European trips in the civilian sector including of course Browning and the US Olympians bound for London in 1948.

The SS America was sold in 1964 to the Greek ocean shipping Chandris Group and renamed the Australis. The Australis provided regular service from Southampton, England to Australia and New Zealand until 1977. The next year she was sold to Venture Cruises of New York and renamed back to S.S. America. It was in a sad state of disrepair. On its first cruise, headed to Nova Scotia, it was overbooked and passengers mutinied and forced the ship to return to New York. After the first cruise to Nova Scotia, the ship was ordered sold at auction to pay debts of $2.5 million in civil claims from passengers. Chandris repurchased the ship for 1 million dollars and renamed her Italis. The Italis had her funnel stack removed and subsequently passed through iterations as a hotel ship, a Mediterranean cruise ship, and then was sold to become a prison ship in Beirut.

Next named Alferdoss, the ship's bilge pipes burst and it was sold for $2 million in scrap. The scrappers defaulted in payment, and the ship was sold again as the American star and re-fitted as a five-star hotel shop off the coast of Thailand.

The ship was being towed to Greece when it encountered an Atlantic storm, which necessitated a helicopter rescue of the crew. The ship was left adrift and ran aground in the Canary Islands where pounding surf broke the ship in two in only 48 hours. The ship slowly sank until in 2010 only about 15 feet of the bow remained above water. It was a sad end for a ship that had contributed so much to history including the 1948 Olympic Games in its 55-year run.

A Third Olympics?

ANTICIPATING A POSSIBLE THIRD OLYMPIC bid in the 1956 Summer Olympics in Melbourne Australia, Browning had a full racing season in 1956.

In March, Browning and Luther Burdelle finished first in a 2- man marathon relay from Annapolis to Baltimore. They ran a combined 2:32 despite a 25 mile per hour headwind and frigid March temperatures.

On Good Friday, March 30, Browning won the 15 mile Hamilton Veterans Road Race for the fifth time in 1:23:04, just seconds off his course record set in 1953.

The following week Browning won the Cathedral 10 mile in Boston in 55:40 despite arriving the morning of the race.

Browning went on to win an Olympic Development mile in 4:21 and a Baltimore three mile in 15:11 also in the spring.

In June of 1956 Browning and Dave Williams traveled to Atlantic City to interview for teaching and track and cross-country coaching positions at Atlantic City High School. Williams turned down the position after determining the 120-mile commute from Gloucester to Atlantic City was too far. Browning accepted a position as teacher and coach at Atlantic City High and resigned from Woodbury High. Shortly after he received an offer from Woodrow Wilson High School in Camden, NJ to teach history and coach the school's first cross-country team.

The Olympic Trials were held in Los Angeles June 28-29 in the Los Angeles Coliseum. Browning received an invitation to take part. The marathon team, which Browning was considering was picked from among the top

Boston Marathon finishers and the AAU National Marathon Championships on September 30 in Yonkers, New York. The 10k runners were to be selected June 23 in Bakersfield California.

Because Browning had just accepted the Woodrow Wilson position, and the Melbourne Olympics were to be held in late November and early December, Browning rejected the Olympic invitation. In his reply, he cited the extended leave he would have to take from his job and absence from family as the reason for not attending the Olympic trials to see a third Olympic bid.

Freed from the pressure of trying to qualify for a third Olympics, Browning won a number of races in a variety of distances every weekend.

He won his fourth straight AAU 10k Championship in 31:29.

Then he suffered what the newspapers called "an accident at home" but still won the AAU 3 ½-mile race despite a bleeding right shin.

Browning just missed an American record on the track in the hour run but won his tenth AAU 10k cross-country championship by outkicking Alex Breckenridge from Villanova (a 1960 Olympian).

The following week Browning outkicked Breckenridge again to win the AAU 25k championship in 1:22.05. The race made all of the Philadelphia sports headlines with a strange twist. "Ross Gains Championship but at a Cost" was a typical headline, as Browning was unable to find his gold watch, presented to him by his 1948 Villanova teammates upon his return from the Olympic, after the race.

The following week Browning won the Woodbury 10 mile for the fourth time in 52:41 and the newspapers reported a happy ending to the watch saga. Much to his embarrassment Browning had discovered his watch tucked in his running shoe after the previous week's race.

Browning went on to win a 5 mile AAU run and was pictured getting hugs from Bonnie and Barry in the Philadelphia newspapers. Next was a victory in a hilly 3-mile cross-country race in Fairmount Park in 15:10 and of course a Berwick victory once again.

Sports of the Times Columnist Ed Phettepace wrote an article about Browning that summed up his running achievements up to the spring of 1956 as Woodrow Wilson track coach. "At the age of 32 he is still competing in major meets and it won't be surprising if Browning Ross is still running in championship form at the age of 50."

The mid-1950's were obviously a far gentler and more positive era in journalism as Phettepace ended the article with an acrostic spelling of Browning:

B reaker of records
R unner extraordinary
O lympic symbol
W inner of medals
N ational fame
I nspirational leader
N ations Cross-Country Ace
G reat Competitor

Sara Marie Herold Cardenas was a student of Browning's at Woodrow Wilson and remembers him 60 years later as her favorite teacher. "I can still see him perched on the end of the desk. He offered great insights, many from his world travel experiences as a runner, and he had a great sense of humor-- but I felt bad because it was kind of wasted on some of the boys in the class who were just interested in goofing around."

Jim O'Hara was a classmate of Sara's and a member of the Woodrow Wilson Track and Cross-Country teams. He recalled, "After one of our meets Browning took us to his parent's house in Woodbury and then to his house. I remember all of his trophies, it seems like hundreds were stored in his parent's house, and he didn't have enough room in his house. Some of the trophies at his parents' house were as high as a horse."

"I remember sitting in English class and I looked out the window at 2 o'clock and saw Browning running laps around the school building during his free period, getting in his workout."

Larry Delaney was a close friend of Browning's, a frequent racer, and a teacher and coach at Cheltenham High School in Pennsylvania before becoming a professor at Rowan University, "I remember we had a meet with Browning's brand new cross-country team at Woodrow Wilson that year and they beat us easily. He had the team up and competitive very quickly but he was the same low-key Browning."

Harry Berkowitz was one of the Woodrow Wilson runners on whom Browning had the greatest influence. Berkowitz bristled under the "General Patton" style of the previous track coach but blossomed into a good runner under Browning and a competitive runner for more than 50 years. Harry said, "Browning always treated me as a friend. I traveled to races with Browning, Kenny Lovell, a Wilson teammate and Tom Osler. Many times, over the years I would be running a race and Browning would drive up and ask me if I needed any coaching. Then he would laugh and drive off. Years later he would show up at the 6 Day Races held at the Cooper River and ask me the same question when I was in my 40's."

Tom Osler attended nearby Camden High and remembered Browning training on Camden Highs' cross-country course, "Browning was in such good shape then that I saw him run the Farnham Park Cross-Country course twice, and each time he ran faster than the course record. The record was extremely fast and was held by an outstanding runner, a high school state champion at the time."

When Browning recalled his teaching days at Woodrow Wilson, he often mentioned being in the office mimeographing papers when the son of heavyweight boxing champion Jersey Joe Walcott (Arnold Cream) was brought to the office for disciplinary reasons. "One of the administrators was saying to him, "Now Mr. Cream you know you have to respect the teacher." I'll never forget his answer, "He don't respect me, I don't respect him." When you really think about it most of the problems people have with each other come down to a lack of respect."

Browning also later remembered another thing about his teaching days, "One of the worst things about trying to train, when you are a teacher-- a kid with a bad cold would come up a few inches away and say to you, "Oh, Mr.

Ross, I feel so sick, cough, cough!" In a day or so you'd be coughing and sick too."

Jim Flanagan was the top high school milers in South Jersey and a graduate of the Camden Catholic class of 1955: "I didn't know Browning then, but it gave you a sense that great running accomplishments were possible knowing there was an Olympian named Browning Ross living just a couple miles away in Woodbury." (Flanagan went on to win age group prizes in his 70's at the Boston Marathon and Broad Street Run in Philadelphia).

The Magnificent
Sao Silvestre Road Race-
Glamour Race of them All!

THE BEST NEWS FOR BROWNING in 1956 was that he qualified for the Sao Paulo, Brazil Midnight run with a third-place finish to Horace Ashenfelter and John Macy of Houston in a "rain-swept" Senior National 10k cross-country championships on December 11. Browning would accept the invitation to Sao Paolo and would always call the Midnight New Year's Eve 7.3-kilometer Sao Silvestre (Saint Silvester) race one of the highlights of his running career.

Browning often said the most memorable race he ran in his career was the Sao Silvestre Road Race in Sao Paolo Brazil. In January 1957, Browning traveled to Sao Paolo to run both the 3000-meter Steeplechase and the 7,400-meter road run. He won the Steeplechase in 9:35 beating an international field and wrote about the Road Race in an article entitled "The Magnificent Sao Silvestre Road Race- Glamour Race of Them All."

"Having been selected by the National AAU to represent the United States in the XXXII Sao Silvestre International road run in Sao Paulo, Brazil, I departed from New York's Idlewild Airport on December 27th via a Varig, (Brazilian) Super Constellation airplane. After a 25-hour trip (with stops at Ciudad Trujillo, Belen, and Rio De Janiero) I arrived in

Sao Paulo with all the fanfare of a visiting dignitary, much to my "sleepy" embarrassment.

Seven of Europe's finest distance runners had arrived a few days previously, and after my arrival at the beautiful Hotel Florida, we became fast friends despite the barrier of speaking eight different languages.

The accommodations at the Hotel Florida were excellent and made us almost reluctant to accept the invitations extended us during the holiday season to dine and visit with our many newly founded Brazilian friends. The waiters in the hotel dining room must have had special training in patience when the eight foreign athletes began ordering their own favorite foods in eight different languages, much to the amusement of the rest of the diners.

Each evening, we all trained together at the beautiful Tiete Regattas Club shaded by tall palms and other tropical trees and swam in the beautiful club pool. Since all of us had left winter weather behind we were especially grateful to the Tiete Club officials, (especially Rolf Eric Haikkola, who had left behind in his native Finland, two feet of snow and below zero weather!)

At approximately 15 minutes before midnight on New Year's Eve, the 7,400-meter road race through the main streets of Sao Paolo began amid a thunderous roar of cheers, sirens, and gunfire, colorful display of fireworks, and a shower of confetti, ankle deep in some places. Up to a million-people strained at the ropes to wish the runners luck with a "whack" on the back! One word- **petrified**, described my emotions! The tumult was even greater immediately after the race when the Brazilians acclaimed Manuel Faria of Portugal, 'The upset winner who pulverized the prognosticators.' The victory was acclaimed as half Portugal's and half Brazil's since Brazil is a Portuguese-speaking nation.

Following the race, the athletes were the guest of the Journal a Gazeta Esportiva, sponsor of the international competition, at a gigantic New Year's Eve Party on the rooftop of the ultra-modern newspaper plant, which also houses their own radio station.

The prizes were awarded on the evening of Jan 2nd. Two of the auditoriums of the Gazeta were needed to accommodate the runners and interested spectators. Faria received approximately 12 prizes, including a gold cup for the Portuguese federation valued at $1800. (For 9th place, I received a beautiful bronze statue trophy, a map of Brazil made of gold coins, a silver medallion, an enormous bag of flour and a couple dozen eggs.)

The 27-year-old likable Faria, who holds all the National Records in Portugal from 1500 meters to 10.000 meters broke down and cried as he received his many and just awards. Last year he finished in 40th place and his one aim all year was to <u>win</u> Sao Silvestre!

Friday night at "Estadio Municipal" at Pacaembu before a good crowd- for a 4-event competition- we competed in 4 distance track races (under the lights). I had the good fortune to win the 3000-meter steeplechase with a sprint in the home stretch but the misfortune to be disqualified later by an Uruguayan official for stepping on the grass after hitting the curb on the dimly lighted bend. (Note: the official's Uruguayan countryman Viterbo Rivro was second). The following morning, I was given a medal by the Athletic Federation of Sao Paulo (whether it was the winner's award or a special award I still haven't been able to determine). Faria captured the 5000 meters, bringing another thunderous ovation and fireworks display from the enthusiastic spectators.

After much urging to stay on in Sao Paulo for another 4 event "Distance Meet" at the Tiete Club on Sunday, Jan 6th I had to comply with the wishes of my employer, Woodrow Wilson HS, Camden N.J. and return to the states.

My deepest appreciation and fondest memories of the finest trip I've ever had under AAU sponsorship go to the Gazeta Esportiva, it's director, Carlos Joel Nelli, race officials Henrique Nicolini and Hop-step and Jumper, Adhemar Ferreira da Silva, my wonderful interpreters Claudia Violani and Eso Murto and many others connected with Sao Silvestre, the most fabulous race in the world!"

Browning finished 9th in the Midnight run in 22:56, his great kick enabling him to hold off six trailing runners who were within 5 seconds of him. He often mentioned remembering carrying all of his prizes-- including the huge trophy and bag of flour while trying to catch a train in Philadelphia's subway system upon his return, and he especially remembered the double takes of his fellow passengers.

Barry Ross, "Mom ended up throwing out most of dad's trophies (that he didn't recycle and give out as prizes) but that big 3-foot vase/trophy always sat in our living room. She always kept that thing."

I Run Just as Fast As I Can

IN THE POST-OLYMPIC YEAR OF 1953, Browning won races every weekend at a wide variety of distances. That winter Browning won the Seton Hall Relays indoor 2-mile race in 9:38 beating Horace Ashenfelter and Gordon McKenzie.

In the spring, Browning won the 12 mile Baltimore run in 1:06. The following weekend he traveled to Canada to win the Firestone Hamilton 15-mile race in 1:23 beating Johnny Kelly by 4 1/2 minutes and lowering the course record by 2 minutes 40 seconds in the process. After the race, Browning missed his plane from Ontario and had to take an overnight train to Buffalo, and then to Boston for the 10-mile Cathedral race the next day. He arrived in Boston just before the race started. Browning still won the Boston Cathedral 10 mile run for the fourth time in 56:22.

Next Browning beat Charlie Robbins by 600 yards to win the Woodbury "Ten Mile Marathon" in 52:25. The race was noteworthy as an example of the prizes given out at the time. Browning won a set of fancy drinking glasses donated by Cap Paine and a bread box. Robbins won a bath scale; the next finisher won a clock and a steak knife. Other top finisher's prizes included a card table, track shoes, motor oil and a wallet. Browning's parents Frank and Olive donated a sports shirt for a prize.

On May 4, 1953, Browning won the Atlantic City Boardwalk Mile for the first time in 4:13.6. The Boardwalk Mile attracted the best runners in the county and offered to pay traveling expenses to the Penn Relays Invitational Milers.

Browning doubled in monsoon conditions an AAU track meet at Olney High School in Philadelphia, winning the steeplechase and then the 3-mile in 14:57 in "a quagmire of mud" on the track according to the Philadelphia Bulletin.

The following week Browning won an AAU mile in Baltimore in 4:33 and then traveled to Downington, Pa to win a two-mile in 9:47.

In the fall Browning took a teaching job at Port Norris grade school. On Thanksgiving, he won the Berwick Marathon for the 7th time setting a course record of 46:38.

A January 1954 Philadelphia Inquirer feature by Art Morrow profiled 29-year-old "curly-headed" Browning Ross and his running career, including his "habitual victories" at Berwick, and the 15 mile Hamilton Around the Bay Race.

The article profiled his training and his new job as a seventh-grade teacher at Port Norris School and illustrated how creative Browning had to be to keep fit. "Ross himself is surprised at the form he has shown. He thought that his job this year teaching seventh grade at picturesque Port Norris at the southern tip of New Jersey would force him to quit.

For a couple of years, Brownie worked as a postman and found the job ideal. All he had to do was load up at 7 A.M. all day, bag on shoulder delivering mail. The trudge ended shortly after 3 o'clock and then Brownie was free to run until dark.

He never liked to run at night except naturally under the lights such as those which illuminate Convention Hall for the Inquirer Mile. Since it is 48 miles from Woodbury to Port Norris, he feared that his training methods patterned after the Swedes' would not allow him to remain in completion. At this time of year, it is usually dark by the time Ross gets home.

But with the help of a fellow teacher in the oyster port, Clyde Chenoweth, who lives in Vineland and rides from that point back and forth with Brownie every school day, the problem was solved. Chenoweth simply gives Ross half an hour's head start after classes have finished then takes off with the automobile after him.

There's a half-mile dirt horse track in Pt. Norris for trotters and pacers—and two or three days a week Ross runs on that too. Browning, the teacher organizes the kids into relay teams and then races them.

"But the main workouts come after school," Brownie says. "People down there don't know what to make of it, but I put on an old pair of pants and a sweatshirt every day after school, and then start down the road. Chenoweth generally catches up to me by the time I've covered anywhere from four and a half to seven miles and I guess that's enough. Every once in a while, whenever I feel like it I sprint from one telephone pole to the next."

This, of course, is in line with the European training methods that have made the Swedes and Finns so dominant, developing not only a change of pace which opponents find disconcerting in a race but also a free-swinging rhythm which spectators may note at the Inquirer track meet. In their go-as-they please style, though, the Europeans advocate occasional stretches of plain walking mixed in.

"Not me," says Ross. "At least not this time of year. I keep running until Chenoweth picks me up. Afraid I'd freeze if I stopped."

In 1954 Browning won the Hamilton, Ontario Firestone race for the third straight time beating Olympian Curt Stone by 1300 meters. When asked about his strategy by the Hamilton newspapers after the race he remarked, "I just run as far and as fast as I can for as long as I can." Browning mentioned another race secret, "When I'm on the road, I eat a couple of Tums antacid tablets with dinner the night before to try to prevent an upset stomach race morning."

His victories at various distances in '54 included everything from an indoor mile in 4:34 to the King Midas 15 ½- mile race in Long Branch, NJ.

On May 29, Browning won the J.Gordon Flannery marathon in Fishkill, NY and he and Sis and welcomed a son Barry the next day. The **Poughkeepsie Journal** interviewed Browning about the new addition, "His wife gave birth to a boy, and the newcomer tips the scales at 7 pounds, 6 ounces. Ross quips, "People say I'll have him running before he can walk, but my wife says no, he is going to be a ballet dancer. Dancing with a rose in his teeth?"

On the Fourth of July, Browning won the 10-mile race in Taconic State Park in New York in 52:43 in front of a reported 75,000 spectators. Afterward, he was asked about his future running plans in the Philadelphia newspapers and said, "I'm 30 now so this is the year I take the marathon seriously. I'd like to try to go to Melbourne in '56 (in the marathon).

Browning won the Senior AAU 30k (18 3/4 mile) race on the Atlantic City Boardwalk with a young Tom Osler in attendance.

Osler recalled the race, "Browning was essentially the first runner I ever saw. I read in September in the newspaper that there was going to be this big race in Atlantic City, the National 30-kilometer championship and it was going to start and finish on the Boardwalk at Steel Pier. I got myself a bus ticket and went down there and stood in front of Steel Pier and waited for this race. Actually, the first person I saw show up for the race was a guy who wasn't dressed to run. This guy, who was about 30, had a leather jacket and sunglasses on. His name was Helmut Gude.

Gude had been on the Olympic team for Germany in the steeplechase in 1952, a great runner who immigrated to the United States and promised his relatives who sponsored him to come over that he would not race anymore because they were afraid he was going to come over and "waste his time." In those days people thought running was a waste of time. He promised to "shake the habit." He never did race. Helmut Gude showed me who all the runners were. He became a good friend of Jack Barry who became a mentor of mine.

Gude showed me, Browning Ross, when he arrived. I remember thinking my hero Browning Ross was smaller than I had pictured. The race was several laps so you saw them come by several times.

The first two laps there was a Canadian champion with Browning, but after that, there was nobody with him, it was just Browning. Somebody got me to hold the string at the finish line and you can see me at the finish line of the picture of the race.

Jack Barry told me the story about how he, Browning Ross, and Gude all went out to Medford Lakes, N.J. to do a workout on the sand trails in the pines by Atsion Lake. Gude made the remark after the workout that if he could train there all the time he'd be the best runner in the United States. Browning looked at Barry and said, "He doesn't realize it but he's already the best runner in the United States."

Browning returned to Atlantic City a few months later to run a 4:23 mile on a slippery boardwalk in heavy rain. In that race, he edged Horace Ashenfelter and John Joe Barry.

Although the races were small in numbers, almost every big race featured at least a couple tough Olympic caliber runners. Browning won the Fishkill "Marathon in Poughkeepsie, New York beating John Kelley.

A profile on Browning in the Philadelphia Bulletin after Browning won a 5 1/2 mile AAU Street Run in Philadelphia in 25:50 stated, "Browning Ross is tough to beat. He can run a 440 in under 50, the 880 under 1:50 and a mile in 4:13. He has more speed than anyone..."

In September, he took a position as a teacher at his alma mater in Woodbury and as an assistant to Cap Paine in track and head cross country coach-- both positions unpaid to preserve his amateur standing.

Browning had such a dominating year in 1955 that he was nominated for a Sullivan Award, the AAU's amateur athlete of the year award.

One of the strangest races in Browning's career took place June 1st in Devon, Pa. Browning and Jack Barry raced against horses in the 50th annual Devon Horse Show on an 8.6-mile course. Barry, the Middle Atlantic AAU marathon champion finished 32 seconds before the first horse, but Browning finished 1 1/2 minutes in front of the first horse running the course from Radnor Hunt Club to Devon grounds in 46 minutes and 30 seconds. Among the many headlines, the next day was "Men Outrun Nags in Race at Devon" in the Wilmington, Delaware, News Journal.

Dave Budd, a 1956 graduate of Woodbury High, a multi-sport athlete who played 6 years for the New York Knicks, remembers watching Browning train at Woodbury High. "The Woodbury base-ball team played on a field in the middle of the track. I remember playing and watching Browning work out, running laps around the outside of the track. Everyone else ran the shortest distance in the in-side lane but to me, that symbolized Browning trying to get the best possible workout by running the longer distance and never cutting corners."

George Fresholn a Woodbury native remembered, "I would al-ways see Browning running through Woodbury along the railroad tracks." There was a lot less traffic from cars along the tracks.

A January 6, 1955, profile of Browning in the Philadelphia Inquirer drew attention to Browning bringing Woodbury High to the Inquirer Games in the mile relay, while he entered the Lawson Memorial Two Mile Invitational. "The curly-headed veteran of 500 board, track, cinder path, road, cross-country and steeplechase races yesterday burbled more enthusiastically over the prospects of his protégés than over his own, al-though he appeared in top form. A teacher at Woodbury Junior High, the 30-year old perpetual motion machine receives no salary as coach at the senior school, his alma mater- but the job provides him with plenty of company in his workouts. He trains with his pupils. "All of them," he proudly reported, "Can run five miles."

Not that Brownie lets them go that far in the daily drills. "Since the tracks and fields are so marshy this time of year, we work out on a hard-packed farm road near here," he explained. "I space them out at various distances according to their events and then take off after them. Instructions are that each man is to start sprinting as I threaten to overtake him. This way they get in some good practice at sprinting."

And so does the coach. Not only did he win National Championships at both 15 and 30 kilometers last fall, as well as the Middle Atlantic cross-country crown, along with a string of first plac-es in other races, but he also posted his fifth straight triumph- his eighth over a longer span in the grueling Berwick Marathon.

The victory came only three days before the national AAU cross-country championships; else in the opinion of most observers, Ross would have won that race too. (Second to Gordon McKenzie by ten yards.)

Still, Ross had no regrets for the season ranked with his best. It was memorable too because the Woodbury High cross-country team carried its winning streak through 23 consecutive meets."

Jim Shea a Woodbury athlete on the 1954 team still remembered about the workouts 63 years later. "Browning took us out there and staggered the workout intervals so we almost all finished at the same time. Also Browning was able to get Adidas running shoes from one of his contacts in Europe so I think we were among the first people in the country running in Adidas."

In April, Browning, along with Jumbo Elliott, Sportscaster Jack Whittaker, and Philadelphia Warriors guard Angelo Musi spoke at the Gloucester Catholic sports award banquet in Gloucester City, NJ in front of 550 attendees including the Gloucester Catholic Drum and Bugle Corps. Basketball was the only girl's sport in the school at the time. Browning would return to Gloucester Catholic as a coach in 1972.

Browning continued to travel and win races at various distances from the mile to 30k every weekend in 1955. He won the AAU 30k on the Atlantic City Boardwalk again in 1:21.45.

One of his regular stops was the Cathedral Ten Mile in Boston. Before the 1955 Cathedral Ten Mile, a Boston newspaper wrote this preview, "Veteran road race men think Browning Ross could be the best American marathoner if he really trained for the distance. The former Villanova star will be favored in the Cathedral race this afternoon, and it will be interesting to learn whether he intends to shoot for the BAA classic and an Olympic spot at the longest distance in the games."

Browning also won a large number of ten mile races that year including the AAU 10 mile Cross-Country Championships in 50:46, and the Camden Vocational and Woodbury ten mile runs in 50:46 for the third time.

Browning won the Reading, Pa. 4-mile run in 19:11. He then looked forward to a showdown with Kansas great Wes Santee in another 4-mile run-- the 33rd Annual Camden Y 4 run.

In early 1955, Santee a Marine Second Lieutenant came close to breaking the four-minute mile running 4:00.6 in Compton California. His intermediate time in the 1500 meters set a world record of 3:42.8. Santee ran 4:00.7 the next night and had three of the four fastest miles at the time.

Soon after, he was then suspended by the AAU for allegedly accepting $1,200 in "excessive" expense money from track meets. The AAU announced they were suspending Santee permanently as an amateur athlete. Santee's coach said the meet's promoters, most of them officials of the AAU, had offered Santee the money. While the AAU debated whether to lift Santee's ban, Browning said he would only run the Camden Y race if Santee were permitted to run. Santee had run one race since the ban but was not permitted to run the Camden Race depriving track fans of a Santee Ross showdown.

The suspension was overturned and Santee arrived by Quantico helicopter for a 5-mile race the following week, but the showdown was not to be as Browning had a 102-degree fever and was forbidden by doctor's orders to run. Santee won the race easily in 27:36.

A year later, Santee was suspended by the AAU again. After a bitter court battle, the New York State Supreme Court found that for a total of seven meets in 1955, he had accepted at least $1,500 in expenses beyond the allowable $15 a day and travel expenses. He was then suspended for life. Santee was profiled in a cover story in a 1956 Life Magazine story. He wrote: "The A.A.U. says it is possible to get by on the expense allowances permitted by their rules. My answer to that is, 'Yes, if you want to become an athletic bum.'"

Santee's problems with the AAU likely deprived him of breaking the four-minute mile and were a presage of Browning's future AAU troubles.

All of the major Philadelphia and South Jersey newspapers, as well as papers in other parts of the country, covered distance running in much greater detail in the 1950's. Mayer Brandschain, a freelance writer for the Philadelphia Inquirer was one of the unsung staffers who covered the sport better than anyone. Bonnie Ross remembers Brandschain calling for her father every Sunday afternoon without fail for an update on those weekends races.

In an Inquirer tribute to his colleague Brandschain, Jay Searcy of the Inquirer wrote:

"Mr. Brandschain seemed to know everybody and everything about everybody in Philadelphia sports. He made his rounds every day, like a fastidious doctor, from tennis clubs to Boat House Row, from the Vet to Garden State Park, to golf courses, and arenas large and small. Almost everyone who knew him attempted to imitate his soft, quavering voice, which barely rose above a whisper. He consistently produced well over 300 bylined stories a year, in addition to hundreds of event results that carried no credit. His car resembled a rolling filing cabinet with his many boxes of file folders, notebooks, and press releases, many held together with rubber bands."

Brandschain profiled Browning after he won the Olympic Development 10k in Fairmont Park in Philadelphia in 30:20 on November 6, 1955. "Ross, 31, ran such a wonderful race, he is prepared for another big bid for a place on the 1956 Olympic team Browning beat Jack Barry by two minutes and 16 seconds to remain unbeaten in cross-country this fall."

Browning Ross wins 1956 Boston Cathedral 10- mile race.

The Most Versatile
Runner of All Time?

"BAREFOOT" CHARLIE ROBBINS, MD, WAS ahead of his time. In 1936 at the age of 15, Robbins started running 4 miles barefoot through nearby farms in Bolton Connecticut to meet his girlfriend Doris at her grandfather's farm.

"Then I thought if I could run the four miles without stopping, I ran cross-country for Manchester High School, and then the University of Connecticut from 1938-42, and had a prolific amateur racing career.

Robbins was one of the first doctors in the country to advocate running and of course he was one of the first advocates of running barefoot more than a half century long before "Born to Run" became the top-selling book in the country. Robbins finished the Manchester Road Race 50 times and the Boston Marathon 20 times.

"In 1947 when I ran in Central Park, a policeman asked what I was doing," Robbins said. "I said, 'Running.'" "Nobody does that in the city," he said, "And you'd better put your shirt on."

"People stopped to say running was bad for my heart. I heard the myth of the 'athlete's heart' in medical school." Robbins said, "That was turned around when one of Dwight Eisenhower's doctors, Dr. Paul Dudley White, prescribed exercise after the president's heart problems."

"Running barefoot seemed natural," said Robbins. "Five million years of evolution didn't include shoes. I run the same or little better speed than with shoes. Sometimes I race halfway with and halfway without shoes. The change feels good." He said his Size 8 mediums have the same footprints as years past, and a good arch. "When you run barefoot, you don't pound," he said.

Robbins won 11 AAU national titles, including five 20-kilometer titles, two 25-kilometer, two 30-kilometer and two national marathon championships between the years of 1944-54.

In 1955 Robbins wrote about "the most impressive runner he had ever seen," a runner he also called "the most versatile of all-time," Browning Ross. Robbins wrote:

"I believe Browning Ross is the most versatile runner of all time. Here are his best times:

100 yards- 10.6 seconds
220 yards- 23.0 seconds
440 yards -50.0 seconds
880 yards- 1 minute 55 seconds
Mile- 4 min 13.2 indoor, 4 min 10.0 outdoor
2 mile- 9 min 8.3 seconds
3000-meter Steeplechase- 9 min 8.3 seconds
10000 meters 31 minutes 3 seconds
Marathon 2 hrs. 43 minutes 10 seconds

Ross's best distance is from 8 to 15 miles on the road, it is unfortunate that races over six miles are run over the roads. Ross ran the Shanahan Catholic Club marathon in 1954 as a goodwill gesture to help us promote the race the first year. He had done no training over six miles for several months previously but he stayed with Ted Corbitt the winner for 23 miles and then walked and ran to the finish. To cap it off Browning ran 9 minutes 8 seconds for an indoor 2-mile six days later!

Here's versatility-- Brownie won the 1500 meters in the last Pan Am Games, qualified for the Olympic 3000-meter Steeplechase twice, and last year won the National 15-mile championship in Binghamton NY and the 30-kilometer Championship in Atlantic City, then he placed second in the National Cross Country Championships by 10 yards.

I first heard of Brownie during the war in 1944. Chief John (Jock) Semple was rumored to have some kid at the Fargo Building in Boston that did remarkably well in the Cathedral 10- mile race. The next that I heard was Boston Marathon results-- Browning, 22nd place in 3 hrs., 19 minutes and 32 seconds. From there he went on to star at Villanova College and later in AAU running. He made one serious try at the marathon distance in the 1952 Boston Marathon after winning all the spring races at 10 to 15 miles. He couldn't have picked a more unfavorable race. It was a boiling hot day, after staying with the leaders for 18 miles, he was forced to walk most of the latter miles and finished completely exhausted in 3 hours 18 min and 48 seconds.

I hadn't realized how exceptional Browning was until I went to Philadelphia to live. I found out that everything down there was measured by how close one could get to Ross. In the two seasons, I competed there, I found out why this was so!"

In turn, Robbins barefoot running seemed to influence Browning. Although he did not race barefoot, Browning often trained barefoot when it was safe to do so, and he often extolled the benefits of running barefoot. He featured barefoot running in his practices throughout his coaching care

Robbins ran barefoot for over 60 years. He reflected on his love of barefoot running: "Running barefoot seemed natural," said Robbins. "Five million years of evolution didn't include shoes. I run the same or little better speed than with shoes. Sometimes I race halfway with and halfway without shoes. The change feels good." He said his Size 8 mediums have the same footprints as years past, and a good arch. And of course--"When you run barefoot, you don't pound," he said.

In an August 2002 New York Times profile of Robbins Bill Tribou, Robbin's college running teammate, close friend and rival said, "I tried barefoot running for about 10 yards, and thought I'd ruin myself for life. I accused Charley of trying to injure me so he'd beat me," he laughed. "Charley's feet are like elephant hide, the only tender parts between his toes."

The article also described Robbins' diet and philosophy: "His diet is spare, with six graham crackers with peanut butter for breakfast, raisin bread with peanut butter for lunch, and maybe a salad, soup, and piece of pizza for dinner. "I have hot water often," he said, "I like the heat. I add a little powdered milk as a token of calcium.""

"I don't give unsolicited advice, which I say is of no use. I don't spout any philosophies, and try to be nonjudgmental."

"When I don't feel well, I go out and run and things seem better," Robbins said. "I think exercise combats neurosis. I used to think a fair amount of brains were involved in living longer. I've grown fatalistic, and now I think its 99 percent luck and 1 percent anything else. And if exercise feels good, do it, it probably is. And if the food tastes good, it also probably is."

Amby Burfoot remembered looking forward to seeing Charlie run Wednesday workouts at Wesleyan University in Middleton Connecticut over the years, "I would have dozens of questions for him: Am I doing this right? How long should I taper? Do you think I did too many 400s this week? He had a stock answer. "Don't worry. It'll all work out fine." And it almost always did." Note: Charlie Robbins passed away in 2006 at the age of 85.

Browning Ross Wins 1951 Berwick Marathon, one of his 10 Berwick Victories.

A Ring for Every Finger

BROWNING FINALLY HAD AN OPPORTUNITY to run his first Berwick race after his discharge from the Navy. On a cold Thanksgiving Day in 1946, Browning, a 22-year-old Villanova Freshman, drove the 138 miles from Woodbury to Berwick, Pa. to run the one race he had most looked forward to while in the Navy.

One of the oldest races in the country Berwick was contested since 1908. The Berwick "Marathon" was actually a 9-mile race that featured a grueling, lung -searing 1.7-mile incline at the two-mile mark. The race was unique for awarding diamond rings to the top 7 finishers.

When Browning arrived, 1945 Boston Marathon winner Johnny Kelley was the overwhelming favorite. Kelley had a string of four straight

Berwick victories, to go along with his impressive five straight Boston Marathon top five finishes. Kelley was quoted before the race, "Except for the Boston and Olympic marathons there is no race that I would rather win than Berwick."

In pre-race interviews, Kelley said that "Ross was going to be a factor in the race." Unheralded, Browning won the race in 48:35 with Kelley third 21 seconds behind.

In 1947 Browning returned to defend his title as the favorite. He won his second diamond ring with a nearly identical time of 48:37. The race finished in front of 6,500 screaming football fans during half time at Crispin Memorial Stadium.

In 1948 Browning returned from a post-London Olympic European racing tour to win his third Berwick in 48:24.

His streak was briefly halted with a third-place finish in 1949 in what is called the greatest Berwick race, as 8 seconds separated Olympians Curt Stone, Horace Ashenfelter, and Browning with Kelley fourth. Babe Ross finished 22nd in the deep field.

Curt Stone, "The distance probably fit Browning's athletic strengths. As to why Horace and I beat him, I would have to say that Browning usually won his races early in the contest, and, he probably ran himself out during the race. The times he beat me, he simply ran away from me somewhere after the first third of the way. Also, the race that year ended on the track and Horace and I were ready for a fast last lap..."

In 1950, future US marathon champ Jesse Van Zandt set the early pace as Browning battled through a side stitch. By mid-race of the courses quick up and down hills in Kasinki Hollow Browning pulled even. The Berwick newspaper accounts said "Ross and Van Zandt were as close as hand and glove" at the half way point. Browning gained a ten-yard lead and then pulled away to run under 47 minutes for the win in 46:50.

The 1951 race was expected to be a rematch of Olympians Browning Ross, Curt Stone, and Horace Ashenfelter along with 1949 Boston Marathon runner-up Vic Drygall. Ashenfelter pulled out when his child was born before the race. Browning won by 150 yards and lowered his Berwick course record to 46:41.

In another outstanding Berwick field in 1952 Browning lowered the record and won in 46:40 for his sixth title.

In 1953, he lowered the course record once again to 46:38 beating 1956 10,000 meter Olympian Richard Hart by 50 seconds with Johnny Kelley a distant third.

In 1954 Browning won once again by 500 yards in 47:15. By this point, Browning's fame as Berwick champ had spread, and it wasn't only sports fans who noticed that Browning was going to Berwick every Thanksgiving to win the race. His house was burglarized and a radio and stereo were taken from the Ross residence.

In 1955 the course was changed back to the original YMCA finish instead of the stadium during the Berwick football game. He won again in 46:43.

In 1956, he out-sprinted Rudolfo Mendez in the homestretch in a battle much like Alberto Salazar's fierce battle with Rodolfo Gomez in the 1982 New York Marathon. Ted Corbitt finished sixth in the race and recalled, "The Berwick sponsor imported at least one top runner to challenge Ross each time-- there was a lot of betting on this race, or so we heard. His main opponent was Rudy Mendez of the New York Pioneer Club. Mendez was ready and thought he could win. He stayed with Ross and Mendez's version of the encounter was that Ross crowded him, elbowed him to get him off or away, stepped on him, and generally roughed Rudy up until Ross eventually ran away to win in 46.39 Ross was one of several top runners who did not like to lose."

In 1957 Browning finished second by 1 second to Canadian two-time Olympian Doug Kyle. Kyle out-sprinted Browning in the last 50 yards to hold on to the victory. Kyle had also ended Browning's victory streak in the Firestone 15 mile run in Hamilton Ontario earlier in the year.

Mark Will-Weber author of "Run for the Diamonds: wrote, "Some of Ross's close race losses are actually more interesting (than his 10 victories). One of those came in 1958 when Bob Carmen from Pittsburgh barely held off "Brownie" in a sprint to the finish.

In fact, Carman needed to summon every ounce of speed his body could muster--so much so that he was unable to veer around a hefty photographer who had parked himself just inside the finish line to get the best possible shot. "I was simply too tired to go around him, so I closed my eyes and banged right into him…" Carman recalls of his 47:33 victory. Browning finished only 4 seconds behind in his last Berwick race.

The Nov 28, 1958, Reading Eagle account of Browning's last Berwick race, "Robert Carmen of Pittsburgh pulled away from Browning Ross of Camden, NJ in the final mile to win the 49th annual Berwick Marathon yesterday in a photo finish, running directly into a cameraman standing at the finish line. Bob Seaman former UCLA star was third, Jack Barry of Philadelphia finished fourth and Johnny Kelley the former Olympic runner from Boston wound up fifth."

Browning finished his Berwick string with 10 first place diamond rings, 2-second places by a combined 5 seconds, and one-third by 8 seconds to two fellow Olympians in 13 years. (The diamond ring count dipped by one a few months when young Barry placed one of the rings in the collection basket in a Pennsylvania church.

The Ross's returned to the church months later, and the ring which was held in safe keeping was returned to the family by the Reverend after the service.

Of course, there are other great victory streaks in major American road races such as Amby Burfoot's 9 victories in the Manchester Thanksgiving Day 4.7-Mile race.

I contacted Burfoot about his Manchester victory record and those impressive victory streaks of Johnny A. Kelley and John J Kelley in road races. Burfoot said that he though Ross's Berwick record was the most impressive, and recommended that I could find Browning's Berwick streaks proper place in American road racing history by talking with Ken Young the statistician for the Association of Road Racing Statisticians. Young is the undisputed source of information on both American runners and races and maintains a historical database of every major American road race.

Young said, "I hate to even attempt to define "major road race." It is a continuum and where one draws the line is subjective." Young than provided objective data-- 16 of the all-time top streaks of major race wins by males and females in American races. The top streaks, not necessarily consecutive wins, included everything from Greta Waitz' 9 New York Marathon victories and Ann Trasons' 14 Western States 100 victories to Mike Slinskeys' 16 New York

K of C 5 mile wins, and of course Browning's Berwick record 10 victories from 1948 to 1956.

Browning's near misses and the caliber of competition he faced every year give his streak additional weight.

On November 23, 1995, almost 40 years after his last Berwick race, Browning was invited back to Berwick as a guest speaker at the Berwick pre-race dinner. He was interviewed by Michael Lester a writer for the Press Enterprise about his Berwick races. Here is an excerpt of the article.

"If it weren't for a friend named Norm Gordon and a deal he made with Browning Ross, Ross would never have established himself as one of the giants of the Run for the Diamonds.

It was 1946, he had recently been discharged from the Navy and he agreed to stay with Gord for a couple of days and go to some "running event" in Berwick.

In return, Morton could get to know Ross a little better in an attempt to attract him to Penn State where Gordon coached the track and field team.

It's no mystery who got the better of the deal.

Ross would go on to win a record 10 of the Berwick races, compete twice in the Olympics and win a national track title, but not at Penn State.

Ross turned Gordon's Penn State offer down, heading instead for Villanova University, a school closer to his South Jersey home, where he became a 22-year-old freshman.

"He was a good friend of mind," said Ross. "He finished second in the 1943 race and he built the race up to me." "I was going to go to Penn State. He said, "Come up and stay and "I'll go up to Berwick with you. I ran the race but didn't go to Penn State."

Ross surprised the field to win in his first run here beating Olympians Johnny Kelley and Scott Rankin who were the cream of the running crop at the time. Ross ended Kelley's string of five consecutive Run for the Diamonds victories and went on to win 10 of the next 11.

"I think he's the greatest to come here," said Berwick Marathon Association Vice President Lanny Conner. "Anybody that can do that is phenomenal. The best part of his victory that day was he came out of nowhere to do it with Kelley heavily favored to win his sixth straight. He was a total unknown; in the paper, a pre-race article just listed his name and number. Everybody thought Kelley would do it again," added Conner.

Everybody was wrong. Ross completed the race in 48:35 on a cold, breezy day and the rest is history. Conner and other running experts liken his string of wins to the consecutive games played streak of Baltimore Oriole Cal Ripken.

An Ironman he was, but Ross had considerably less to work with when training in those days. While competing at Villanova and later in the Olympics Ross typically ran 20 miles a week—all speed workouts in his canvas Converse sneaks.

"I had good speed. I could run the quarter mile in under 49 seconds on the Villanova relay team. I just stuck with the pack and kicked at the end."

During his Berwick reign, Ross broke the course record four times and became the first to run the nine-mile course in under 47 minutes. He was also involved in what most consider the finest run in the race's history in 1949. Running against Olympians Curt Stone and Horace Ashenfelter- both of the ironically Penn State stars- Ross came in third, with the three separated by only eight seconds. Stone edged Ashenfelter for the win.

That's when another buddy enters the picture. Ross blames that loss on Berwick native Joe "Bells" Colone, who went on to play professional basketball and teach at Woodbury High School where Ross was a Social Studies instructor.

"After I lost I blamed it on him. His father made his own wine in the cellar. He started giving us this wine and I was getting bombed… the night before the race."

Ross learned his lesson, going on to win seven in a row from 1950-56. He ran again in 1957 and 1958, his last year of competing, and finished second both times. The 1957 race also among the most memorable saw Ross edged by Michigan native Doug Kyle by a mere second in a race decided in the last 50 yards.

"The last year I got second and I thought I was over the hill," said Ross. "We (Browning and Sis) were due for a third child, so my wife said no more, that's it. I took off Thanksgivings (from then on)."

But he'll hardly be forgotten in Berwick.

"I don't think anyone will ever match him," said Conner. "But you never say never. You never know when a ringer is going to get in it."

Like Browning Ross."

Young Tom Osler is on the left at the finish line as Browning wins the AAU National 30k in 1954.

In the Long Run

it's the

Long Distance Log

VOLUME 13   FEBRUARY, 1968   NUMBER 146

Tom Osler winning National R. R. C. 50 Mile Run, Poughkeepsie, N. Y.

Tom Osler on the cover of the Long Distance Log.

The Long Distance Log

BROWNING ROSS FOUNDED THE *LONG Distance Log,* the first national American Running Magazine in January 1956. It cost 15 cents a copy or $1.50 per year. There had been attempts at putting together national coverage of distance racing results before the Long Distance Log, but the publications often had limited regional readerships and lacked nationwide distribution.

On the Road Runners Club of America website, in a section dedicated to the Long Distance Log, Tom Osler mentions one such publication: "In June 1953, Austin Scott of the New York Pioneer Club began circulating a self-made publication he called the *Distance Running Journal.* It was mimeographed on 8.5 by 14-inch paper and each issue was about 12 pages. It contained race results, schedules of races and other items of interest to long distance runners. A one-year subscription was $3.00. Sadly, Scott died one week after finishing fourth in the 6 Mile Race of the 1954 National AAU Track and Field Championships in St. Louis, MO on a terribly hot night."

"*The Log* was a successor to Scott's *Distance Running Journal* and initially had the same physical appearance. It was a monthly publication that carried the complete results of nearly every road race held in the USA as well as some track races and important international races. In addition, it carried editorials by Ross, letters to the editor, minutes of the RRCA as well as RRC chapters, relevant magazine articles and other items of interest to long distance runners. *The Log* first appeared in 1956 and ended in 1975."

However, Browning was receiving a publication called "The Midwest Long-Distance Log" which was published from the late 1940's through at least 1953. This quarterly publication was also a 12-page mimeographed compilation of distance results, editorials and commentary and was compiled and distributed by Robert A. Craib of Los Angeles, California. It is likely that Browning received the publication from Craib because his victories are so prominently featured in the results. One December 1952 headline, "Ross Takes Two National Tests in Eight Days." (Browning won National AAU 25k and 30k titles.)

In all of the publications, there is no mention of a subscription cost but requests to submit results from around the country. In a September 1953 issue, Craib states, "It was a slack period in the Middle Atlantic region, but whenever Penn AC's Browning Ross did run he was first at the finish."

In another editorial Craib apologizes for trying to get too big too fast, an attempt at a 29 page Midwest Long-Distance Log caused a long delay in the usual quarterly publication schedule. Besides road races, the Midwest Long Distance Log also covered national high school state championships and major college cross-country races before it folded.

Scott's publication, possibly because of his relation to the New York Pioneers seemed to loom large in runner's memories than Craib's even though

Browning simply dropped Midwest from the title when starting the Long Distance Log.

Curt Stone: "I remember when Browning started editing the Log in 1956. I recall there was a runner, Austin Scott from New York who died in the hospital with kidney failure after running the AAU 10,000 meters. It was terribly hot that day. He had been turning out a running publication. After his death Brownie took over (publishing). I actually tried to help Brownie by typing out the names of his subscribers. I wish I had saved some of the sheets of paper with gummed labels that he sent me. According to the records, there were about 140 names, and I presume Brownie had to lick each one. Nothing like the nice white gummed labels available today. I also recall writing an article for the Log on a talk by the Australian coach Percy Cerutty. Percy was an unusual person, very intense but quite likable. I had met him in Oslo after the 1952 Olympics and he offered to lecture the US team members in the Olympic Village. He took Horace Ashenfelter and me around Melbourne as a courtesy, his fame came later. At any rate, about a year later Brownie found another way of labeling the publication. He sent me a form to sign and a request for funds for the Log. I joked with him that I thought I deserved some free copies for my typing assistance. Browning was trying to get the business of the Log off the ground."

Tom Osler: "*The Log* was a one-man production. Ross typed all the pages. He was teaching at Woodrow Wilson High School in Camden he used the mimeograph sheets available at school for the log. Sometimes he glued articles from newspapers and magazines to his master copy. When finished at 28 pages he delivered the master to a local printer who then made a few hundred copies. Ross then addressed these copies by hand to his 200 subscribers. In the years 1956 to about 1970, long distance running had very few, but very enthusiastic participants. Readers of *the Log* often immediately devoured every word on its arrival. In spite of this, *The Log* never made a profit for Ross but remained a labor of love for him. It had about 200 subscribers for the first 12 years and lost money every year. In fact, Browning had a debt of $500 from putting out the Log.

In the summer of 1967, I wrote "The Conditioning of Distance Runners. At this time, there was really very little running literature available. In a library, you could find maybe five running books, and some of them might be 35 years old. I had a friend who was a runner and a printer, George Braceland. He told me if I could get my book "The Conditioning of Distance Runners" printed up; he'd print 2000 copies at ten cents a copy for $200. We advertised the book in the Long Distance Log for $1 a copy.

George didn't expect to make any money on it, and I didn't expect to either. But Browning put a little ad in the Log saying that my book was available for one dollar. In a month I sold 200 copies, getting back my investment.

I was worried about losing my amateur status and being considered a professional by the AAU for sales of the book because in those days they didn't like anyone making any money from anything connected with running. As soon as I broke even I took all boxes of books to Browning's house and left them on his porch. He wasn't even home. I left a note that said "They're all yours Browning. Use them for the Log." That's the last I saw of the books." Sales of "Conditioning" erased the debt and Browning was able to double the size of the Log through proceeds of the book. He featured me on the cover of the expanded Log after I won the National 50k Championship."

Joe Henderson was an excellent high school and college (Drake University) runner who went on to write more than 30 running books. He also wrote for Track and Field News and was editor in chief of Runners World: "Browning Ross wasn't just a father of modern distance running. He was one of my own running-writing fathers. My first words in a running publication appeared as a letter in *Long Distance Log*. Breaking into the *Log* took no skill. All I needed in was an envelope and stamp for mailing a handwritten note. It began, "I am 17 years old and a senior in high school. If it is possible, could you include a few articles about the training methods employed by the great runners to give boys like me an idea of what it takes in training to be a good long-distance runner?

Browning printed this letter, not because it said anything special but because it helped fill space. That was the beauty of the *Log*. Anyone, writer or runner, could break in there.

The other magazine of the time, *Track & Field News*, was different. It had high standards even then, both editorially and in the performances, it listed. *T&FN* told of running at its best. The *Log* covered all of us – and I do mean *all*, right back to the last finisher and often even the DNFs. A magazine could do that then without being a thousand pages long.

The early *Logs* were printed on the backs of old test papers. Browning was a teacher at Woodrow Wilson High School in Camden at the time. He'd graduated to semi-standard magazine format by the time I arrived as a subscriber. But the *Log* never grew beyond a hobby for him and never was accused of being "slick." Its format was small, the size of a paperback book cover instead of standard 8½ by 11 inches. The photos were always black and white, and often a hazy gray. Browning was known to run the same cover two months in a row.

Publication schedules depended on how much material had accumulated and how busy he was elsewhere. He might mail a month early or a month late, and he never put any statute of limitations on the age of race results.

My pilgrimage east in 1964 took me to see where long- distance dreams were born. I traveled to the East Coast by Greyhound, first to visit Drake teammate Rich Vehlow and his family in Queens, New York. The second visit was with Browning Ross. The Long Distance Log he published put me on the long road to the marathon and beyond. If asked to name the fathers of modern U.S. Road racing, I'd think first of Harris Browning Ross. He was a terrific runner himself. A runner works for his own good, though, and Browning worked for the good of all who ran. He never sought glory for his publishing and organizing, never was widely celebrated for it, and probably never realized the breadth and depth of his contributions. The Log was the first to link the small and scattered band of road racers.

Now I had a chance to meet him. I didn't try to visit the magazine's offices because there was none; he worked from a spare room at home. I didn't expect a job offer because he did everything himself. No, I came to his hometown of Woodbury only to see him. We met for the first time at a summer camp that he operated, as he was cleaning the pool. He put down the debris-collecting pole and sat to chat. We hadn't talked five minutes before he said, "Would you like a summer job, helping me here at the camp? He made this offer to someone he knew nothing about, except that I was a runner who read his magazine. For him, that was a good enough recommendation. I would always regret turning him down in favor of summer school back at Drake."

Nike co-founder Jeff Johnson placed Blue Ribbon Sports shoe ads on the back of the Log which helped immensely with the Logs printing costs. For example, Blue Ribbon running shoes were available from $8.50 to $9.95 with a 75-cent shipping charge in the late sixties, and more varieties were available for close to $20 in the bigger edition of the Log in the 1970's.

Browning's daughter Barbara remembered almost being responsible for a delay in one issue of the log. "I was little and was jumping up and down on the bed where Dad was assembling the Logs. He almost went into shock when he saw them but mom came to the rescue by ironing out the wrinkles with an iron and then they were mailed out."

Amby Burfoot the 1968 Boston Marathon winner was also an editor of Runners World, he said, "The Long Distance Log was my first serious connection with the larger world of distance running, and I read every word many times. Of course, I subscribed probably from 1964 onward. One of my great regrets in running is that I never met Browning Ross. I probably revere him more for the Log than I do for his great running career. He was a path setter. We owe him more than people realize. I didn't save copies of the Log. I wish I had."

Browning once said this, "It (The Long Distance Log) was a lot of work for one person. I can remember typing for one long stretch when my son Barry, probably five or six looked in at me and said: "There goes Tommy Typer at it again!" I knew it was time to take a break."

On December 23, 1975, Browning in response to a query from NYRR, wrote that the December 1975 issue of the Long Distance Log would be the last. "Too much of a hassle," Ross wrote. But Browning had published *his* last issue of the Log in August 1974.

The United States Track and Field Federation took over publication of the magazine with the September-October issue. The USTFF dedicated the November/December 1974 issue to Browning.

They also put Browning on the cover of the January/February 1975 issue before finally ceasing publication with the November/December 1975 issue. At the time of its demise, a yearly subscription to the Log was six dollars and a single issue was 50 cents.

In 1966, another runner, high school senior Bob Anderson from Overland Park Kansas published a black and white mimeographed magazine called Distance Running News. Anderson gave out free copies of his 28-page publication at area races and offered a two-issue yearly subscription for one dollar. By its second year *Distance Running News* had 850 subscribers. *Distance Running News* quickly grew to a semiannual publication and passed the Long Distance Log in circulation. Distance Running News focusing more on "how to train" articles and running shoe review than the Log quickly grew to over 3000 subscribers.

In 1969 Anderson renamed the publication "The Runners World," dropping out of college to publish it full-time. In 1970, he moved Runners World to Mountain View California. Runners World later went monthly in 1973 and offered a $75-lifetime subscription offer which was quickly accepted by 1,400 subscribers. Circulation would top 100,000 subscribers in 1977 and was purchased by Rodale in 1985. As a result of the running, boom subscription reached an estimated peak of 1 million subscribers.

Bob Anderson, founder of Runners World. "I subscribed to Track and Field News and there I learned about Browning's Long Distance Log. I subscribed to both and read every word many times over. In high school, I was already writing runners from around the country. I got their addresses from Browning Ross...I started asking people like Ted Corbitt and Arne Richards for training advice. They gave me more names and addresses. My senior year, in 1966 I published two issues of a magazine I called "Distance Running News". Runners started sending me a dollar for a one-year subscription and some runners like Tom Osler send me another extra $5.00 to help out." Osler remembers "I sent him extra money and a note warning him that this idea of a national running magazine would never work. I told him that there were just not enough runners out there to make it profitable, and he shouldn't get his hopes up. Boy was I wrong! Distance Running News, of course, became Runners World and had an enormous number of subscribers at its peak."

Anderson recalls the two of the biggest boosts to Runners World's subscriptions being Frank Shorters' Gold Medal in the marathon in the 1972 Olympics and Jim Fixx featuring a chapter about Runners World in his best-selling 1977 book "The Complete Book of Running."

Unlike Browning's one-man operation producing the Long Distance Log, Runners World had a full staff including of writers including first employee Joe Henderson and Hal Higdon. Anderson took his responsibility to runners and Runners World seriously.

Vince Phillips, I wrote a letter to Anderson letting him know that I was unhappy that Runners World was missing some of the results (that the Long Distance Log would have probably covered), and that sometimes they were taking two months to get the results to press. I also complained about them taking on automobile ads-- the natural enemy of the runner in a big portion of the magazine." Phillips received a personal letter back from Anderson that started with a bit of analysis, "Mr. Phillips you are obviously a person that does not enjoy running..." At that point, at least Runners World still had the personal touch.

Tom Osler, "In the late 1970's Runners World was really popular. Its cultural impact was such that it hosted a National Running Week between Christmas and New Years in Palo Alto, California. They flew in a who's who of well-known runners as well as running coaches and writers for a panel discussion. Two of the panelists included me and Bill Bowerman, the Oregon coach. Bowerman was a real gentleman and down to earth guy. You would never have known he was a famous track coach. A few years later I met him again at the Houston Marathon. Before the race, I was taking my sweats off and looking around and he said, "What are you doing?" I said I'm looking for someplace to hide my sweat suit so I can find it when I finish."

He said, "Give it to me and I'll hold it for you." I looked at him and said "Wow! This will be a story to tell. An Olympic Track Coach holding my sweats while I run the race. He just laughed. A couple of months later, at Christmas time my doorbell rings and there is a mailman with a big box. I open it up and there's a big Christmas wreath on top. Inside are several pairs of different Nike running shoes, shorts, shirts, and different Nike apparel that Bowerman had sent me as a gift."

At this time interest in running publications was cresting. Running Times and other regional running publications such as Runners Gazette grew in popularity and popular, and other competing national running magazines were launched including, Running(featuring writers such as Hunter S. Thompson), and The Runner(published by George Hirsch, and staffed with major running writers like Hal Higdon). Some of the magazines have folded, but thanks in large part to Browning Ross's efforts the running publications that have survived, like Runners World are a far cry from the days of mimeographing results for the 200 or so interested runners in the country.

The Road Runners Club of America patch was based on the
British RRC patch and imported from Britain.

Founding of the Road Runners Club

IN THE FALL OF 1957, Browning Ross founded the first chapter of the Road
Runners Club of Philadelphia. It became the Middle Atlantic RRC. In
February of 1958, the national version of this club was started and called
the Road Runners Club of America. The RRCA's purpose was to promote
long distance running, which was so small at the time that there were only 9
marathons in North America in 1958 and less than 300 Americans running
in marathons.

Ted Corbitt biographer John Chodes: "1958 may have been the most important year in the history of American distance running. It was the year

the Road Runners Club became a reality in the USA. Within a decade this organization revolutionized long distance running; instead of five marathons a year there would be over a hundred. It was this kind of widespread competition that made it possible for Frank Shorter to emerge and win the 1972 Olympic marathon.

Browning's idea for the American Road Runners Club was based on the existing British model of the same name.

In the August 1957, Long Distance Log Browning had first proposed the idea for the Road Runners Club in an editorial:

"Wouldn't it be great if we could emulate the Road Running Clubs of England South Africa, New Zealand, and Sweden etc. and institute an organization within the USA with the object of the encouragement of running, particularly road running? This organization would include not only runners but also officials, race sponsors, coaches etc. This type of organization could exercise full control of our branch of the sport.

Representatives from each district could attend Council meetings periodically to propose fundraising techniques such as annual banquet, annual dance, raffles, selling of uniforms, shoes etc. to make out the coming season schedules of races to recruit new sponsors etc. I know—it would be difficult. Especially with our districts so far apart, but local Road Runner clubs could appoint members to serve on the National Committee and look out for their own interests. All the long-distance races now obsolete could be revived (One hour run, track races of over 10,000 m, long relays etc.)

A club publication could be started. Let's kick it around a while and hear the pro's or cons from readers of LDL. It's something to think about—I know the idea has me enthused!"

Chodes: "Browning Ross transplanted the RRC idea to the USA. He was the perfect man for this: one of America's greatest track/road runners and an enthusiastic promoter of the sport. He had also been national AAU Long

Distance Chairman and editor of the first worldwide long distance running coverage magazine the Long Distance Log. While competing overseas, Ross joined the RRC of England greatly impressed with the way it had revitalized the sport there. The RRC of England promoted the "spreading of the Gospel" (of running) to other countries. Ross became a zealous missionary."

The first Road Runners Club of America was held February 22, 1958, at the Paramount Hotel in New York City with ten interested "founding members in attendance. Ross was named the first acting provisional president.

Tom Osler remembers the founding meeting: "Browning invited Harry Berkowitz and me to New York to see the National Indoor Track Meet at Madison Square Garden. As a sideshow, Browning had asked representatives from other districts to get together before the Meet to talk about the Road Runners Club. We went to the Paramount Hotel to meet. The Paramount had a second-floor balcony that overlooked the lobby. We saw some chairs and pulled them all together into a circle and that was the meeting. It lasted about an hour and we decided to start this club.

Some people were concerned the AAU might get upset about it. It turned out we operated within the laws of the AAU. It allowed you to form clubs within the AAU. Like the Penn AC, and the Shanahan Catholic Club, the RRC now became such a club within the AAU. You were permitted to hold events that were for your club. So, you joined the AAU, then you joined the RRC, and you could run all the RRC races and not risk losing your amateur status."

Hal Higdon missed the meeting in the balcony while resting up for the three-mile run at that night's meet but caught up with the group later as they continued to meet and wrote about the meeting for Marathon and Beyond: "The group continued to meet in Browning's room, so small that it barely accommodated a single bed, much less many chairs. Even after 50 years, I remember sitting on a radiator in the window and hearing Browning talk about the Road Runners Club of Great Britain, a country where the sport flourished, producing top distance runners on the track and on the roads. He felt we needed such a club to promote our sport in the United States. Thus, the Road Runners Club of America was founded, now an organization of more than 774 clubs and 175,000 runner-members."

Besides Ross, Higdon, Osler and Berkowitz attendees at the first Road Runners founding meeting included Kurt Steiner, Harry Murphy, John Sterner, Dick Donahue, Bob Chambers, Lou White, Bob Campbell and Joe Kleinerman. Olympian Ted Corbitt was not at the meeting, although he would become a key figure in the spread of the RRCA as the New York Chapters first President. Corbitt missed the meeting because he ran a 30-mile training run for the Boston Marathon early in the day, and spent the rest of the day watching the track meets at Madison Square Garden.

Ted Corbitt recalled, "The first club meeting of the New York RRC was a talk and coaching session at Van Cortland Park (the Bronx in New York City) featuring Australia's running Coach Percy Cerutty who stayed with us for a week on his way to the Commonwealth Games."

Ironically, several months after the founding of the RRCA, Corbitt's entry to the Boston Marathon was rejected when he failed the pre-race on-site doctor's physical exam, mandated by the AAU for a high heart rate. Corbitt had a heart murmur and was nervous about it being detected and failing the exam, leading to a temporarily elevated heart rate. He ran unofficially, starting at the back of the pack and finished an unofficial sixth. Higdon notes, "No ombudsman existed at that point to stand up to the Amateur Athletic Association (AAU) with its archaic rules that often prohibited running as much as it promoted it. The RRCA would soon change that."

A similar situation had occurred in Boston 48 years previously. Clarence Demar ran the 1910 Boston Marathon and was warned by the examining physician at race site he would die if he were ever foolish enough to ever try to run 26 miles again. "You have a bad heart," the doctor said. "You shouldn't even walk upstairs. Demar, of course ultimately ignored the advice and went on to win Boston seven times between 1911 and 1930. Partly due to the warning, with no running ombudsman on his side, he skipped Boston 9 times during some of his peak running years. "I've always insisted that the physician was listening to his own heart, not mine," Demar was fond of saying. (Demar continued to race in more than a thousand road races, running his last race, a 15 kilometer in Bath Maine only a few months before passing away from cancer in 1958 at age 70.)

From 1966 to 1976, the RRCA conducted its annual meeting in conjunction with the Boston Marathon.

Higdon remarked on the subsequent growth of road racing after the initial meeting "Thanks to Browning the first seismic rumbles of what a decade later would be identified as the running boom had begun to be heard. Races began appearing even in relatively small cities, where there previously had been no history of competition."

Chodes: "(Ross) explained the Road Runners Club idea to athletes in various parts of the country asking them to help form regional associations." John Sterner asked Ted Corbitt if he would be the first New York Metropolitan area President. Corbitt at first declined and then accepted. Chodes noted: "Some runners were suspicious and refused to join. As individualists, they distrusted organizations."

Tom Osler would later preside over the Philadelphia chapter of the RRCA and was an eyewitness to the frustration Browning faced in his own hometown in trying to overcome local running politics to get the Road Runners Club off the ground as Ross tried to start the RRC with a series of races in the Philadelphia area.

Tom Osler, "We met at the Penn Athletic Club where Browning had been a member for some time. The running part of the club was run by Jack St. Clair, Senior. Jack Sr. was loud and sometimes drank too much. At one meeting Browning, who spoke very softly, was trying to organize the Road Runners Club by describing its benefits and Jack Sr. came in-- he appeared drunk and was causing a ruckus yelling how they didn't need the Road Runners Club. Browning stopped, and then patiently started to speak again. Jack Sr. started yelling, drowning him out once again. Browning got very angry--which you seldom saw--but angry in a quiet way and he got up, looked straight at St. Clair, and said, "I quit." And Browning walked out. St. Clair started crying, "Why did he have to quit?" Browning was the star runner of the club. Browning never went back--he started his own club, the Delaware Valley Track Club.

I started out in the Shanahan Catholic Club because Jack Pyrah introduced me to it. The next club I joined was the Delaware Valley Track Club.

Browning asked me to join. Then later he formed the South Jersey Track Club. We (the Mid-Atlantic Road Runners Club) listed our upcoming races on a postcard and sent it out to all the Mid-Atlantic Road Runners Club members."

The South Jersey Track Club under Ross hosted a number of MARRCA races in South Jersey including regular races in Cooper River in Pennsauken, New Jersey, and in Browning's hometown of Woodbury New Jersey. Browning would often direct the races, sometimes run in them, and publish the race results in his Long Distance Log magazine.

In March of 1984, the IAAF World Cross Country Championships were held at the Meadowlands Sports Complex in East Rutherford, New Jersey. Browning had been the manager of one of the early US teams that participated in the World Cross Country Championships in 1969 in Tunis. Browning was eager to the see the World Cross Country Championship so close to home, only an hour and a half drive from his hometown of Woodbury, NJ.

After the race, Ross drove the nearly exactly half marathon distance from the Meadowlands into New York City to revisit the Paramount Hotel in New York City with a few friends. He slowly pulled up outside the hotel, found a parking spot and stopped. From his car, he pointed to the balcony where the first RRCA meeting had taken place, remarking that he hadn't been back to the site for many years, and then he slowly drove off for the return ride to Woodbury.

Note: shortly after Browning passed away in 1998, runners took a new look at Browning's accomplishments. Ted Corbitt led a discussion about Browning's influence on American distance running and especially his founding the RRCA. Some runners wondered if (and when) a national running organization similar to the RRCA would have been eventually founded by someone else. Harry Berkowitz addressed this topic in a letter to Ted Corbitt:

Dear Ted,

It is always interesting to speculate on what might have happened if a particular person had not been present. In my opinion, not only was Browning uniquely responsible for starting the RRCA but without him, there is a good chance that long distance running in the US today would still have the same organizational structure and the same small number of participants that it had in the 1950's. I believe that Browning provided the following:

1. He had the foresight to establish an organization to get around the AAU bureaucracy and allow runners to organize races that they wanted to run.
2. His achievements as a runner gave him credibility among others in the sport.
3. His personality, namely his lack of interest in grabbing power or of making money off others, allowed him to work easily with other people.
4. His publishing of the <u>Long Distance Log</u> provided a means of communication among those interested in having more races, and in allowing runners to improve.

The first point was important because the AAU was mainly interested in being involved with elite competition. It did not provide any foundations for sports for the average person. One of the ways the AAU controlled running was the use of travel permits to restrict people from competing outside their home districts. The stated reason was to control expense money paid to athletes. But anyone with any sense of reality should have known that most runners did not receive money for their expenses from the race organizers.

Browning wanted to provide running opportunities for as many people as possible, but he wanted those people to be involved in the organizing of the events. It was his prodding of others around the country to organize, and then to form a rather loose alliance that, I believe, contributed to the early success of the RRCA.

A few AAU associations did provide several local races throughout the year, but most of the country did not. The Long Distance Log contained the results of most of the country's races. The Log allowed people to see what others were doing. Browning glued things together and made no money from it. His interest in building the RRCA was based on pure interest in and love for the sport. It allowed him to start an organization without creating jealousy towards him.

I think that it is just as conceivable that without Browning there would be no organization such as the RRCA. There would be just a few races a year throughout the country, no professional road races, and no athletic shoes except those mad of canvas, no NIKE— Michael Jordan would be wearing black Converse shoes, and would only be paid for playing basketball.

However, it is more likely that people would have started running for health and there would have been a running and exercise boom. But there may not have been an RRCA, or the great number of races that currently are held in the US today.

Thanks for asking for my thoughts, such as they are. I hope to see you at some of BUS's summer races. I plan to run them all.
Best Wishes,
Harry Berkowitz June 3, 1998

Tom Osler summed up the discussion. "Some runners speculated that Browning might not have been the only American runner to correspond to Jim Peters and John Jewell, the Presidents of the British Road Runners Club during the 1950's. They also speculated whether any of these other runners may have eventually started an organization similar to the RRCA given enough time. Well, Browning is the only one who got off his rear end to actually accomplish it. We runners continue to benefit from his tremendous efforts. Once Browning started the RRCA the national mechanism was in place for running to grow by millions of runners, and thousands of runners during the running boom. All that was necessary was to expand the size of the fields."

In 2013, the RRCA reported over 1200 running clubs and over 200,000 members involved in running events with over three million participants each year. As Ross envisioned, the RRCA provides a national infrastructure for the development of youth and adult running clubs and promotes running as a healthy lifestyle and positive social activity for runners of all ages throughout the United States.

A plaque in the Fitness Center of the Paramount commemorates the founding of the Road Runners Club at the hotel.

Around the World—and then Some on Foot

In 1957, Browning decided to do something he had been thinking about since his student days at Villanova and the start of his relationship with Sis-- convert to Catholicism.

Browning did this with no parental support. Because Browning's mother had grown up in an anti-Catholic atmosphere in her father's household, Sis did not feel completely welcome when and would often stay with a Catholic neighbor when stopping over to visit Browning.

Browning wanted to surprise Sis and started attending weekly RCIA (Rite of Christian Initiation of Adults) classes on Thursdays without telling her why he was not available on Thursday nights. After a few months, Sis began to wonder if Browning was having an affair.

On December 20, 1958, Browning was baptized in St. Patrick's Church in Woodbury as a Catholic.

After the baptism, Bonnie remembers, "I was about 7 and couldn't wait to burst into Grandma Ross's house with the good news, "Grandma, did you hear? Dad is a Catholic now!!" I still remember the look of complete shock on her face. She didn't look too happy, but she accepted it."

Bonnie continued, "We went with Dad to church as he made his first confession as a Catholic. We were in the pew and dad and the priest were in the confessional when we heard dad's voice echo loudly through the church as he recited the first part of the confession, (which is supposed to be said quietly to the priest):"BLESS ME, FATHER, FOR I HAVE SINNED..." At that point, the priest told him to tone it down. Dad always got a laugh when we would remember that years later."

Browning continued to win a variety of races every weekend including a 7.6-mile race at Cooper River in Pennsauken, NJ, a Baltimore 10 mile in 51:51, breaking the course record by a minute.

In the spring Browning returned to Hamilton for the Firestone Race and John Girling, the dean of Canadian track and field reporting, and an Ontario road race course certifier in a pre-Firestone race article predicted "Browning Ross could challenge the marathon world record of 2:18. In checking race times of Browning Ross, Jim Peters (Great Britain) and Zatopek of Czechoslovakia, it must be remembered that Ross usually wins races by a country mile. With this in mind, it's hard to say how fast he can go with his effortless machine-like stride. Who can beat him or extend him? Your guess is as good as mine. Somebody we haven't seen like John J. Kelley of Boston University (Kelley would win the Boston Marathon that year) or Olympian Curt Stone. The article turned into a bit of a jinx as Browning lead the whole race but was hobbled in the last 200 yards and passed at the finish by Canadian Olympian Dough Kyle. Browning's time of 1:25:18 would have won the 1950-54 races.

In April Browning returned home to win the 3 mile AAU track meet at Villanova in 15:07.

In May, he won the AAU 25k Championship in 1:27:56 on the Atlantic City Boardwalk. He returned the following month to win the Boardwalk mile in 4:20, and then a Malvern, PA hilly 7-mile cross-country race in 37:56.

Browning was also focused on the Long Distance Log, printing the Log on the back of old test papers from Woodrow Wilson. The LDL featured a letter from world-renowned coach Percy Cerutty to Fred Wilt highlighting various aspects of distance running training; and training contributions from Jock Semple, Harry Groves of Penn State and Fred Wilt.

The January 1959 LDL contained letters from two running founding fathers detailing the RRC's struggle with the AAU. The first was from Hal Higdon, whom a Long Distance Log reader noted: "was a good enough writer to write for the New Yorker." In fact, Higdon would go on to write for Sports Illustrated, Runners World for over 50 years, and to write 34 books. Higdon wrote, "From what I can tell the AAU people are afraid of the road running clubs because we can run races that are now restricted to members of road running clubs. To this I say so what: colleges run races that are restricted to collegiate runners. We may have to fight against the politically minded bigots in the AAU for a while, but eventually, if we continue to push our cause I feel that we can accomplish some good for the sport."

Ted Corbitt wrote in the same issue, I had heard about Mike Portanova's defection at the Convention-- it is apparent that the objectors in the Met (NY) AAU "got to him" and the others. They promised to do so. The bit in the Convention Bulletin covers all arguments (the AAU) threw against us when they rejected our application for membership. The RRC can still do a service by sponsoring Open races. But will the AAU cooperate in this?"

Browning's editorial in the same LDL spelled out the RRC's impact on distance running in its short existence. "Since its inception last year, the RRC has doubled the number of distance races usually held in the Middle Atlantic AAU area. It is vital that the RRC movement and its current problem with certain AAU people be cleared up and allowed to continue if improvement is to continue in our sport. Politically minded people and Olympic trip aspirants in the AAU, currently holding back the progress of the RRC, surely must realize the real reason for our decline in world-class distance running--lack of continuous competition and lack of clubs interested in furthering distance running. AAU men have advocated this before and now that it's a reality they censure it??? Our second national meeting will be held in New York City on February, 21st, everyone will be contacted and Met AAU officials will be invited. Please arrange to be present to state the progress or problems in your particular area."

In November, Browning earned headlines in the New York Times for defending his AAU cross-country title in 31:33 in Fairmount Park. "It was the twelfth time since 1942 that Ross, representing Penn AC, had won the championship. The minute and 2-second margin was Browning's most decisive."

The New York Times reported Browning returned to Fairmount Park in December to win the AAU 10k handicapped cross-country race in 30:46. The Times noted that Browning beat two outstanding runners who were refugees from Hungary. World famous Hungarian Track Coach Mihaly Igloi had fled the 1956 Hungarian revolution along with some of Hungary's top runners.

Igloi, known as a tough coach and stern taskmaster, would later coach American Bob Schul, to the 1964 Olympic gold medal at 5,000 meters. He also coached world-class milers Sandor Iharos, Laszlo Tabori and outstanding American Milers Jim Beatty and Dyrol Burleson.

In four years under Igloi's coaching, Beatty would later become the first sub-four-minute miler indoors (3 minutes 58.9 seconds in 1962) and ran 3:55.0 outdoors in 1963. In an issue of the Long Distance Log, it was noted that Igloi liked to compare his runners to violin players preparing for a concert, repeating a piece over and over.

In 1958, the Philadelphia Bulletin's Earl Eby interviewed Browning for about his training while also providing a nice summary of his career up to that time.

"Around the World" not in 80 days, but "On the Run" is the title of a story Browning Ross might yet write.

At 33 years of age, the Woodbury, NJ history teacher is a classic example of what the modern method of training can do for a runner. "Browning Ross Wins" was a stock headline on the sports pages of the 1940's. "Browning Ross Wins" is still a stock headline while all the runners who opposed him in the 1940's have long since hung up their spikes.

In the 19 years, he has taken running over the hill and dale, in the streets or on the cinders; he has covered a staggering total of mileage.

The circumference of the earth at the equator is approximately 24,902 miles. Since 1946 alone, Ross has pounded out 24,964 miles. In 1946, he began his current schedule of training 40 miles a week. And he's not even tired. "I find it less exhausting to train today than I did 15 years ago," he says.

"I follow the interval system developed in Europe." In that system, you don't run at an even pace. You break it up. You run fast and slow. It depends on how you feel. But the secret is to run day in and day out." Ross believes he is in better condition today than he was in 1950 when he was picked for three events on the AAU All-American team.

Nineteen years ago in Woodbury, Ross a rather frail youth, stepped out on his back porch just in time to see his next door buddy make a mess of trying to vault over a clothesline using his mother's prop as a pole. "That sport is for the birds," young Ross decided. "I'll try running."

Run he did four years at Woodbury High, competed for the Navy in World War II, represented various athletic clubs, and starred under Coach Jumbo Elliott at Villanova for four years. His Woodbury coach was Cap Paine. At the Penn A.C. club, he represents his tutor is John St. Clair.

"I also received good advice from Pop Haddleton, the Haverford College coach who died last week," Browning says. "They all helped me."

He has won eight national AAU championships. In 1950, he won the 15k, 25k and 20k titles. He has won the Berwick Marathon ten times, the Mid-Atlantic AAU senior cross-country championship 12 times. He was a member of the 1948 and 1952 Olympic US Steeplechase teams. In 1951, he won the Pan-American 1,500-meter title. He won the indoor mile title in Washington D.C. in 1948 in 4:13.7 setting the Washington Star meet record. He has been clocked in 9:08.7 on the boards but loathes indoor running.

His travels have carried him, in addition to all over Europe to Argentina, Chile and other South American countries. "Browning Ross Wins" appeared on the sports pages of all those countries but in Spanish. Ross who teaches American history at Camden's Woodrow Wilson High is considerably more articulate than most athletes. In machine gun fashion, he answers questions on running with fine intelligence.

When asked about runners in the past he replied: "Runners were just as good 50 years ago as they are today-- that is physically. The reason why they are making faster times today is because present day runners have profited by the experience gained in the past. There are new training methods which had they been employed by old-time runners would have resulted in a sub four-minute mile years ago. "

"George of England would have broken four minutes. So would Gunder Hagg the Sweden."

When is Ross quitting the sport? "Maybe next year he says. "Jack Kelly Jr., however, told me to keep running as long as I'm winning. We'll see--I feel pretty good." Ross lives at 306 West Center Street in Woodbury with his understanding wife Rosemarie and his two children, a daughter Bonnie 6 ½ and a son Barry 3 ½.

Ross like all husbands is human. Upon entering the house after one of his running jaunts home from school Ross balked when Rosemarie said she needed a loaf of bread. "Do I have to go all the way to the store?" moaned the suddenly exhausted Ross."

In March of 1958, Browning won the Middle Atlantic AAU 30k championship in 1:43.54. In April, the New York Times gave billing to the "First race of its kind in this country as Browning Ross ran a 25:11 five-mile anchor split in a 20 mile AAU cross-country relay championship to lead a Penn AC quartet to victory over a team of US Marines from Quantico, Va."

In May, Browning won the 25k Riverview Park race from Wilmington, Delaware City Hall, over the Delaware Memorial Bridge, to Riverview Park in Pennsville, NJ in 1:27.48. Newspapers featured a picture of 3-year-old Barry joining in at the end and running in with his father.

One of the RRC's first sponsored races in the summer of 1958 was the first Avalon Beach 5 mile in Avalon NJ. Browning won the first race. The Avalon race would continue for over 30 years.

Browning's picture made the front page of the Philadelphia newspaper sports sections again in October when he won the 4 1/2 mile AAU cross-country championship in Fairmount Park. Browning managed to run 23:11 despite losing his shoe 50 yards from the finish. In the picture, Browning is "consoled" at the finish by a dog named Blackie.

Browning had to skip the AAU 20k championship with a sore Achilles tendon, but he returned to win a 15-mile Wilmington, De. Race in 1:27.48; a

Municipal Games 6 mile in Baltimore and an 11 ½-mile race at Cooper River in New Jersey the following week.

He also won the Mid-Atlantic AAU 15k championship in October in 47:20. Despite spending more time with the Road Runners Club, publishing the Long Distance Log and occasionally directing and timing races, Browning put a string of 20 race wins together.

In 1959 Browning went to teach at the Cinnaminson, NJ Middle School where he promptly started a fitness and running program. Browning, now 35, decided to cut back on his travels to races as the RRCA was creating many more racing opportunities close to home. Browning finished first in the popular "married men versus single men" race at Cooper River (the AAU was still prohibiting women from racing distances.)

In April, Browning was a close second in heavy rain in the Quantico Relays, Va. 10,000 meters to Penn State's Fred Kerr. Later that month Browning won an AAU 6-mile race against a tough field in 30:49 in Wenonah, NJ.

In one of his best races of the year, Browning set an American record in the one hour run, running 17.927 kilometers in Cheltenham Maryland in May breaking Hal Higdon's record from the previous June.

Browning was invited to Whitinsville, Massachusetts in June for a world record attempt on the 10-mile run. John J. Kelley won in 50:51, settling for a new American 10-mile record.

The AAU had approved the United States versus Russia track meets in 1958 and 1959. Browning officiated the finish line of the 1959 meet at Philadelphia's Franklin Field in front of 54,380 fans and found himself a witness to one of the most controversial track meets in US history.

The Meet was held in extreme heat and humidity, leading American Bob Soth collapsed on the track in the 10,000 and had to be hospitalized, then other runners started collapsing on the track. American Max Truex broke the tape in the first place only to have the Russians incorrectly claim that Truex had d previously been lapped by their runner Parnakivi who was lying collapsed on the track. With Parnakivi lying on the ground, Truex was forced to run an extra lap to earn the third-place point before collapsing himself. Browning had counted Truex's laps, knew that he was not lapped, and declared Truex the winner. He was overruled by the other officials. Truex went on to finish sixth the following year in the 1960 Olympics in Rome.

In September, Browning won an RRC sponsored 7-mile race in Malvern, Pa. The race consisted of 4 1.7 mile loops and started at the then common mid-afternoon time of 2:30 pm. Two weeks later Browning won the Woodbury ten mile (9.4 miles) run in 51:10 for the seventh time in eight years.

Browning Ross wins a rainy Atlantic City Boardwalk race in 1955.

2 Leagues from Atlantic City

PETE LEAGUE, " DURING THE late 1940's or early 1950's my dad, Ed League, an Atlantic City fireman, founded and directed the Boardwalk Mile in Atlantic City, New Jersey. I was just a 12-year-old in 1949, and just beginning to develop an interest in running when I first heard the name, Brownie Ross. The Atlantic City Boardwalk Miles were started as an attempt to provide the best mile runners in the United States an opportunity to be the first to break the four-minute barrier for the mile (Note: The Penn Relays mile winner was offered a ride and expenses to run the Atlantic City Boardwalk Mile. Roger Bannister the Penn winner in 1951 was thought to have declined this offer because he had to return to Great Britain.)

The Boardwalk Mile was a straightaway mile race which started and finished either at the Steel Pier or the Convention Hall (depending on the favorable wind direction). I recall names like Horace Ashenfelter (1952 Olympic Gold Medal winner in the Steeplechase), Bill Ashenfelter, Johnny Twomey, Fred Wilt (FBUI agent and Olympian), and Browning Ross (1948 and 1952 Olympian) competing in those early Boardwalk Miles. I suppose that is also the first time I became aware of Villanova University, the college in Philadelphia for which Browning competed during his college days.

There was an interesting turn of events during one of those early Boardwalk Miles, my dad arranged for Pacers to lead the runners during each of the two half-miles. Alex Breckenridge of Villanova the pacer for the first half mile started at the same time as the field of milers. Instead of dropping out at the half-mile point (near the Central Pier) Alex continued on. And he beat the entire field including the second-half-mile pacer. Since he had not officially entered the race, he was not declared the winner. The media made a big deal of all of this.

In 1959 Browning, Dick Donahue, Bob Chambers and I went to Central Park in Bob or Dick's Ford Thunderbird to run the Milk Run, which was 15k in Central Park. Browning and I were overwhelmed by the price of a hamburger in a downtown Manhattan restaurant: $3.00! That was a small fortune in 1959.

Brownie and I were the two officials for a rather thin officiating crew for the first Atlantic City Marathon in 1959. It is believed to be New Jersey's oldest race.

During the summer of 1963, I came back to South Jersey during summer college break. I intended to find a job in Atlantic City, but Browning called me and told me he wanted to work for him during the summer as a camp counselor at the Salem YMCA he directed. It was an opportunity to do some real running during the summer. I worked at the camp during the day, ran many miles each evening with Browning, and raced on the weekends.

Browning took me to a race in Maryland one weekend. It was really hot. Browning won the race and I finished and picked up a trophy. What I remember most is the ride back to South Jersey. We were really hungry and saw a McDonald's sign: 10 hamburgers for $1.00. We wolfed down those ten dime hamburgers in no time flat. It was quite a difference from our trip to New York City four years earlier.

During the late 50's and early 60's Browning and my dad managed swimming pools in Sea Isle City. Browning, Sis, and the kids rented a small place and I would come down from Pleasantville every once in a while, and go for a run with Browning. During these runs, he taught me how to breathe properly while running. During one run, as we crossed the toll bridge linking Sea Isle City with Avalon, the fellow in the toll booth gave us a verbal lashing for running over his bridge, "Where do you think you are, on a race track or something!!" On the way back we really picked up the pace as we came charging back across the bridge maybe an hour or so later. Again, the fellow came to his window and yelled at us again. Browning would chuckle over that for years."

When my mom passed away in 1962 Browning and Sis invited me to their home in Woodbury for dinner. Browning and Sis were such loving people and I will always remember that thoughtful and compassionate gesture.

"306 West Center Street Woodbury, NJ"--Ask any runners who were active and involved in running during the 1950's and 1960's about that address. They knew it by heart and many like me stopped by for a to Browning and Sis visit when they were in South Jersey."

Bonnie Ross remembered the summers in Sea Isle. "Before we found a place to stay we stayed in a small pool house. I remember there was a small handicapped boy who came to visit dad in a wheelchair at the pool every day. Dad was always glad to see him and he followed dad around, the two of them chatting during the day."

Pete League, "I recall talking with my dad the day we learned of Roger Bannister's four-minute mile (May 6, 1954). He was skeptical, but soon realized it was true. The next year (1955) the Boardwalk Mile shifted from being an invitational event to an open event (I ran it in 1955, that first "open" year; being the first high school student to do so). I have no idea of how fast (or slow) I ran.

I have a theory on why a four-minute mile was not run on that straight-away stretch of Boardwalk. I believe the course was long. My reasoning: I was in Atlantic City for the 2008 AC Marathon (we were having a little family reunion) and my wife and I walked in the two-mile walk from the Convention Hall to Steel Pier and back. The course for the Boardwalk Mile started at the dead center of the Convention Hall and finished at the fire hydrant on the Convention Hall side of the Steel Pier (or, depending on the wind, in the opposite direction), and it ran on the rolling-chair lane closest to the ocean (there were two rolling-chair lanes). I recall having heard my dad say something to the effect that the city survey team had measured the course.

Well, in that 2008 two-mile walk, we turned around at the one-mile mark which was a loooong way from that fire hydrant. Given today's careful and reliable measuring techniques (thank you, Ted Corbitt!!), I would assign more reliability to today's course measurement standards. I'm proud to say that when I recently looked at the list of the first 25 marathons to have been "certi-fied" as having been accurately measured (Gary Corbitt, Ted's son, sent the list to me), I realized that I had measured four of those courses."

The Philadelphia Bulletin featured an article and this cartoon on Browning being pulled over by local police so many times.

Police Skeptical of Morning Rambles

BRYANT HEISINGER IS AMONG THE many runners whose running career from youth to masters, was enriched by Browning. Heisinger recalled, "I heard about Browning at a very young age, probably 7 or 8 in the mid-1950 when Browning was mentioned in a story about the police stopping a man for running down the road at 6 am. They figured if someone was running down the road they must have done something wrong! My parents and I lived in Woodbury until I was about 6. My mother was and is a big sports fan, and Browning lived about four blocks away. She knew Browning from his running down the streets of Woodbury when we lived there. When the story appeared, my mother pointed out to me "That is the man we used to see running in Woodbury-- Browning Ross!"

The first time I actually met Browning I was about 10-- he had sprint races for the kids at the Woodbury Fourth of July Fireworks at the high school track. For winning one of the races I was handed a "recycled" medal (red and white ribbon, 1st place, emblazoned on the back and my name was in the paper but it was spelled "Bob" Heisinger.

My freshman year, I ran his Junior Olympic races at the Salem YMCA in the 1960's, and later I ran in Browning's All-Comers track meets at Deptford High. Browning was a one-man track meet--clerk, starter, official, awards presenter of weekly track meets and road races. In his "All-Comer" meets an eight-year-old might line up next to a runner over 70.

My senior year at Deptford High School, the Deptford track team started its first of 10 straight undefeated track seasons, and Browning was the speaker at our Deptford Sports program. I coached with him at Gloucester Catholic a year or two before you arrived there.

As a track athlete, coach, official and meet administrator I have talked to hundreds of athletes (male and female) who credit Browning with getting and keeping them interested in track and running. Most of them have a medal or trophy first won by Browning and recycled as a prized possession.

Despite giving tons of medals and trophies away, Browning still had an attic full of large trophies and medals. He had some nice awards like the 15 identical "Loving Cups" from winning one local town's "Founders Day" race through town 15 years in a row.

Years later someone mentioned to Browning that he should get his remaining trophies appraised. He tossed five or six medals and trophies into a paper bag, drove over to Philadelphia and plopped his '50's era awards on the dealer's counter. He walked out with enough money to take his wife Sis on a vacation. Turns out most good medals from the 40's and early 50's had high gold content. Browning lived a very modest lifestyle, so that was an unexpected windfall. No one was more deserving than Brownie Ross!"

Another neighbor, John Stratton John Stratton grew up in Woodbury near the Ross family, "Barry Ross was my best friend growing up. When we were about six years old I had a little globe pencil sharpener that I really liked and Barry was over my house and we were playing with it. Barry went home and I noticed it was gone. I begged my dad to go to the Ross's to get it back. Reluctantly my dad took me over to their house and Browning answered the door. My dad sheepishly said, "I think Barry might have accidentally left with John's globe pencil sharpener." "He didn't accidentally leave with it, he took it!" I yelled.

Browning just laughed, he thought the whole thing was comical and got a kick out of watching me and Barry. Then he asked Barry if he had it and I got it back. My dad was mortified. As we were leaving he said "Don't you ever do that to me again, embarrass me by making me come over here. That Browning Ross is the nicest man in the world." Barry and I ran track for Woodbury and Barry went with Browning to a lot of his races, then when Barry got tired of going, Browning took me to a lot of the races with him."

Browning said, "When Bonnie and Barry were small, I was driving down Browning Road in Bellmawr at night when Barry asked me if Browning Road had any connection to me. I said 'Sure, and sometimes they still recognize me when I drive on it.' I briefly turned my lights off and thee next three or four cars flashed their lights at me (to get me to turn my lights on) and Barry said "Wow, you're right!".

On March 18, 1964, George Kiseda of the Philadelphia Bulletin wrote an article about one of Browning and other runner's biggest problems before the running boom. The article was titled, "Police Skeptical of Morning Rambles. Ross Runs to Relax; Still Wins at 40"

Here is an excerpt: "Browning Ross may be the only athlete in the country who has been stopped more times by the police more than Sonny Liston.

What's more, Ross has records in Pennsylvania, New Jersey, Florida, California, Texas, Ohio, Illinois, and Utah etc. Ross' problem with the cops is persuading them that he's a runner. He runs six days a week through the sand trails west of Woodbury N.J. where he lives with his wife and three children.

Morning, noon or night you can find the lonely hooded figure of Ross plodding through the brush along Route 130. Neither rain nor snow nor sleet or temperatures 20 degrees below freezing nor the Deptford Township police have stayed Ross from his appointed rounds. The Deptford Township police have come the closest.

"They used to stop me regularly," Ross said. "They'd ask where I was going, what I was doing, who I was running from. They'd look at me as if I was off my rocker."

There are Jersey hunters who share the police department's doubts. On several occasions, they've fired away at a shadowy figure only to discover it had two legs; once three of them flushed Ross out of a brush. They seemed disappointed to discover he wasn't a rabbit.

Ross will be 40 years old next month. He has run for 25 years, 40,000 miles, and 600 medals, cups and watches and is not ready to abandon the loneliness of the long-distance runner. Just the other day he won a five-mile race in Woodbury. All of this he finds perfectly normal for a 40-year old. "Some people like to hunt," he said. "Some people like to go out and parade in string bands. I think they're the ones who are nuts."

He said he runs because he likes it and because it relaxes him. "It takes the tensions off our everyday work," he said. It's just a method of relaxation. It's better than taking tranquilizers. When you get tens, go out and take a run."

It's easy, he said. "All you have to do is go out and put one leg in front of the other," he said. "If you do it every day, it's not going to hurt you."

The curious thing about Ross, aside from the fact that he's running at all at his age, is that he's running better than ever. His five-mile time of 24:54 at Woodbury was a career record. The reason is, he said, that he's in better shape than he was at Villanova (class of '51) or at the Olympics in London in '48 and in Helsinki in '52 or when he was winning eight national championships.

Like everybody else who is breaking down track barriers, he has learned that you can't over-train. He runs seven to ten miles a day, 50 miles a week. Four-minute Milers like Tom O'Hara thrive on 100 miles or more a week.

"We didn't know how to train," Ross said. "When we were in college you'd consider a mile and a half over distance. Nowadays they do 10-15 miles. They wouldn't even consider a mile and a half. That used to be Jumbo Elliott's theory-- a mile and a half for over distance work. But he's changed since Ronnie Delany came in there and taught him a little."

Ross Fulltime job as a physical director of the Salem County YMCA occupies about nine hours of his day but he still has time-- between dodging cops and hunters -- to pursue an avocation to his avocation. He is the publisher, editor, circulation manager and advertising manager of "Long Distance Log." The subscribers include track coaches, long-distance runners, and even some "normal people."

Turtle Tom Osler
is Now a Hare

BROWNING WASN'T THE ONLY RUNNER to have his training interrupted by suspicious protectors of the peace in the 1960's.

1963 Pan Am 10,000-meter gold medalist Pete McArdle once said, "Dogs and police were usually our biggest problems in the '60's when we were out training."

Tom Osler, "Sometimes when I was out training on the roads I was followed by police cars wondering what I was "up to" out running. Around 1964, I was running through the Cooper River Park in Cherry Hill. I came down a hill and was face to face with a police officer who yelled "We got him!" and proceeded to grab me and put me in the police car. Now, most people did their running on tracks then and it was rare to see anyone running on the streets except for street races. I was running in a pair of green pants like you'd see a workman wear, and I had on a sweatshirt.

I told the cop "You're making a big mistake buddy. You better let me go or you're in a lot of trouble." He told me they had reports of young people stealing cars in that area. When they saw me running towards them, fitting the basic description they grabbed me. The thought was there was no reason a sane person would be running on the streets then unless he was up to no good, running away from something. He eventually called in and checked my address and information and they let me go. It was quite common to be stopped and questioned by the police while running then.

While Bill Bowerman was tinkering with running shoes in Oregon on the West Coast for what later became Nike, Browning was doing the same on the East Coast. Osler: "The shoes Browning made were terrible. This was before Tiger shoes were available and they were out about 1966. So, Browning's shoes were out in around 1963 maybe. They were professionally made. Apparently, in Browning's mind runners were cheap, and they didn't like the idea that their running shoes were wearing out so fast so he got these shoes that wouldn't wear out. The bottoms were so hard that you wore out first before the shoes. They wouldn't give."

The shoes were available in red or white. Pete League, " I purchased some shoes from Browning that he had designed, believing that he had designed a pretty good shoe after considering the input of so many runners that he knew. I thought they were pretty good shoes, but in retrospect not nearly as good as the shoes we have today. It's amazing how shoe technology has changed. Tom Osler used to run in Hush Puppies or dress shoes for crying out loud."

In the 1960's running was still a small community where everyone knew everyone else. Race fields were usually small, (usually averaging 30 runners), young and of course mostly male.

Osler, "In a ten-mile race the winner may run 52 minutes, the next few runners were all under 60 minutes and you would have most of the rest of the field running around one hour and ten minutes. The fields in the races were very fast. Most people in that era were training to try and win championships and not for fitness."

Even the Boston Marathon field was small.

Osler recalled, "I met George Sheehan at the Boston Marathon in 1964. Boston had 200 runners then tops, and we all stayed at the Lennox Hotel. You knew a lot of people there, a sizable fraction of the field. Runners have always been a fairly upscale group of people. Professionally educated people--it was that way then too. A group of us met in the lobby and decided to get together the night before the race at a really nice Italian restaurant. There were really quite a few of us-- 15 or 16. I happened to be sitting next to George Sheehan, who I had never seen before. I guess George was in his late 30s and was still relatively unknown.

We're sitting there--a fairly impressive group of people, one runner is an engineer, Ted Corbitt, a Physical Therapist, and here's George Sheehan who's a heart specialist. We were sitting there eating, having a nice discussion when all of the sudden George goes "Whahhhahhahhhhhhh!!!"-- (a Tarzan yell). We all stopped and looked at him and George said: "I just get so excited at these events!"

I thought here's another one of these crazy guys... I sure at that moment everyone thought we won't hear much from him again.

Of course, George goes on to become a great running guru. Of course, he became the most read and talked about runner of our time. He spoke for runners in his writing. He really seemed to hit the pulse of running. He was a very good writer and a very nice man. He had a dozen kids and was always very down to earth. He drove a little old car and always dressed in jeans and a casual shirt. George was the sweetest guy in the world. When I wrote my Serious Runner's Handbook, he was at the time the most famous running author.

Occasionally George and I were the featured speakers at a major race and George, Kathy, and I would go out to dinner. We were close, we got along really well. I later found one of my Boston Marathon entries-- the entry fee was 25 cents!"

Osler won his first national championship, the National AAU 25k Championship in Rochester NY 1:27:09. That year he also became the Mid-Atlantic RRC President and won 28 races at various distances. "I wasn't a champion in High school so it was a nice surprise to win those champion-ships (also the National AAU 30k in 1967) after running for ten years. I won 2 of the 3 National Championships wearing dress shoes not running shoes. They were light and flexible and probably better than most of the running shoes you can buy today. Browning was my biggest supporter and even took me to a lot of those races. I often trained with Jack Barry (no relation to Irish Olympian John Joe Barry), Barry was a championship caliber runner, espe-cially in the marathon and was my mentor.

I started to follow Lydiard's training methods and improved dramati-cally from someone in the middle of the pack to someone who was actually a threat to win every race. Browning gave me the nickname "Turtle" and Hugh Jascourt once wrote an article that "Turtle Tom Osler is now a hare".

I documented my training findings that led to my breakthrough in the "Condition of Distance Runners" booklet. A lot of people bought the book or read it online but I always doubted how many people actually followed it's advice."

"As I got better, and Ed Dodd and other top area runners got better, and Browning got older, we used to get together to talk about the day we'd finally be able to catch up to him. We could see ourselves getting a little closer. He was in his 40's and we were in our peak years in our 20's. That day finally came in a track race, 6 miles in Penns Grove in 1965. Browning had a bad day and I had a good day. I trailed him and finally caught him and passed him.

At the finish, I went bananas. I don't know what overcame me but I started jumping up and down, "I beat Browning! I finally beat him! I did it!" I turned around and Browning was a few feet away calmly looking at me. He didn't say a word. I felt about six inches tall. I felt totally humiliated by my outburst and the surprised but gentle look on his face.

In 1966, I became a Mathematics Instructor at St. Joseph's College in Philadelphia. I used Browning and his gentle, patient nature as a model for what a teacher should be like. Long before the t-shirts appeared WWJD? ("What Would Jesus Do,") I thought-- what would Browning do in this (teaching) situation. How would he treat this student? That has been my guide for 50 years of teaching."

In 1967, the year of Jock Semple's' unsuccessful attempt to strong arm and remove Katherine Switzer's number, Osler ran the Boston Marathon in 2:29:04, finishing 19th. He also captured a second national title, the National AAU 30k championship in 1:40.40 in Maryland.

Later that year, Osler self-published a seminal work on running, the 32-page classic, "The Conditioning of Distance Runners."

Osler, "George Sheehan and I became good friends. He and Dr. Tim Noakes stopped over our house in Glassboro for a visit. Browning, Ted

Corbitt, and George Sheehan were friends and examples of the great people you could only meet through running."

Dr. Tim Noakes (author of "The Lure of Running") said, "Conditioning of Distance Runners" remains one of the absolute classic training books of the world. Tom Osler's great contribution was to emphasize the importance of peaking in training. He was the first to verbalize that in a way that was really understandable to most athletes. Most importantly, he was absolutely correct in what he proposed. Our own research undertaken [in South Africa] shows his principles to be absolutely correct. The principles Osler described withstood the test of time and are unquestionably real physiological laws."

Osler also published the "Serious Runner's Handbook" in the 1970's. The question and answer format training book was a big seller during the height of the running boom. Osler went on to run over 2700 races.

Back to Competition

Browning continued to run but "retired" from competition in 1960 because he was working two jobs, as a teacher and as a Director at the Salem County YMCA. This enabled him to concentrate on the Long Distance Log and directing RRC sponsored Road races. The Log had a publisher's imposed limit of 30 pages and he was swamped with submissions, letters, and results from around the world.

The winter of '61 was the second snowiest in Philadelphia history. In January 1961, the second of three major storms hit the East Coast destroying and sinking the United States Air Force Texas Tower 4 Surveillance Radar Station off the coast of New York, sinking it and killing all 28 men aboard.

Browning returned to competition in February after his year long hiatus from competition. President John F. Kennedy launched a national Physical fitness initiative, and the American Heart Association and Vesper Boat Club recruited Browning to run and publicize their "marathon" race to promote physical fitness. It is worth noting that the race was not a fundraiser like most races today, but was one of the first races to associate itself with a cause-- an awareness of physical fitness in line with the President's program. Of course, by choosing the 18+ mile distance only runners who were very fit could participate. Because there were so few runners the race focused on the few who could complete the distance rather than stressing mass participation like fitness runs do today.

Browning was profiled in a Philadelphia Bulletin article in February 1961 on the eve of the race titled "Browning Ross Likes to Run 10 Miles Daily to

Escape Colds." Here is an excerpt that mentions Browning's training and his return to competition:

"This has been a tough winter for Browning Ross and many millions of others in this section of the country. Browning's idea of a good time is to run about ten miles a day in the open, but running in snow up to the hips, or at least to the knees is no fun, even for this veteran marathoner who, figuratively and literally has run all over the world. Ross feels his physical best when he is running ten miles regularly every day. Despite the weather, he has had a sufficient number of workouts to believe he is in good enough condition to run almost 19 miles Sunday in the Vesper Boat Club Heart Association 18 ¾- mile race. With customary caution, Ross wanted to be sure he was in shape so he ran a nine-mile road race last Sunday. He was the winner, so he knew he was ready. The upcoming Mid-Atlantic AAU title marathon will be the first championship in which Ross, who is a school teacher in Cinnaminson N.J. has competed in two years. "After that race (two years ago) I thought I was getting too old to stay in competition. I laid off completely-- no running at all.

That was a mistake. I'm sure of that now. I got cold after cold. I never felt so bad physically. I started exercising regularly again starting with short distances which I increased gradually."

He's up to ten miles a day when weather permits.

"I know there are few who have the time to run a distance like this upcoming 18-Mile race, or even ten miles," he said, "but everyone should participate in some form of exercise regularly. That's the idea we're trying to put over for the Heart Association. I'm convinced I feel better when I'm working out regularly, and I think all athletes will tell you the same."

Some time ago Ross estimated that he has run 24,902 miles, which is more than the circumference of the earth.

It isn't likely that the veteran runner will ever stop running again after his recent experience with colds, although he may not compete much longer. Some time ago Olympian Jack Kelly, Jr. advised Ross not to quit so long as he continued to win.

That may have been Kelly's way of saying he should never stop."

In March, Browning ran 25:05 to win 5.2-mile cross-country race in Woodbury, lowering the course record by two minutes and beating Irish Marathon Champion Willie Morris by six seconds.

A week later, he won the Mid-Atlantic AAU 25K Championship in 1:22.05 The Philadelphia newspapers noted Browning's 2 minute and 27 second margin of victory, but headlines also declared the victory "AAU Title a Costly Triumph to Ross." "The 36-year-old school teacher discovered his gold wrist watch missing from his locker in the Vesper Boat House after the race. The time-piece was a priceless possession for Ross since it was the gift of fellow Villanova University students upon his return from the 1948 Olympic Games."

The "costly" story had a happy ending the following week when Browning won the RRC sponsored Cooper River ten mile in 53:30, and sheepishly admitted that he had found the watch in his running shoes when he returned home after the race the week before.

Browning continued to either director or run in the additional race opportunities provided by the RRC. In the summer, he set a record in The Penn AC 6 mile run in 30:41, and in November he won the 4 1/2 mile AAU hilly cross- country race in Fairmount Park, Philadelphia in 24:00. He also set a record in a six mile Penn AC run in 30:41.

Browning continued to race and win through 1963, but the big story for Browning and Sis in 1963 was the birth of their third child, daughter Barbara in May.

With three children and increased racing opportunities provided by the RRCA, the 39-year-old Browning won a number of major races in 1963. He won the Mid-Atlantic RRCA 5-mile Championship in 24:52, the 9 ¼-mile AAU Road Race in 49:35 at Philadelphia's Bartram High, and a 9.3 mile AAU race in 49.56. He also won the Middle Atlantic AAU 25K Championship over an emerging Tom Osler in 1:25:50.2.

All of these race victories were a prelude to one of the greatest years in his career, his first in the newly formed master's category promoted by the RRCA in 1964.

I Got Us This Far

In 1962 Browning left teaching and went to work for the Salem, (Penns Grove, NJ) County YMCA as a full-time Program Director.

Jim Cheney was 16 at the time and remembers, "I began hanging around the YMCA at the time (Browning was hired), and Browning got me hooked on distance running. Some of my buddies started running with me and soon we had about 8 guys running every night after school. In those days, there was no cross-country team at Penns Grove High. Just about every Sunday we would pile into Browning's 1963 Mercury Comet and go to a race.

I remember one race, in particular, that was hosted by Hugh Jascourt, then the President of the RRC. The race was a 10k through the suburbs of DC after the race started everyone proceeded to get lost. By the time everyone crossed the finish line it was late. We stopped to eat on the way home, which made it even later. As we traveled home north up 95, the transmission fell out of Browning's car and I had to call my dad to pick us up 2 am in the morning. Browning always had a smile on his face and was always glad to see you. He was also willing to sell you a pair of shoes from the supplies he kept in his truck (when running shoes were hard to find.)"

There are two oft-told stories of Browning's days working at the Salem County Y involved trips to 1960 Olympic Pole Vault Gold Medalist Don Bragg's Green Acres Camp near Batsto in the New Jersey Pine Barrens (The camp was later named Camp Olympik). The first involves Muhammad Ali, then known as Cassius Clay. Ali was a 1960 US Olympic boxing Gold Medalist and teammate and friend of Bragg. Bragg was born raised in the Y's town of Penns Grove, NJ, a Villanova graduate and a good friend of Browning. Ali appeared at the Camp with Bragg to put on a boxing clinic and both 1960 Gold medalists clowned for the kids in the camp. Bragg did his patented Tarzan yell while Ali mugged with and shadow boxed the young campers. Browning said, "Ali was a good sport and probably one of the greatest athletes who ever lived, one of the most famous athletes of the 20th century but I noticed he couldn't play basketball. As graceful as he looked boxing, he looked almost uncoordinated dribbling and shooting a basketball. The kids were talking about it when he returned to the Y and I said, Look, this is a lesson for you-- no matter how talented you are at something; no one is great at everything."

Bob Romansky, a runner and also a native of Penns Grove remembered accompanying Browning on one of the day trips to Green Acres. "The bus driver was Max Weeks. Max took the kids to Don's camp by a long circuitous route involving a lot of extra mileage or so Browning thought. Upon completion of competition between the Salem YMCA kids and Don's campers, Browning came up with a new plan: "Max, I know a shorter way through the woods on the sand roads that will save us a lot of time going back home. I can take you on these back roads and we'll end up within site of the Batsto Historical area." "Sounds good," replied Max.

So off they went driving the big bus with 30 kids along the narrow, winding sand roads, the bus banging against the low-hanging branches of the trees lining the road. Finally, just as Browning had said, they came within sight of Batsto. However, there was one minor problem. There was a chain linked fence stretched across the road! Browning never missed a beat. "OK Max, I've got us this far, you can take over now!"

**Browning, far left sets American Masters Mile record of 4:43.
Dr. George Sheehan is in field fourth from left.**

Masters Records

By 1964 THE AAU WAS lessening its resistance to master's races for runners over 40. The RRCA had pushed for racing opportunities for women and masters since its inception, and finally saw the fruits of its efforts. Browning turned 40 in 1964 and although he continued to win open races, like a five-mile race in 24:51 in February, the RRCA provided more racing options for masters, and the Long Distance Log's coverage helped boost the profile of master's races in the country. Cardiologist Dr. George Sheehan was among the many runners whose interest was renewed by masters racing opportunities. Sheehan had been a track star at Manhattan College and returned to racing 25 years later after first training in his backyard in Rumson New Jersey.

1964 was also an Olympic year and Browning was asked to help publicize the US Olympic effort before the team left for Tokyo. Browning brought the Olympic Torch into Franklin Field during halftime of the Eagles "Olympic Day" game. Browning and other Olympians including Jack Kelly Jr. put on a foot race display, while Mr. America put on a weight lifting display. In the Philadelphia Bulletins description, "the Eagles spent the first half running like marathoners after Norm Snead's passes. Unlike the losing hometown Eagles, the Olympians received polite applause but the crowd's biggest ovation of the day was reserved for Miss Pennsylvania who was escorted by Jack Kelly, brother of Princess Grace Kelly..."

Browning won a running Pentathlon in Atlantic City's Bader Field in 1964 consisting of a 9-mile road race, a mile, a 2-mile steeplechase, an 880 and a 440 by finishing first in first 3 races and second in the 880.

Within the space of a couple of weeks in May Browning lowered a course record by two minutes in running 53:22 and winning a 10-mile Cooper River Parkway race by 800 yards. He then won a 7-mile West Deptford race by 25 seconds, and ran the fastest ten-mile leg in 52:52 on a 20-mile two-man relay from Woodstown to Mullica Hill and return to bring his team from fifth place to second.

In October, Browning at the age of 40 won the inaugural Caesar Rodney Half Marathon in Wilmington Delaware in 1:07:24. The Caesar Rodney course is extremely hilly, and many believe the race has to rank among the top of Browning's many career victories. The Wilmington News Journal gave the race major coverage with front page pictures of Browning winning, "The slender, blond, squinty-eyed, two-time Olympic Steeplechaser ran a perfect race in winning the first annual Caesar Rodney Half Marathon. Lou Coppens his nearest competitor was about 200 feet behind. After it was over, the 5 foot 6 inch, 136 pound Ross gasped, "I don't think I could have gone another mile. Believe me, this was a very tough course, lots of hills. Very picturesque though; well planned and laid out. As soon as I get home I'm going to get in the bathtub and soak for a few hours. Anytime I run in any race over 10 miles these days it takes me three days to get over it!"

In 1965 and 1966 Browning continued to race and usually win both open and masters races. For example, he finished first in a Mid-Atlantic Road Runners Club sponsored 10k in 1965 and first in a Mid-Atlantic Road Runners Club Masters 5 mile in 1966, and first every year in the Wenonah Woods 5 mile races. In 1965 Browning ran a 5-mile MARRC race in 24:51, but was outkicked by an emerging young runner, a recent college grad from Burlington County in South Jersey named Herb Lorenz.

Lorenz was born in Cologne Germany, and much like Browning was able to parlay his 49 second 400 speed to win races at a wide variety of distances from the mile to 25 kilometers. Lorenz would usually win his races pulling away from the field early. If Browning was in the race, however, Lorenz would rely on his kick. Lorenz outkicked Browning in the MARRC 10-mile championship in 1967.

Neil Weygandt accompanied Browning to many of the races and recalled, "In 1966 and 1967 Browning was still frequently winning races, sometimes beating much younger (by two decades) and faster racers by using his speed, wiles and knowledge of racing strategy. There were some really good runners like Lou Coppens and Herb Lorenz that he was still able to beat on occasion."

Herb Lorenz outkicked Browning in the last few yards of a 10-mile race Mid-Atlantic AAU Championship in 1967 but often recalled a race in Wenonah Woods against Browning in the same time frame as his favorite memory. "There was a race held every year in the Wenonah Woods that Browning often won. It had a lot of turns, and I wasn't sure where I was going so I stayed right on Browning's shoulder. He would signal an upcoming turn by shooting out his left or right index finger in the direction of the turn. Suddenly he sped up a little and I did too, then he stopped dead. Browning yelled back, "That was the finish line!" He was first, and I was second. We both laughed, no one knew those woods better than Browning. If you couldn't stay with him you had no idea where you were going."

In January 1968, Browning toed the line with some of the best Masters racers in the country at Cornell for an Indoor Masters Mile. The race included George Sheehan and Olympian and fellow master runner Ted Vogel. Browning, hen 43 set the American Masters record in the mile, winning the Cornell Invitational Masters Mile in 4:43.

The wire service write-up of the race was covered in all the major newspapers and headlined,

"Ross wins First Eastern Staging of Masters Mile in Record Time: "Twenty-one senior men (40 and over) ran in the first Masters Mile to be held in the East. The original field was picked some two months ago but due to a last-minute flood of entries another field was added and two sections were run. Smooth striding ex-Olympian Ted Vogel took command of the first race at the starting gun and ticked off eight laps of the 220-yard track in 5:01.6.

The late section got underway with Jim Hartshorne breaking into the lead at the gun and holding this position until Browning Ross took over the pace at the first quarter. These two maintained their relative positions throughout the race and gradually moved out from the main pack until the last lap when George Sheehan exploded out of the main body of runners and cut down the lead of the front runners to but a few seconds as he finished third.

The first four men finished under 5 minutes and Ross' 4:45 shave 2 tenths of a second off of Jim Correll's West Coast U.S. Masters mile record. Silver trophies were awarded to the five best times for the combined sections. There were two watches on every man with at least three of the winners of each section."

The Cornell Daily Sun reported the next day, "Really pushing on the last lap, Ross set a new record with a time of 4:45. (For comparison) the college freshman race was won in 4:34.6. George Sheehan, 49, doctor and father of 12, finished third with a very strong kick at 4:51.5.

Ted Vogle a 1948 Olympic teammate of Browning in the marathon won section II of the event with a time of 5:01.6."

In 1970, 45-year-old Browning won another indoor master's mile the Inquirer Relay Carnival directed by Jumbo Elliott in 4:55.8.

It was a flashback to twenty years earlier with Jumbo waiting at the finish line as Browning broke the tape. Interviewed by the New York Times after his victory Browning, the executive director of the Woodbury YMCA said, "I've been keeping in shape by running around the swimming pool at the Y," he said. "It's 80 yards around and I can get in about 20 miles a week. I used to run about 20 miles a week in those (Olympic) days," he said. "Now guys like Liquori and Jim Ryun run 130. Running is all mental. They broke the four-minute mile barrier and now they know they can do anything."

A number of master's races also sprung up along the Jersey Shore and Browning won the Cape May masters two-mile in 10:34. The Atlantic City Press race write-up mentioned that "Browning had competed in Norway, Belgium, France, Canada, England, Finland, Italy, Ethiopia, Tunisia, Zambia, Morocco, Scotland, Ireland, Czechoslovakia, Holland, and Kenya. Of course, there was also Brazil, Cuba, Chile as well as most of the United States."

Coach Browning Ross and the 1968 US World Cross-Country Team

World Cross-Country Team Coach

THE FIRST OFFICIAL INTERNATIONAL CROSS-COUNTRY meet, consisting of the four countries in the United Kingdom was held in Scotland in 1903. France joined the meet and the International Cross-Country Union in 1907, and several the additional other Continental European countries joined in the 1920s.

When Tunisia, the first African non-European country joined the Meet in 1958, followed by the other French Colonies of Algeria and Morocco there was an opening for other countries to compete. Browning wrote a letter to the International Cross-Country Union requesting permission for the United States to enter a team in the meet.

Permission was granted and the first US team consisting Tracy Smith, Doug Brown, Eamon O'Reilly, Tom Bache, Michael Kimball, Herb Lorenz, Bruce Mortensen, and Bob Scharf traveled to Rabat, Morocco to compete against 14 other nations in the 7.5-mile race. Tracy Smith's third place finish paced the Americans to a fifth-place finish. Olympian Oscar Moore and Bob Reddington were also named to the team, but did not compete.

Fifty years later, Oscar Moore recalled the circumstances of making the first International Cross Country team while running for Southern Illinois, "I must have qualified for the (1966) team by either finishing second to Tracy Smith in an indoor 2-mile championship or by winning an AAU cross-country meet in Wyoming. In those days, someone would tell you that you qualified for a championship team while you were warming down after the qualifying race, or they would tell your coach while you were warming down and he may or may not tell you, depending on how it fit into his plans for the team. I remember qualifying for a two-week trip to Africa to race back then, but I didn't want to go because I figured adjusting to the food in Africa would throw off my diet and my training."

Browning was named to coach the men's 1967 International Cross Country Championships held in Barry, Wales with a women's event held for the first time. When the AAU refused to fund the team, Ross tried to raise the funds for the team to travel to the meet by soliciting donations from readers through the Long Distance Log. All donors had their names listed in the Log, but the $5 and $10 donations did not generate enough funds for the team to attend the Meet.

American Doris Brown Heritage did make it to the race and won. John Kissane wrote about the 1967 race in Running Times Magazine:

"A fortuitous development for Brown Heritage was the staging in 1967 of the first women's international cross country championship, held on a cold and windy March afternoon outside the coastal Welsh town of Barry. After touring a three-mile course through muddy athletic fields and cow pastures, Brown Heritage entered the quarter mile homestretch all alone. The best European harriers were nearly 200 meters back when Brown Heritage crossed the finish line, the first of a record five consecutive victories in the event.

"To win that, because it was the first world championship for women, was a pretty awesome experience," Brown Heritage says. "I remember the feeling—I can see it and taste it and smell it—but I don't know how to put it into words." More than her own victory, Brown Heritage valued the entire experience and what the event held for the future of women's distance running. "I had a feeling," she recalls, "that my winning would make a difference to the AAU [Amateur Athletic Union], that maybe the U.S. women would get to have a team the next year." Indeed, in 1968 the AAU did send a women's team to the meet. Brown Heritage won again and Falcon teammate Vicki Foltz finished second, and the U.S. defeated England by a single point. The downside was that everyone had to pay their own way to the competition; the level playing field hadn't been conceived just yet."

Brown would win the event four more times.

The US State Department under the direction of two-time Olympic 800-meter Gold medalist Mal Whitfield stepped up and sponsored the 1968 team with Browning as Coach for the race in Tunis, Tunisia. The State Department picked up all transportation expenses, while the AAU agreed to pay clothing and other expenses.

With team sponsorship in place, Browning turned to picking the team. Neil Weygandt remembered Browning turning races at Boat House Row in Philadelphia into mini tryouts for the team by placing pommel horses on the course to test the mid-race leaping ability of runners interested in trying out for the team.

The men's team consisted of Bill Clark, Herb Lorenz, Don Lakin, Tom Heinonen, Doug Wiebe, Bill Reilly and Moses Mayfield. Clark's 26th place finish and Lorenz's 34th place helped lead the US men to a 7th place finish.

The State Department also scheduled stops for the team in Ethiopia to promote goodwill through running and asked only that the team brief the State Department on their return on what they had seen on their travels through Africa.

Doris Brown and Vicki Fultz finished first and second in Tunis to lead the U.S. women's team to a first-place team finish. Ironically, women would not be able to officially enter the Boston Marathon for another four years.

Tom Heinonen remembered, "The 1968 trip team was selected primarily by the AAU Cross-Country Championships in Chicago Washington Park) in November 1967. Mal Whitfield was working in Africa for the US State Dept. With the championships in Tunis in March 1968, he wanted to take the team on a month-long tour in Africa, doing clinics and races.

No serious Olympic team contender was willing to go to Africa for a month, so the team spots went begging. I finished 13th at 1967 AAU's and was the sixth person to accept the invitation. The team must have been eight men.

Moses Mayfield, a black steelworker from Philadelphia was added to the team. He hadn't run in the AAU's. As I recall, he and Browning kidded a lot and seemed to know each other before the team got together.

Moses was vision-impaired, had extraordinarily thick glasses. (Browning worried how Mayfield would deal with the cross country obstacles.)

The team included several military guys who were glad to be in Africa, not Viet Nam.

The day of the championships in Tunis was my graduation day (end of winter quarter) at the University of Minnesota. I remember having to apply to graduate "in absentia."

Browning must have served in World War II in North Africa or in France. I remember him laughing about speaking French. He tried to tell us that GI's pronounced thank you very much (merci beaucoup) as "murky buck-up".

Browning was a delightful guy, very self-effacing. There were officers among the military guys on the trip. He was more than willing to let them take charge of things.

After Tunis, where Gammoudi won the race in front of the king, we flew to Rome for a couple days and then flew via Cairo (I saw MIG-15s with Russian red stars on their fuselages, sitting on the tarmac) to Addis Ababa.

Abebe Bikila, among others, met us at the plane wearing a military uniform including pith helmet.

We raced 10km in the streets of Addis Ababa. The Ethiopian team, led by Mamo Wolde, waxed us. I was the top American finisher in 10th place.

I'd been in Alamosa, Colorado, the previous summer in a study conducted by Jack Daniels, so I was the only US runner with serious altitude experience.

We spent a few days in rural Ethiopia trying to conduct a couple of clinics, but all distance runners, we were pretty inept and ignorant in the other track events.

Next, we flew to Dar es Salaam, Tanzania, and stayed overnight. I saw a sign that said "Tanganyika Crocodile Company". We stayed a plush hotel right on the Indian Ocean and I remember eating "T-Bone Steak Texas Style" in their restaurant.

Next day we flew to Lusaka, Zambia. We drove far north in Zambia to an area near the Katanga province of what had been the Belgian Congo.

There had been a massacre there not long before, but that was north of us, across the border. I recall two geographic names Nchanga and Chingola in Zambia, where we were. I don't recall if they were towns or a province.

Everyone was getting sick sometime during the trip. I recall eating a couple of "Heath Bars," and later that day being violently ill. I haven't touched one since. Do they even make them anymore? (To the author,)Did your family own the company?

There was to be a cross country race there between us and local runners. A couple of days before the race, word came from the US that Martin Luther King Jr. had been assassinated. The local newspaper wanted to know what Moses Mayfield thought. They interviewed him but made up quotes, things that he hadn't said with words he didn't use. And they said he probably wouldn't run the race, as a protest. As I recall, that made him even more determined to run, although he'd been ill too.

The team ran. I sat out, still sick. There was a stream with steep banks. If you jumped far enough, you got across. If not, you slid down the side into the water and had to find a way up and out. Several people, including Moses, spent a lot of time down there.

The next day, we drove back to Zambia to Lusaka. We'd heard that there were thousands of people protesting in front of the US Embassy.

On the trip, we skirted the central square of a couple towns where people had gathered. I don't recall protests in Lusaka by the time we got there.

We flew home from Lusaka. It had been a month.

None of us made a dent in the 1968 Olympic team."

After returning from the trip, Browning sent a postcard to the team members asking for their thoughts on the trip for inclusion in the Long Distance Log. Bonnie Ross, I remember dad saying he was terrified of Ethiopian Emperor Haile Selassie's pet lion. He had to cross in front of it to get around at the palace."

1968 was an Olympic year and also a year of fierce competition between Puma and Adidas for top athletes. Rumors ran rampant. Vince Phillips, "On the trip, Herb Lorenz said his roommate, a veteran of the US team told him if he left his shoes outside his hotel room door, sponsors would stuff cash into the shoes during the night. Herb opted out, but the roommate put his shoes outside and the next morning they were gone."

Browning saved Tom Heinonen's essay on the Ethiopian portion of the International Cross Country trip titled, "How to acclimatize in seven easy days, or show me and American and I'll show you a loser." Heinonen's essay, reprinted here gives an in-depth account of the team's week in Ethiopia and its humorous style is reminiscent but predates the movie "If it's Tuesday this must be Belgium," by a year.

"They called the first competition a 10,000-meter cross country race. It turned out to be a 5 1/2 mile fiasco. The second effort was a track meet. But why were all of those guys kicking a ball around the infield for thirty minutes between events?

We heard the reason later. An official said, "Oh yes, this is a track meet. We're just having the soccer games to attract a crowd."

The American cross country team flew into Addis Ababa, Ethiopia on Wednesday, March 20, hoping to learn something about high altitude. (They claim Addis is at 7200 feet but no one knows for sure.) Mal Whitfield, who's been with the USIS in Africa for many years, had two races set up for us. The first was a cross-country race the following Sunday.

In order to find out how bad altitude really is, I convinced most of the team to run a 1 1/2 mile time trial on the track (6 x 400 meters) on our second day in Addis. Bill Clark did 7:10, Bill Reilly 7:19; I staggered in through a 7:24. Doug Wiebe jogged off the track after three laps, saying "there ain't no way..."

It's a real ego smasher to run that slow and feel so bad. But it seems to be the best way to learn respect for high altitude.

Watching some of the Ethiopians work out, we realized they weren't hackers. So we all ran pretty hard in the days before the race, knowing it wouldn't make much difference whether or not we were tired on Sunday.

We were right. At the start, there were twenty of them and seven of us. At the finish, there were eight of them before ANY of us. I got ninth in 28:23-- not bad for 10,000 meters on the roads at 7200 feet, huh? We agreed it was about 5 1/2 miles.

Because I spent eleven weeks last summer at 7500 feet in Alamosa with Jack Daniels' study, and none of the others had any high altitude experience, at least one conclusion might be drawn: some degree of previous experience is beneficial to performance upon acute exposure to high altitude.

I shudder to think of the conclusions the Ethiopians drew after we had spent the previous three days showing them how to train.

The second race was on the following Thursday although no one seemed sure of when the Meet would start. It was either at two, four or six P.M. We all went over to the stadium at six, hoping it had been at two or four.

The crowd looked surprisingly large for a track meet.

Programs listed the 800 and 1500 both for 6:05 P.M., the steeplechase at 6:35 and the 5,000 at 7:05. Maybe the schedule would be filled in by other events for the local people, we thought. Then two junior football teams scrambled onto the field and we were enlightened. Sure, it was a track meet, with the events between halves as a sideshow.

The first event, the 800 meters, got off at halftime of the first game. Herb Lorenz was the lucky or unlucky American on the basis of his 49.7 quarter two years ago, though he'd done no speed work for months. His 1:55 was a creditable third.

The 1500 meters came between games although the officials initially wanted to run it *simultaneously* with the 800. After warming up twice for false alarms, Bill Clark was in no mood to race anyone. He ran about 4:20 while Bill Reilly got second in 4:04 which was a pretty fair effort, all factors considered.

Don Lakin ran about 9:50 for third in the steeplechase during halftime of the second game. An Ethiopian who looked to be about thirty-five years old ran 9:06 in his first ever steeplechase-- a good demonstration of the raw talent in Ethiopia, that will probably stay undeveloped until the educational and sanitary problems are solved.

I can attest to the sanitary problems myself. After several days of constant diarrhea, it takes no imagination to figure out what type of personal disaster struck me in the 5000. (I finished in 16:10.)

Dough Wiebe did 15:27 in the 5000 which was run at nine o'clock, two hours after its scheduled start. Converting Wiebe's time to about 14:55 for three miles, it was perhaps the best altitude effort by any of us. Mamo Walde won easily in 14:40.

We hightailed it out of Ethiopia the next morning, having manifestly shown that, come October, a lifetime at 7000 feet will beat the hell out of a week there."

Bill Clark finished second in the 1968 Boston Marathon the following month.

After the Championship race in Tunis, and the week in Ethiopia, the team continued its international tour and stopped for races in Kenya, Zambia (a new country at the time), Turkey and Greece.

After returning from the trip Browning ran and won a Masters Mile race in Cape May, NJ, and was interviewed about the trip through Kenya, Tanzania, Zambia, the Congo and the Republic of South Africa.

Browning remembered the Congo having the toughest course. "The 6k course was in the first place located 120 miles inside Bush country and consisted mainly of lumpy clay. We knew it was going to be trouble when we saw one of the local runners being carried back with a broken ankle and the rest covered with scratches. They told us the course was murderous. After we ran over the lumpy clay, we ran on into the bush, then over sand dunes, and through corn fields. That was the easy part. The next obstacle was a river, where it was necessary to slide down a muddy bank and the swim across. On the other side, you had to haul yourself up by grabbing onto little bushes and their roots. We continued on through corn fields where the runners approached and frightened native women carrying harvested corn on their heads.

For some reason, they were frightened and dropped everything and ran. Again, the course swung back to the river, here about 15 feet across. The African runners simply jumped across the river but I and some of our other runners took a dive.

The purpose of our trip after the International Cross- Country race was to conduct running clinics for African high school runners. The high school students we came in contact with were older than those in the U.S. The average senior we saw was 25 years old.

Bob Shryock of the Woodbury Times also interviewed Browning a few days after his return from the 1968 tour. "The International Championship race in Tunis was a difficult 7-and-a-half-mile course. The US team was not a member of the International Cross-Country Union and finished seventh. We could have done much better with our top runners, guys like Tracy Smith, Billy Mills, and Gerry Lindgren. The Tunisians used the barriers they had for horse races and combined it with a figure X in the infield. There were over 10,000 spectators there."

Browning ran in several of the teams' races only because some of his runners became ill during the trip. It takes about six months to get properly acclimated to the altitude, "The Ethiopians and Kenyans were some of the best runners in the world when we went over to "teach them about running." They listened to us politely and then went on to dominate all of the races under some rough conditions. We gave a three-hour speech to a police sports unit in

Addis Ababa and they just stared at us and no one said a word. We found out later that of the 20 people who were there only two spoke English.

I remember startling some of the villagers carrying water on their heads when we ran through their fields. We got to Ethiopia earlier than expected and there was no one to greet us so we went to our hotel. The next morning, we had to go back to the airport for our "official greeting."

Before we left Ethiopia we had another snafu, they presented us with a carving that had special significance to them. Somehow the handoff was fumbled as they presented it to us and the carving crashed to the ground and broke. I remember the Ethiopian soldier who presented it not being too happy as we left!"

Heinonen, Clark and Tracy Smith traveled to Clydebank Scotland to represent the 1969 U.S. team at the World Championships.

In January 1970 Browning, anticipating the difficulty of fielding a competitive team, sent a letter to the head of the IAAF (International Association of Athletics Federation) proposing that the United States be allowed to join the International Cross-Country Union. The IAAF had closed the Union which controlled many of the best international cross country meets to 12 nations. In order for a new country like the United States to be admitted a country in the Union had to drop out. Portugal was rumored to drop out and Tunisia jockeyed for another African Country to possibly replace Portugal, while Great Britain favored the United States.

Browning returned as coach of the 1970 U.S. Cross Country team that competed in Vichy, France. The team consisting of Charles Messenger, (Villanova, Kenny Moore (Oregon and 1972 U.S. Olympic Marathoner) Tom Heinonen, (Minnesota), Cliff Clark, (California), John Loeschorn (NYU), Bill Norris, (Boston College) and Tim Hendricks (Peru State-Nebraska). Again, without most of the top American runners, the team managed only a disappointing 13th place.

In his role as AAU National Long Distance Chairman from 1969 to 1971, Browning used the national office to promote cross- country. He proposed forming a new Western Hemisphere Cross Country Union with IAAF approval, consisting of the US, Canada, Mexico, the Caribbean and

Central American countries with a championship to be run in December after the Western Hemisphere cross country season ended instead of March at the height of the African and European cross-country season.

Ross wrote: "Why compete in an event almost foreign to us-- 7 ½ miles of hurdles, barriers, sand etc. without our top collegiate and AAU athletes who find it difficult to get away from their jobs at great expense to compete at the height of their cross-country season.

Our cross-country championships in November are also not held at a time conducive to selecting a team for a championship event in late March and in the past we have selected the top indoor two and three-milers who have flopped in the grueling International Cross Country." Ross's proposed Western Hemisphere Cross country championships would have prospective sponsors in New York or with the Sugar Bowl in Louisiana.

The U.S. senior men did not compete in 1971, 1972, 1973 and 1974 meets. The 1972 Meet was the last competition organized by the International Cross Country Union (ICCU). The organization of the event was transferred to the IAAF as recommended at a meeting of the IAAF cross-country committee that year in London.

The world championships were continued as the IAAF World Cross Country Championships starting in 1973. From then on, the event was open to all IAAF members whereas before, Non-ICCU members like the United States were only allowed to compete after special invitation.

The United States senior men's team returned to the meet in 1975.

For a 50 year span, from his days as a Woodbury High School Cross-Country State Champion, to his AAU National Cross-Country Championship, to his promotion of cross country races as a result of founding of the Road Runners Club of America, to his publishing national and international cross-country meet results in the Long Distance Log, to his days as the U.S. National Cross Country Coach and as a high school and college cross country coach-- few have done more than Browning Ross to promote the sport of Cross Country in the USA.

1968 USA Cross-Country team's Tom Heinonen and Bill Reilly
confer with the Ethiopian team before a race.
Olympic greats Mamo Wolde and Abebe Bikila were on the Ethiopian team.

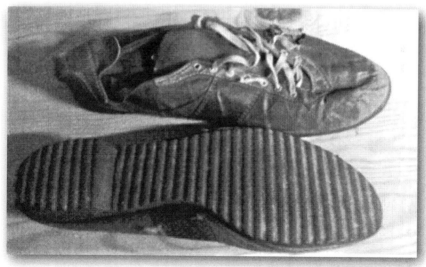

Browning Ross designed running shoes were short-lived.

THE MAGIC ELIXIR

In 1968 the Mid-Atlantic Road Runners Club compiled a booklet similar to Fred Wilt's "How They Train" books featuring the training schedules of top area runners. Browning was 44, and reflected on his present and past training:

> "I train all year around, 5-6-7 days a week except for breaks due to injuries and when my Achilles gets especially troublesome. I'd like to find something new in training, something the others haven't got... The same elixir perhaps which all the athletes of the world are seeking. It used to all click when I was training. It was flowing even though I only used to run 30 to 40 miles a week. Training was a joy. At Villanova in my peak years, they knew nothing about training and usually I was lucky to average 20 miles a week."

Here was a typical week of training for him at the time:

> Mon: 5 1/2 miles through the woods
> Tues: 5 1/2 miles on the track
> Wed: 6 1/2 miles through Wenonah Woods
> Thurs: 5 1/2 miles through woods
> Fri: 5 miles on the track
> Sat: 4 1/2 miles on the track
> "Browning considered his running pace as slow steady but it was relatively fast."

Tom Osler: "I couldn't train with Browning; even in his forties his usual training pace was much too fast for me."

Bonnie Ross, "I remember one time we were waiting for dad to come home from a run in the woods for dinner and he never showed up. We were really getting worried because that had never happened. Then a few hours later he finally came home. He had stepped on a nail while running, it went through his shoe into his foot and he blacked out. When he finally recovered he jogged home. That was the danger of training in the woods, there was no one around."

Barry Ross remembered a similar incident, "Dad stepped on the spike running down the railroad tracks. His foot blew up, and he went to the hospital. When he was released the doctor gave him strict orders not to out to run until the foot healed. Well, since the doc said not to "go out" and run he decided he would run 500 times around the dining room table. Ten times one way, ten times the other till he got to 500. Mom thought he was a bit eccentric, to say the least."

In early April of 1968, a terrible event ended one of Browning's favorite races for good. Tom Derderian, "In April 1968 I hitchhiked from UMass in Amherst to run the Cathedral Race, but when I got there I couldn't find it. Martin Luther King's assassination led to a cancellation that I didn't know about. It was never held again."

In September of 1969, Browning accepted the Gloucester County YMCA director position to open the new YMCA building in Woodbury. An excerpt from Stan Boody's interview with Browning in the Woodbury Times spotlights Browning's efforts to improve youth fitness through incentives:

"If you want to run a smooth business hire a smooth runner.

The new YMCA building on Red Bank Avenue will soon be open for business with former Olympian Browning Ross as the physical education director. "They have been very good to me in Salem County during my nine years there, but I couldn't pass up this opportunity. This has been my home for a good many years."

Ross was teaching school and working part time at the Salem County YMCA in 1960. Working two jobs became too much of a strain so he had to make a choice.

"It wasn't a hard choice to make," said Ross. "I didn't especially like teaching that much, but I've been interested in the YMCA ever since I was in grade school. My job at Salem gave me an opportunity to work a program out for myself. I tried various things out and I had as many failures as successes but I feel we had a good program. (Ross's job was to set up athletic programs throughout Salem County.)

"Our physical fitness program in Salem County was very successful. The kids had to go through a series of 19 tests. Each time they reached a higher level they received a different color T-shirt. It was a thrill to receive a red T-shirt which designated a youngers as All-American, but the big goal was to get a gold T-shirt. That made the wearer an Olympian. It may not seem like such a big deal to some people, getting a gold T-shirt for top achievement, but our winners were just as excited over that piece of cloth as a gold-medal winner in the Olympics."

Browning's job will be to oversee the entire athletic program. Plans call for a learn-to-swim campaign, competitive swimming, and a series of gym and fitness classes."

In 1970 and 1971, Browning was still running fast enough to win both Open and Masters races.

He finished first in a Masters mile in 4:55 in Convention Hall in Philadelphia, first in a Philadelphia Masters 3 Mile in 17:52. He also finished first in the Atlantic Coast 5 mile Masters Championship in 28:39. He also won the Cape May 2 mile road run in 10:34 at 46 years old.

Neil Weygandt: "About this point, Browning seemed to tire of racing. He was easily winning the master's races easily, but I don't think the Master's races were challenging enough for him. In fact, I asked him about that. We were driving to a race together and he was going to help time the race but not run. I asked him if he was a little bored with running master's races and he said something along the lines of, "Yeah, it is kind of hard to get that excited about trying to win a masters division in these races when you've traveled around the world and run in so many races for so long."

Browning soon found a new challenge-- a return to coaching.

Jock Semple, Browning's Navy friend and Boston Marathon Race
Director with Amby Burfoot 1968 Boston Marathon Champion.

Browning Ross is a Pro?
Trouble with the AAU

"Have courage for the great sorrows of life and patience for the
small ones; and when you have laboriously accomplished your
daily task, go to sleep in peace. God is awake." Victor Hugo

THE MAY 7, 1969, PHILADELPHIA Bulletin, featured a large picture of
Browning running by Independence Hall in Philadelphia in a charity event
to raise money for the 1964 US Olympic team. The picture was accompanied
by an article written by George Kiseda about Browning's increasing conflicts
with the AAU. Francis (Frank) Carver had contacted the AAU numerous

times to request that Browning be banned from competition, and be considered a professional. (Kiseda later wrote for the Los Angeles Times and was called by Hall of Fame writer Bob Ryan of the Boston Globe "the greatest NBA writer of all time".)

"Browning Ross a pro? Somebody say it isn't so. There were always certain truths nobody could deny. De Gaulle got his mail at Elysee Palace... Sam Jones wore a Kelly-green uniform, black low cuts, and made bank shots, Joe Kuharic wore white socks, drank from a water bucket and seven times a year would show up at Franklin Field on a Sunday to be booed...and Browning Ross was an amateur. Now, what is there left to believe in? Next, somebody will announce that Raquel Welch is a boy. Browning Ross a pro? "It's ridiculous," Browning Ross said.

"He has to typify the real amateur of the world," Villanova Coach Jumbo Elliott said. "I don't think you could be more of an amateur."

According to the Middle Atlantic AAU, Browning Ross has been capitalizing on his fame as an athlete by selling track shoes, and that is against the rules. Browning Ross is so famous that he is constantly besieged by people seeking his autograph. "I get about one request a year," He said.

Browning Ross, 44, ex-Villanovan is the loneliest of long distance runners. He has been running for 30 years, picking up a medal here, a trophy there, sometimes a ribbon, sometimes nothing but a good sweat, frequently paying his own expenses. He has accumulated perhaps the world's greatest collection of useless silverware ("My wife doesn't want the trophies in the house, so we stick them in the attic.")

Twice an Olympian, a gold medalist in the 1,500 meters at the Pan American Games in Buenos Aires in 1951, eight times a National champion, he has long ceased to be a world class competitor. But until the local AAU found him breaking the rules of amateurism he still competed in assorted road races—for fun.

Ross lives in a modest three-bedroom home in Woodbury, N.J. wife his wife Rosemarie, two daughters 17 and 5 and a miler son, 14.

He drives a four-year-old Pontiac and he works for the Salem County YMCA in Penns Grove, N.J. Yesterday he ran six miles around the neighborhood. Tomorrow he will do the same. He likes to run.

The man who turned him in is Frank Carver, 26 ex-Notre Carver, a competitive runner himself, chairman of the Middle Atlantic AAU long distance running committee. Ross is chairman of the National AAU long distance running committee. Carver is scandalized that national chairman would do the things he says Ross has done. Other people are scandalized that Carver would say such things about Ross.

"To the best of my knowledge," Carver said, "he should be ineligible. He is selling track shoes. He is using his association with sports to make money, which is professional. He's been tied in with a sporting goods store in Woodbury ever since I've known him-12-13 years." (Lie! Browning wrote in the margin.) "Everybody's kind of overlooked it for a long time. He sells track shoes at track meets and cross-country meets to other runners.

"I think all the money he makes is tied in with athletics. I'd say at least half the income for his family comes from athletics. (Lie! Browning wrote again.)

"I'm still trying to unravel this thing. A couple of weeks ago (it was April 19) he ran in an AAU race in Fairmount Park. He finished second or third. I think they entered some fictitious name in the results, which is a flagrant violation of the rules. It was done as a joke, but it's no joking matter. A professional isn't supposed to be in an AAU race. He could jeopardize everybody else in the race. He's the national chairman, and he's perhaps the biggest violator of the rules." (Note- Browning ran the race under the name "L.D. Log")

Ross admits that technically he has broken the rules, but a pro?

"If I was making a fortune on these shoes," he said, "It would be different. "But this is just a part-time thing. The whole thing is ridiculous, I don't think I ever made a penny out of athletics except for these shoes and even there it is not that much money, just enough to keep the magazine going."

AH, THE MAGAZINE, another source of irritation for Carver.

Ross is the publisher, editor, advertising director, circulation manager, production chief, copy reading department and reportorial staff of Long Distance Log, a monthly magazine dedicated to promoting long distance running in 28 pages of fine print.

"This is another thing he got away with," Carver said. "What would have happened if it had been financially successful?" The worldwide circulation of Long Distance Log is between 1,200 and 1,500. Subscriptions are $4 a year. Ads are $60 a page. There was one ad in the February issue.

The ad was for Tiger track shoes, the Japanese brand Ross sells. "What I'm selling the shoes for is to finance the magazine," Ross said. "Printing expenses got so high. I was $1,300 in debt."

Ross estimated it has cost him about $30,000 to be an amateur long-distance runner- an average of $1,000 a year.

Nobody has been more active in recent years promoting distance running. Ross stages road races and even whole track meets, donating his own trophies as prizes. "I remember this one meet," said a New Jersey man whose teenaged son came home with one of Ross' trophies, "Browning Ross ran the whole meet. He brought his trophies in a cardboard box. He stood there with a clipboard taking down the names of all the contestants. He fired the starting gun. And I swear he was at the finish line holding the tape. Who does more for track than Browning Ross?"

Ross said he has received hundreds of letters from other runners across the country expressing amazement at the AAU's action.

Carver said he has noticed some of the other athletes giving him black looks. "I guess I probably am a villain," Carver said. "I feel I'm right. I feel the AAU rules have to be supported. People kind of closed their eyes to him for a decade. Somebody once called him the father of distance running in this country. HE IS one of the masters at establishing the sport here. "But that doesn't give him the right to violate the rules."

AAU officials point out that Ross has the right of appeal- all the way up to the National AAU convention- but has not exercised that right. They may not have to wait much longer.

"I'm gonna go up there with some of the bills from the magazine," Ross said. "I don't give a damn about Carver. But I want to show them the money isn't going into my pocket."

Browning, unfailingly tranquil, saved the article and felt strongly enough about it to make the one-word "lie!" notes in the margins of the article next to each of the accusations.

As Browning's suspension held in the summer of 1969, the running community rallied to inundate the Mid-Atlantic AAU office with letters supporting Browning's amateur reinstatement. Representative of the passion of the correspondence was a July letter from Edward O'Connell of Tufts University's Fletcher School of Law and Diplomacy. It was addressed to the Chairman of the Mid Atlantic AAU. O'Connell was also the President of the Road Runners Club of America at the time:

"I am astonished to learn that the Middle Atlantic Association of the AAU has initiated action to deprive Browning Ross of his amateur standing. It appears that this is a course of action that reaches ludicrous proportions.

Surely, anyone even remotely familiar with Browning Ross and his life-long dedication to amateur sports must realize that in fact he is the epitome of the true amateur. For over a decade with tremendous inputs of time and energy and even of his personal money, he has subsidized the publication of the Long Distance Log. As every enthusiast of long-distance running knows, the Log is a service publication, not a profit-making venture. Probably more than any other factor, Browning's hard work in this area has contributed to the phenomenal growth of distance running as a sport through our country. He took a sport that had largely been limited to activity on the East coast and in California and made it truly national in character.

How could Mr. Carver or anyone else look into his heart and accuse Browning Ross of being a professional shoe clerk? We all know that if he were money oriented he could improve his personal fortune much more readily by devoting whatever leisure hours he may have to truly commercial and remunerative activities. If Browning Ross performs a service for young athletes by advising them of what is proper footwear for running and this service in any way defrays the cost of publishing the Long Distance Log, I say bully for him! This is the kind of initiative our sport so sorely needs.

It occurs to me that no one ever raised any dispute when Browning Ross lent his name and fame and carried the torch through the streets of Philadelphia raising nickels, dimes and quarters for the U.S. Olympic Team. Here is a man whose devotion to the highest standards of amateur athletics has indeed been exemplary. To punish him for his zeal and devotion would not only be short-sighted and vindictive but would do a great disservice to the sport of long distance running, probably one of the few remaining sanctuaries of amateur athletics as espoused by the AAU. Whoever heard of a marathon runner capitalizing on his fame? The idea is absurd!

Browning Ross has reached a stage in life where he is no longer a threat to win national championships. He wishes to participate for the sheer joy and zest of competition. As a competitor of his, I miss him in the field. No runner ever found it a shame to finish behind Browning Ross.

As President of the Road Runners Club of America, speaking on behalf of hundreds of amateur athletes across this country, I earnestly request that you consider restoring Browning Ross to his full and deserved status as an amateur. To do less that this would be a dishonor to one of the finest persons it has been my privilege to know in my thirty years of experience in organized athletics.

I am enclosing an extra copy of this letter which I would appreciate making available to Mr. Frank Carver.

Sincerely yours,

Edward F. O'Connell

President, Road Runners Club of America

Ironically, Carver's road race victories were featured in articles written by Browning in the Long Distance Log before he assumed his administrative position with the AAU. Most Mid-Atlantic AAU area runners were confused by Carver's persistent pursuit of Browning. It seemed to many that Carver was playing Inspector Javert to Browning Ross's Jean Valjean. Carver could sense the resentment from other runners when he went to a race.

Neil Weygandt, "Carver was highly respected as a good runner, but many runners lost respect for him because it appeared he turned on Browning and was hounding him."

Vince Phillips remembers Herb Lorenz mentioning how he and other top runners would see Carver at a race and point and say, "There goes Fran Carver, the guy that keeps trying to get Browning in trouble."

Many tried to guess at Carver's motivation, some thought he had designs on the National Long-Distance Chair position that Browning held, but the reason may have been less concrete— a matter of principle rather than one personal gain.

Carver was also a member of the Penn A.C. and married one of Jack St. Clair's daughters Kathleen. St. Clair had coached Carver at Cardinal Dougherty. Carver was quoted in the Philadelphia Inquirer's obituary of St. Clair in March 2007 crediting St. Clair with helping him to get a scholarship to Notre Dame, "Jack helped scores of people like me who would never have had a chance to go to college," Carver said. "Eventually any runner who "The Saint" recommended was accepted by Notre Dame sight unseen."

In the fall of 2016, I contacted Frank Carver about his role in Browning Ross's suspension by the AAU, and he graciously agreed to speak with me.

Question: I know that you were Philadelphia Catholic League Cross-Country Champion, and the state half and mile champion at Cardinal Dougherty, and won a number of other races at Notre Dame. How did you start running?
FC: I started running with a Penn A.C street run in 1956.

What was your relationship with Browning before you called the AAU to report him?
FC: I had no relation with Browning besides seeing him at races. As far as runners go there was Browning Ross and there was everyone else. He would usually run the race, win it and leave so I had no social relationship with him.

Tom Osler talked about being present at the Penn AC meeting when Browning tried to start the Road Runners Club of America. He talked about your Jack St. Clair, your father in law, who was an AAU official giving him a hard time while he was speaking until Browning gave up and left and quit the club. Did that incident influence your call to the AAU about Browning? Were you trying to support your future father in law?
FC: Well, let's put it this way he (St. Clair) didn't try to stop me from calling.

At the time you were both AAU Chairman, you were the local AAU Chair and Browning the National Chair. Did you have any interest in replacing Browning and becoming the National Chairman?
FC: No, I didn't care about that. I did think that because Browning was the National Chairman he had the responsibility to hold himself to the highest amateur standards.

You were aware though that your phone calls would likely result in sanctions for Browning including suspension from running races?
FC: Yes, of course. I'd been sanctioned by the AAU while running for Notre Dame for running in the Ohio Relays without a permit and I was suspended for a season of indoor races.

Were you prepared for the reaction you received from the other runners after you reported Browning and he was suspended?
FC: It was hard to go to a race and get hear negative words or get the cold shoulder from the other runners, but I did what I thought was right at the time in my position (of Mid-Atlantic AAU Chair.)

What was Browning's reaction to you?
FC: I had no contact with him besides seeing him in races.
He was right behind me in one race, and I know he could have easily gone by me and pulled away but he never did.

OF course, Browning always maintained the accusations were baseless. Did it bother you that Browning didn't seem contrite enough, or that he was defying the sanctions after you made the accusations?
FC: Yes, it did. It bothered me that he kind of made a joke about it continuing to run as "L.D. Log" and continuing the running activities he was involved in.

So what was your motivation, if not personal, for going through the trouble to contact the AAU? It made Browning's life a lot harder and obviously your life as well because of the reaction you received from runners.
FC: My main motivation was I thought the Road Runners Club that Browning was starting was going to hurt the AAU, dilute the number of races we were able to put on. The AAU sponsored about a race a week, and I saw the RRCA as a threat. I thought they would be in competition with each other and runners would end up having fewer races to run with a weakened AAU.

Do you think Jack St. Clair felt the same way, that the RRCA was a bad idea that would threaten the AAU?
FC: Yes, I believe so.

Looking back, do you feel your efforts to have the AAU sanction Browning and the resulting consequences were a good idea? Would you do the same thing again?
FC: Of course not. The Road Runners Club, of course, turned out to be a good thing for runners. It played a huge part in actually expanding the running world-- both a number of races and runners. I felt strongly about it at the time, but in hindsight, I wouldn't do the same thing, it was a mistake. Browning, besides being a great runner himself, made huge contributions to the growth of the sport through his founding the Road Runners Club and by publishing the Long Distance Log.

Browning never complained, but he paid a personal price for all of the contributions he made to American Distance Running. Suspensions from the AAU for permitting women to run races, for carrying running shoes when they were almost impossible to find, for coaching and for publishing a national distance running magazine and indirectly for starting the Road Runners Club of America. These were all things that greatly improved the sport of running.

Hockey Hall of Famer Bobby Hull once said, "Well, pioneers always suffer. I don't care who is the first to embark upon things-- they went through hell doing it, but it had to be done."

Browning Ross lights Olympic Torch at Baltimore's City Hall after winning special Maryland Day run from Annapolis to that city. With him are (from left) John St. Clair, PAC Track Coach; Phil Jackelski, Nat'l AAU Walking Chrmn.; Al Whitle (wearing badge), former AAU President; and Mrs. Jackelski.

Browning lights the 1968 Olympic torch passing through Baltimore.

The Browning Ross Affair – A Happy Ending

LUCKILY FOR BROWNING, FRANK CARVER, and the rest of the American running world affected by the sanctions placed on Browning by the AAU, the suspension was amicably resolved in December of 1969 at the AAU National Convention in Atlantic City.

The details of the resolution follow in a letter published at the conclusion of the Convention by Bill Marmot:

"The "Browning Ross Affair" as Track & Field News recently described this situation came to a happy ending on Wednesday, Dec. 3,

1969, at the meeting of the National AAU Registration Committee at the 82nd Annual National AAU Convention held at the Marco Polo Hotel in Miami Beach, Florida.

Two-time U.S. Olympic runner (steeplechase, 1948 & 52) and 1951 Pan American Games 1500-meter gold medal champion, Browning Ross was suspended by the Middle Atlantic Assoc. of the AAU early in 1969 due to a personal misunderstanding between Ross and Middle Atlantic AAU Long Distance Running Committee Chairman, Frank Carver, ex-Notre Dame star. Ross, former Villanova star, holder of 10 National AAU Championships, founder of the Road Runners Club of America in 1957 and its first President; editor & chief of the Long Distance Log, a monthly publication of race results published since 1956; and National Chairman of the AAU Long Distance & Road Running Committee and the pioneer promoter of long-distance running in the United States explained in detail in a letter to Mr. Arthur Toner, Chairman of the National AAU Registration Committee that this whole unfortunate affair stemmed from a personal matter between himself and Carver.

Ross was suspended by the Middle Atlantic AAU in November of 1968 that Ross was a pro because he was selling Tiger shoes in the Long Distance Log. Ross stated in his letter to Mr. Toner and to the Middle Atlantic AAU that the financial rewards received were to help pull the Long Distance Log out of the red, and that he was selling the shoes for the whole purpose of paying off the Log, a publication Ross has spent quite a sum of money out of his own pocket over the years.

Runners all over the U.S., as well as friends of Ross, rallied to his support and many newspaper articles were printed defending Ross stating that although Ross would never compete again on a serious basis as he is 45 years old, the important issue is the principle of the whole affair.

The 7th Annual Eastern Regional Meeting of the Road Runners Club of American at Atlantic City, N.J. on Sept. 27th, resolved that the National AAU Long Distance & Road Running Committee, such that many are members of that committee should contest this situation and come to the aid of Browning Ross since the Middle Atlantic AAU was putting the whole affair in the hands of the National AAU Registration Committee. At Atlantic City, former National AAU Long Distance Running Committee Chairman Aldo Scandurra started the ball rolling by agreeing to contact Mr. Pincus Sober, National AAU official, and attorney.

I, Bill Marot had a long talk with my old friend, Mr. Ed League, the new President of the Middle Atlantic AAU and a close friend of Browning Ross who said he would do everything possible to help Ross.

When I arrived in Miami Beach on Nov. 29th I started at once to lobby support for my friend Browning Ross. I had an informal meeting with my friend Jerry Hardy, a member of the National AAU Registration Committee; Dr. Myles Barton; Mr. AAU himself, Dan Ferris and Mr. Arthur Toner. I was most encouraged when Dan Ferris told me he was familiar with this situation as was Track & Field Administrator Ollan Cassell, who I also met with.

On Wed. Dec. 3rd I presented Ross's appeal to the National AAU Registration Committee, as Ross did not arrive until Dec 4th as he was delayed due to the fact he started a new job in Woodbury, N.J., his hometown as director of the YMCA. Aldo Scandurra was tied up in men's Track & Field so he asked me to intercede for Ross.

After presenting the case to the Registration Committee and answering quite a few questions by committee members this case came to a vote. May I also add that former National AAU Long Distance Chairman, Marv Thomas from the Central AAU, and Mr. Bill Dowling from the D.C. AAU were also very helpful and then (Olympian) Mr. "Jack" Kelley the AAU 2nd Vice President, from Philadelphia and the Middle Atlantic AAU testified on behalf of Browning Ross.

Thus, after hearing the facts, it was the nearly unanimous vote of the National AAU Registration Committee that Mr. H. Browning Ross was reinstated to full amateur status. And may I add everyone concerned was very glad that the "Browning Ross Affair" ended on this most happy note! And on Friday morning, December 5th the National AAU Board of Governors upheld the decision of the Registration Committee to reinstate Browning Ross thus making their recommendation official.

On Thursday, December 4th, Browning Ross was reelected to his third straight term as Chairman of the National AAU Long Distance & Road Running Committee and on Saturday, December 6th at the Awards Luncheon in the Persian Room of the Marco Polo Hotel, Mr. Robert DeCelle of Alameda, Ca. (a Co-Chairman of the National AAU Long Distance & Road Running Committee) presented the 1st Annual Award for the person over the past 20 years contributing the most to long distance running. The award went to Browning Ross. The silver tray award was accepted by Browning Ross in a most modest fashion. The tray was inscribed…. "AAU OF THE U.S.A., AWARD OF MERIT, TO, H. BROWNING ROSS, FOR OUTSTANDING SERVICE AND CONTRIBUTION, TO THE SPORT OF LONG DISTANCE RUNNING, 1969."

A very happy ending. Only at a National AAU Convention could a man be reinstated and given an award at the same time…

Sincerely,
Bill Marot
Wilbraham, Mass 01095
Member-at-Large National AAU Long Distance and Road Running Committee

14 Today's Sunbeam, Salem County, N.J., October 13, 1976

NEW COURSE RECORD. Gloucester Catholic's Jack Heath crosses the finish line with a new course record in cross country at Penns Grove yesterday afternoon. Heath ran the better-than three-mile course in 16:28, breaking the old mark of 16:42, set by Melvin Robinson in 1975. Heath led the Ram runners to a 27-30 victory over the Devils.

Browning Ross led the 3 high school cross-country teams he coached (Woodbury, Woodrow Wilson, and Gloucester Catholic) to their best ever season records. His 1974-1976 Gloucester Catholic teams won 48 meets.

Coach Ross- Running for Browning

"Don't you ever think no one's better than you".
Chris Rea, "God's Great Banana Skin."

In June 1972, Athletic Director Jim Carr of Gloucester Catholic High School, a small, coed school in Gloucester City, New Jersey, reluctantly accepted the resignation of Father Dan Norton as track and cross-country coach. Father Norton was leaving teaching and coaching at Gloucester Catholic to become a missionary in Brazil.

Cross-country and track coaches were especially hard to find in a Catholic school, and Carr had only a few months before school started in September to find a replacement coach for two sports.

According to a June 1972 article in the Woodbury Times, Carr wracked his brain and soon thought of Olympian Browning Ross who he had met at Sports East while ordering athletic supplies as Athletic Director and also Gloucester Catholic baseball coach.

Carr took a drive to Sports East to pitch the dual coaching job openings to Browning. Browning mentioned that he hadn't coached high school in years, since Woodbury in the 1950's, and would have to adjust his Sports East work schedule, and would have to think over the offer.

Carr told Browning he was his first choice to coach and would wait to hear back before contacting anyone else. Browning talked it over with Sis, a 1942 Gloucester Catholic graduate and decided to take the job. Besides Sis's connection to the school, another positive was Gloucester Catholic's location-- only five miles away from Browning's home, and his store Sports East in Woodbury New Jersey.

Browning's Sister-in-law Pat Avis remembers talking to Browning soon after he accepted and his being "very happy that he had accepted the coaching positions at Gloucester Catholic."

In September of 1972, when Browning started coaching at Gloucester Catholic High he knew he was not exactly inheriting a powerhouse track and cross-country program. The programs were still boys only, and they had not won more than a single track meet, or multiple cross-country meets in years.

Dave McCollum a sophomore runner at Gloucester Catholic in 1972 remembered: "We heard that Browning, an Olympian, was going to be our coach when we got to school in September. The cross-country team never got the bus. When school started, one of the seniors, Larry had a car and took part of the team from school following Browning's car to practice in a woods course in Deptford, NJ. Browning stopped for a school bus and Larry ran into the back of Ross's Skylark. In our first meet against Paul VI, Paul VI's entire team came in before our first runner. Their first 11 runners came across the finish line holding hands." Browning never got mad. The year before our coach was a priest, Father Norton who would get really PO-ed when we lost. "The course that Browning designed in the woods in Deptford was across from where the Deptford Mall now stands. It finished with an uphill finish through deep sand. Our team finished 5-14 that year. Ross believed the best practice was to run a race. I did see him show emotion when we lost to Clayton High School, a team we should have beaten. He told us to run back to school but picked us up a couple of miles later. We should have won that meet."

Because Gloucester Catholic was not in a Conference, did not have its own fields, and not produced many distance runners of note since Dave Williams, a 1937 graduate who was the best runner in the Philadelphia/ South Jersey area at that time. Many of the top cross-country teams in South Jersey from various conferences called the school to schedule meets looking for an easy win. The large number of meets in the season-- more than 20, posed a challenge. Ross made the best of the situation and responded by training the team easily between races on soft surfaces and by finding scenic places to run. Ross said, "The Athletic Director thinks cross country is like the baseball team and can compete every day. I'm surprised he hasn't scheduled us in a double-header yet."

Ross could have had his pick of a lot easier places to coach where he would have been successful immediately. He did not mind the challenge of taking over a program on the bottom. Why coach at Gloucester Catholic? The connection to the school for Browning was that his wife Sis was a graduate. Sis recalled Gloucester Catholic's closest brush with running greatness was when 1936 Olympic 1500-meter silver medalist Glenn Cunningham visited the school to give an inspirational talk to the student body in the 1940's.

McCollum: "Browning put on one winter track meet that year and held it in the Gloucester Catholic gym right before a dance, and there were lots of kids there to watch. There were only a few events. I ran the mile and we ran in the hallways and came through the gym doors near the stage for the finish. I won the race to the cheers of a couple of hundred kids. It was the only time I ever beat our top runner Ken McHugh in a race, but I was lucky that a couple of hundred people were there to see it. "

McCollum: "The Cross-Country team the following year was not good. We went 4-12, not an impressive team. However, the crux of the team came out the following year and then things started to improve." Within four seasons, Ross would turn things around and guide the best track and cross-country teams in Gloucester Catholic's history. His cross-country teams would also evolve from a doormat to one of the top cross-country teams in South Jersey.

In March of 1974, my freshman English teacher Dave Coghlan invited me to stay after school to play a pickup basketball game. On the way to the gym, I saw some classmates headed to a classroom to sign up for track. They invited me to come along. When we got to the classroom one of the upper classmen who was assisting with the sign ups said, "The track coach is a great guy, Browning Ross. Mr. Ross was a two-time Olympian and won the Pan Am Games." This was the first time I had ever seen or heard of Browning. When I got to the front of the line he had each student sign their name and the events they were interested in.

The boy in front of me, who Browning knew, signed up for the two-mile. I was surprised there was an event that long and pictured trekking to a major road called the Black Horse Pike and back from my house-- a distance of two miles. I wasn't sure how anyone could race that distance on the track. When it was my turn to sign I looked at Coach Ross and asked, "Do you have any-thing that doesn't involve running? He chuckled and I noticed he seemed very approachable.

His blue eyes seemed to twinkle and he said, "Sure, you can do the long jump and high jump, to name two events." I signed up for those to events. I had no idea that what seemed like a random coincidence-- an invitation to stay after school to play basketball on the same day as track sign ups would change my life.

A few days before our first practice meet, I asked Browning what event I should run. The rainy spring had left little time to practice the long or high jump. The Cloud 9 inflatable pole vault and high jump pits at Gloucester High were deflated all spring leaving no time to practice those events. All spring there were safety problems with the pumps not inflating enough air, and with the electrical connections not working due to the rain.

The day before the first practice meet I had no idea what event I should do and approached Browning for a suggestion.

"You look like you have decent speed-- run the 220," Browning said. I ran the 220 in baseball cleats, and was surprised to beat some runners, so I assumed I would run that event again for our first official meet.

A few days later we had our first official meet. After the meet's first event I was surprised to see Browning approaching me, "Jack, I want you to run the mile." I asked "Are you sure?" and he nodded yes. I remember saying a quick prayer that I would finish the race without stopping as the gun went off. I found myself in third with a lap to go and tried to stay in front of two runners from the other team who were right on my heels-- one with a full beard and another who breathed like a freight train.

As I came across the line, Browning immediately ran over to me, gave me a big hug and said, "Atta boy Jack! Great job! You're going to be a good distance runner!" Browning's words at that moment would have a huge influence me. I can't remember if he ever encouraged another runner at the end of a race the same way, but his words and that hug certainly altered the trajectory of my life in a positive way. Of course, a 5-minute mile was not a world-beating time but Browning saw potential in me that I had no idea I had.

Looking down at the baseball cleats my feet he said, "I'll bring you a pair of running spikes from the store."

I started accompanying the distance runners at practice and was finishing a run on the track when Browning called me over. "You have nice form but you toe out on the right side." I wasn't sure what that meant. "With every foot plant, your right foot points slightly outward. The most efficient form is to run in a straight line-- almost pigeon-toed." I asked what I could do to correct it. "Every chance you get, run in a straight line. Straddle the sideline on a football field for example." I practiced running in a straight line all summer. Browning remarked the first day of the next season that I had corrected my form and was running in a straight line.

Browning, long a proponent of girl's track, and cross-country worked by himself with both the first girl's track team and the boy's team. He coached every event was constantly all over the track and on the field with the throwers in practice. I noticed him showing the sprinters how to start, when I looked up again he was working with the hurdlers and urging 3 steps. He also worked with all of the field men. Somehow, he still had time to talk to everyone on the team.

The track team that year did not have an official uniform. Athletes on the team wore a hodgepodge of uniforms from past teams, Gloucester Catholic gym clothes or an assortment of concert shirts or shirts from local pubs. Luckily, Browning was able to provide spikes and track equipment from his sporting goods store Sports East. Ross was also able to provide expert coaching advice on a multitude of events including the weight events and pole vault.

Besides the problem with the Cloud 9 airflow pits—which were later discontinued for being unsafe, were often deflated due to problems with the pump, despite the difficulty in practicing the vault and high jump, Ross quickly developed a handful of capable pole-vaulters.

Bill Thompson, a long-time South Jersey official usually oversaw the pole vault at major meets and remembered Browning's expertise on all the events: "Browning really knew the field events too-- he had started off as a pole-vaulter at Woodbury High. Once Coach Cap Paine saw him win some races, he asked him to put down the vault and concentrate on running." I later found out that Browning had participated in many of the events scoring points for Villanova and on his international trips and had corresponded with his fellow Olympians on technique on just about all of the track and field events.

I quickly discovered while Browning had a low-key personality he also required commitment. Halfway through the season, he called the boys team together. "You may have noticed our best athlete, _____ missed our last meet. He has also missed practices. I talked to him and he didn't have an excuse for missing, just didn't show. I thought about dropping him from the team but I am going to let you, his teammates vote on whether he should be allowed to stay or not." The vote, to allow the best athlete on the team to stay, probably was no surprise but it got the message through to the athlete-- your team depends on you."

When we started to make friends with athletes on other teams we were surprised that unlike Browning their coaches often forbade their athletes from reading anything about running, or from entering races in the off-season. That had the whiff of a cult or at least control to us. Browning urged us to compete and to learn as much about the sport as possible.

Besides coaching by himself Browning's job was made more difficult because of the lack of buses to transport us to meets. Seniors on the team were especially valuable because many of them were drivers who could squeeze half dozen kids in their cars.

It never occurred to me that there was anything unusual or illegal about a car load of students holding javelins and pole vault cases outside the window alongside the car as we drove to meets. The local police forces must have known, "That's the Gloucester Catholic track team, and they don't have buses to lay out their equipment like other teams." I don't remember us ever being stopped on the way to a track meet.

There was only one time I remember a bus and not Browning or teammates taking us to meets. Three South Jersey Catholic High Schools Gloucester Catholic, Paul VI, and Camden Catholic joined together my junior year to share a bus to the state meet. For insurance and other reasons, I don't think that happens very often today, but we enjoyed the experience of bonding with fellow athletes on a bus to the meet.

When I interviewed Browning's runners from different generations for this book most had the same memory that involved driving in Browning's car to meets.

I would sit next to him up front, and although I had complete trust in his driving I experienced firsthand why people recalled this memory. At some point while driving Browning would discuss an interesting meet he had read about in the paper that day. For some reason, the paper was always directly behind him. "Clearview and Kingsway finished in a tie, broken by the fifth man..." at this point he would turn completely around fishing for the sports section to the horror of the other passengers in the car. I had seen this so many times I was completely relaxed and knew he would turn back at the last second, paper in hand to easily avoid the car barreling in the opposite direction.

Late in the 1974 season, Gloucester Catholic was losing a track meet against a Salem County school, but almost miraculously was winning the mile relay as the anchor runners rounded the last curve on the last lap. As the Gloucester Catholic anchorman came around the last lap those present were shocked to see the runner from the other team cut directly across the infield of the track and enter the track in the lead.

The Gloucester Catholic runner slowed down, probably in shock and the other runner finished first with a big smile awaiting a disqualification that never came. There were no track officials present at the meet but the Gloucester Catholic runners howled when they saw the runner would not be disqualified. Browning said, "The heck with it," and he started to pack up the shot and disc and the other meet implements.

It took me a while to figure out why Browning was so calm and didn't insist the runner be disqualified. Obviously, the score was lopsided and the mile relay wouldn't have affected the meet results. It dawned on me however that Browning was probably disappointed in his runner giving up and show-ing no fight when the runner suddenly appeared next to him. I thought to lose the race was probably a better lesson for our runner to learn to overcome adversity and to fight to the end. Jogging through the finish, and having the race awarded to him on the disqualification wouldn't have taught our runner much about heart.

At the end of track season, Browning held a brief meeting and asked all of the middle and distance runners to run 300 miles over the summer and come out for cross-country in the fall.

Like a modern-day Daniel Boone, I notched every mile I ran on a tree in our yard. (The following year Browning would give me a paper training log to fill out!) Browning was disappointed to see most of the runners who came out for cross-country in the fall of 1974 had not run over the summer. "Well, you only have to tell a good athlete once to do something and he or she will," he noted.

We ran our cross-country meets in the Deptford New Jersey woods. Waiting for rides home after practice one day we were stunned to see hun-dreds of acres of trees knocked down in a straight line like bowling pins as if a meteorite or heavy wind had leveled them. The next day we saw rollers and asphalt trucks, the Deptford Mall was being constructed. The Mall would at-tract more stores and housing developments that would soon force us to find another cross-country course.

Gloucester Catholic did not have its own fields, and the farms of South Jersey were being so quickly being developed so Browning had to find new courses for use to use every few years. In a 15-year period, the Cross-Country team ran on 6 different home courses in 5 towns.

Browning was very approachable even to a shy 15-year-old. I remember getting up the nerve to call him and tell him I had just run 5 miles in training for the first time. He seemed as thrilled as I was and was always glad to hear from his runners and to talk running.

As the cross-country season ended, Browning asked if I would like to go with him to run in the Sunday 5-mile winter races at Boat House Row in Philadelphia. I would go to 8 o'clock mass and then jog a half mile to wait in front of Ponzio's Diner to get picked up by Browning. Because I was wearing sweats I sat in the back of the church. It was still the era where someone, most likely a senior citizen was liable to "tsk tsk" you for not being formally dressed up in the church.

I had a similar problem when I arrived at the diner to wait for Browning. Waiting outside of the diner in a sweat suit some of the patrons entering the diner looked at me as if I were a panhandler. One older man accompanied by his wife shook his head in disgust as he passed me every Sunday.

When Browning picked me up I told him how much this weekly reaction bothered me: "I'm sitting in the back of church because I don't want to offend anyone, and then I get to the Diner and have this guy shaking his head at me every week." Browning asked me if I said anything to the man. "Yes, today I finally said, 'Hey, why don't you take her somewhere expense and then you won't have to see me out here,' I'm waiting for a ride! Then he hurried in real fast..." Browning laughed and said, "People are something, who died and left him in charge? Some people really like to lord it over people, especially young people. You're doing the right thing-- going to church and then running a race-- how many people are doing that on Sunday morning? I've learned over the years to just ignore people like that."

From that moment I realized what a great person Browning was to talk to about running and non-running matters that concerned me. Sometimes someone on the team would tell him about something that didn't go as planned and he would say, "Well it's a great life if you don't weaken." The quote from Scottish writer John Buchan was one of his favorites.

Browning was never late when he was picking us up for a race or practice. If you arrived 2 minutes late, he was already gone. I think it was a result of his time served in the Navy-- if you are late in the Navy, the ship has already pulled out of port and is long gone without you.

Browning did forget to pick me up for a Sunday race one time, but it turned into a fortunate occurrence for me. I was waiting in front of Ponzio's a few minutes past the pickup time with a feeling that he wasn't coming. He had in fact forgotten to pick me up and drove by.

I saw a short man with a mustache running towards me at what looked like full speed. I suddenly stopped and said, " You're waiting for Browning, aren't you? He's not coming. If he's not here on time, he's not coming. He forgot. He took me to Boathouse Row about 6 years ago and forgot to pick me up once too. Where do you live? I'll run you back."

The runner was Larry Schmelia. Schmelia was soon the Junior College National 5000-meter champion. He was also a scholastic track and cross-country champion from Gloucester City and the best runner in South Jersey for about a decade. Our chance meeting started a long friendship. Schmelia would also win the Gloucester Sportsman A.C 4 mile that Browning directed for about 10 years straight.

During the 1975 spring track season, we had a meet with Maple Shade that provided Browning with one of his biggest laughs and a story he would often tell at banquets. I was running shoulder to shoulder with a stocky Maple Shade runner in a two mile. Neither of us were savvy racers. I would pass him on a straight away and he would catch back up and pass me on a curve. This continued for 6 laps until Browning yelled, "Come on Jack, and beat that fat kid!" The Maple Shade runner yelled, "Fat kid my ass!" and took off like a flash. After the race, the angry runner approached me and said, "Where's the old guy who called me fat? I'm not fat, I'm a wrestler!" Browning laughed every time he recalled the incident and how it had backfired. "Well, that sure backfired! I thought I would discourage him if he started thinking about his weight but it fired him up."

Before a practice, Browning overheard one of his top runners Jim Plant mention that he was tired from attending a Who concert. Browning did his best Abbott and Costello imitation with Plant who was not familiar with the "Who's on First?" skit.

"Which concert did you go to?" "The Who." "Who?" "Yeah" "Who?" Plant and Ross went back and forth for a few minutes before the exasperated Plant exclaimed, "I saw Tommy Dorsey!" and pantomimed playing trombone. Browning laughed hysterically and would often recall the moment to other teams.

Browning had a few expressions that he used to combat negativity from nervous runners. For those asking what to do about sudden illnesses that "struck" moments before a race he would say, "Rub peanut butter on it."

This was his panacea for sore muscles, sore throats, and other known running maladies. Eventually, runners stopped complaining knowing there was only cure suggested. Many of the new runners did carry around the scent of peanut butter instead of muscle analgesic.

If someone complained about that day's practice-- "Mr. Ross, why are we running hills (or speed work or distance) I hate hills!" Browning would answer, "That's funny they speak highly of you!"

Browning would also take out his handkerchief when someone started to sing the blues about being tired or sore-- dab at the corner of his eye in mock sadness and then say, "Go on, I'm listening."

If someone on the team mentioned he was going out to dinner later that night Browning would always ask which restaurant and then inquire whether he could "press his nose against the window outside while you are eating?"

For some reason, some members of our team never seemed to be aware of who we were racing: "Mr. Ross, where are we running at?" His first response was usually, "Never end a sentence with a preposition." "No, I mean who we running against? "After the question was suitably modified Browning would usually answer, "Little Sisters of the Poor."

Browning frequently gave us input into our practices. Someone once asked Browning if we could run from Gloucester Catholic to the new Deptford Mall a distance of five miles.

Specifically, they were interested in running to Farrell's Ice Cream in the mall. "Mr. Ross, if you mention it's your birthday you get a free Sunday. "Is it your birthday?" "No, but they don't know that." About four runners ran to the mall with Browning following in his car. After a second birthday gambit with water and sundaes, the runners tired of the practice.

When I became aware of Browning's running accomplishments my senior year I asked him what he thought about before his races.

He said, "You have to think, I'm Browning Ross, these guys can't beat me, or in your case, I'm Jack Heath, these guys can't beat me. You can't go into a race thinking anyone is better than you if you expect to win." I followed his advice.

Because of Browning's sane training methods, we were injury free despite having to race 2 or 3 or meets a week. Gloucester Catholic was not in a conference, and the top track and cross-country teams from every conference in South Jersey scheduled meets with Gloucester Catholic looking to pad their won-loss record. Browning made the best of the schedule he was handed-- 23 meets many of it against top schools. "Our Athletic Director thinks cross-country is like baseball where you can just race every day. He has no idea what a race takes out of you.

In cross-country, Ross led his team to its first ever winning season in 1974, and then 18 and 19 win seasons. Gloucester Catholic under Ross was no longer an easy mark.

A few cross-country meets in 1976 stand out as examples of Ross's easy going but an effective leadership style. We traveled to Penns Grove, New Jersey for a tough meet. While using the bathroom, we noticed the Penns Grove coach had hung up a recent article the Woodbury Times had written on our team for motivational purposes. Responses in the article that seemed innocent at the time like: "Yes, I would like to go undefeated the rest of the season and hopefully we can win our remaining meets," sounded like great motivational material for the other team on their locker room billboard. I quickly found myself trailing two runners who went out like a shot the first half mile. As we looped past the start I was wondering what Browning's reaction would be and if he was concerned to see me trailing early in the race.

As I passed Browning I noticed he had a big smile on his face and he simply said, "Atta boy Jack! Perfect, you got it." This gave me a rush of confidence that he believed I would win. I passed both runners and went on to set the course record. That particular race was the biggest influence on my coaching style and the race I reflect on the most when I think about Browning.

Browning's quiet confidence was in contrast to many of the opposing coaches who seemed to feel they could motivate their runners by screaming or trying to control the variables of the race.

We had a race against Gateway High School that finished on the track. As I approached the finish in the lead I was surprised to find the opposing coach blocking the entry to the track and pointing off in the distance. Surprised, I hesitated briefly before pushing the coach enough to create space to enter the track and finish. Before I could ask Browning if he saw the interference I saw him hustle after the opposing coach. He returned a few minutes later. "Unbelievable. He said he didn't think anyone could beat his runners by that much and didn't know what came over him. After I talked to him for a few minutes he apologized. Some of these coaches want to win so badly, but what does it teach their kids to want to win that way?"

One of Browning's main prerace philosophies was never to walk the away course. He believed walking used up the runner's store of energy needed for the race and sometimes psyched out the less fit runners because the course inevitably seemed much longer than 3 miles when walked-- especially on a hot day.

This was a good strategy for the most part and usually worked out well for me. In one particular tri-meet against Woodbury and Pennsville, the strategy did not work out so well. Even though it was an away meet for our team the Woodbury course was only a couple of blocks from Browning's Centre Street home and very familiar to him. He was busy with pre-race timing duties but mentioned the course was different than his five-mile snowball course in Woodbury. I asked him to describe the three-mile course. "It's easy, just remember to turn on the street with the fire box..." and then I heard him mention something about "and the street with a college name..." and he was sending runners to the start.

For the past few weeks of races I had felt in a good groove, and this felt like my best race of the year so far. Browning pulled up to me in his car, "You've got a big lead. You should get the course record easily if you can keep it going for the last three-quarters of a mile! I've got to get back to the finish!" A few moments after he zoomed off behind me to time the finish I realized I wasn't sure where to turn. Every street had a firebox. I heard yelling behind me and turned around to see the second and third place runners turning into a street several blocks back. I reversed direction and did my hardest running of the season just to finish second. I was disappointed because I wasn't sure if I would feel that good again and had lost the win and possible course record because I wasn't sure where I was going.

Browning sensed my disappointment and said, "Oh well, you still ran great, and we won both meets..." While I was mulling over whether I should be mad at Browning for not explaining the course in more detail before the race, or myself for not taking the responsibility to take the time to it, Browning said something totally unexpected that took my mind off my disappointment and made me laugh. "I forgot that this was the dumbest team I've ever coached," he said. "Next time I'll have to take that into account."

He always knew the right thing to say to inspire confidence or to keep his runners from getting too carried away with themselves. After a record-setting performance, Browning would slowly repeat the runner's time as if he was trying to recall something. "15:30? That's about what I was running in third grade, not too bad." Or "I think Woodbury has an eighth girl that can run that fast." Behind the gentle ribbing, which we looked forward to we could tell that Browning was pleased with our performance.

While other coaches were cramming their runner's heads with last minute instructions that were impossible to follow, Browning liked to ease the pre-race tension with humor.

While on the starting line of a major 2-mile race I was deep in thought visualizing my race strategy and the strengths of the runners next to me when I heard Browning call my name. "Jack, did you just get a haircut?" "A couple of days ago," I answered. "There's nothing like the smell of a new haircut, I've got a quarter here," he said and pretended to take a step towards me. He would say things like that which would make you laugh, relax and take your mind off the race. When he was the race starter and timer he would say, "OK, let's get the good-looking guys (or girls) up front." Then he would call out some names, "Jack, Mike, Jim-- get in the back!" That broke the pre-race tension every time I believed it helped us to run relaxed and faster.

While Browning did not make his runners nervous with the absorbing a pre-race strategy, he was frequently thinking of ways to make his runners better. On a practice run to neighboring Brooklawn, four of his runners waited for a break in traffic to cross the street. One looked down at the "Apt for Rent" sign and remarked, "The next time we do this run I'm bringing a permanent marker and changing that "t" to an "e"..." As the other runners looked at the sign Browning pulled up alongside in this car. "Hey, our fifth man is way back as usual. His being so far back is killing us in the big meets. I want you guys to slow down on the rest of the run to force him to keep up with you. If he does it in practice maybe he'll do it in the meets. It's called "fifth man syndrome," they think they should always be the same distance behind the fourth man even if he is walking!"

To Browning's dismay, that's what happened. As the four runners slowed the pace the fifth runner slowed proportionally until all five were barely moving.

"Heck with him," said Browning a few days later. He's not going to stay with you guys, no use ruining your workouts too."

One of the hardest workouts I can recall in high school was a workout with Browning. We ran eight miles on a warm humid day along the railroad tracks from Gloucester to Woodbury. After about 3 miles the other runners on the team had drifted off and turned back. At the four-mile mark, Browning and I turned around at a package good store on the Woodbury border and headed back. At that moment I saw a classmate, Jim coming out of the store and we exchanged quick waves.

The next day in class Jim said, "Jack who was that older gentleman you were racing yesterday?" I explained it was Browning, my coach and we were running a workout together.

"Damn, you guys were flying. I was going in the same direction. Every time I would catch up to you guys I would get stuck at a light and you guys would pull away again."

Browning scheduled a few unique winter track dual-meets with other local schools that used the parking lot of the hosting school. He measured out distances and held a modified meet outdoors under the lights. It was a great idea as the school parking lots were snow and ice free and lit at night-- unlike the school's track. The meets were cold and the athletes were allowed to run in sweats, hats, and gloves. The competition was a great preparation for spring track.

In the middle of track season, we went away for our senior trip to Disney World and Orlando Florida. Not wanting to miss a week of training, I woke up each day before breakfast and ran for 15 minutes through nearby orange groves.

We returned from the trip late Friday night and I finally fell into bed at 2 am. It felt like only minutes later that I was awakened by my father's voice, "Jack, Browning's here."

"In Florida?" I replied, not yet awake. "No, in our living room!" my dad responded. I quickly got changed.

"How was Florida?" Browning asked. "Did you get any workouts in?" I answered yes. "Good, because I entered us in a meet, the Moorestown relays and you in the steeplechase while you were away." I was familiar with the race because Browning ran it in the Olympics but I had never practiced the Steeple barrier or hurdles. "You'll do fine. I also entered a mile relay team, how about if we stop and pick up your friend (also a senior just returned from the trip) he only lives a couple blocks away right?"

My friend's father did not have any luck rousing his tired son. Browning simply stopped at another runner's house in town, a freshman on the team, and we had four for the mile relay.

I remember thinking on the way to the meet, "I didn't know it was an option to tell Browning no."

For close to a year I had looked forward running a meet barefoot on Moorestown Friends grass track. Browning usually asked me before every race how I felt and my answer was always, "Great!"

This time he looked at me and said, "Well, you don't look so good. Do you have a cold?" I nodded. "No mile or two-mile today. I only want you to run the half and the mile relay." Relieved that I would still get a chance to run barefoot I removed my shoes and enjoyed racing. I believe most other coaches would have insisted on running the races that earned the most points without regard to how I was feeling.

On the way to the car after the conclusion of the Meet, Browning spotted some members of the team smoking victory cigars. I'm not sure what was more disappointing to him-- what looked like an attempt to show up another team, or the fact that they were smoking. He chewed them out and let them know they were suspended and would miss the next meet. He got his point across. More than missing the next meet, the worst punishment for anyone on the team was knowing Browning was disappointed.

It might have been karma but we lost our next meet by a couple of points to a tough Maple Shade team. The victors broke into a sing-song wishing us better luck next time. The chant was soon drowned out by an R-rated pirate like shanty that had been passed down to our team by previous track teams. The sing-along froze the other team in their tracks and brought Browning running out waving his hands.

"Hey, you can't do that! You represent a Catholic school you can't be saying those off-color things..."We were looking down at our shoes thinking this is two meets in a row we disappointed him when he continued, "Besides your chant wasn't that good. The one I heard Norfolk's team use when I was in the Navy is much better. "Norfolk, Norfolk! We don't drink or smoke, Norfolk!" He handled the situation perfectly getting his point across with humor.

As the season warmed up, our assistant track coach handed out salt tablets to the team to be used for running in the heat. Before taking them, I consulted Browning. In the previous cross-country season, I listened to the coach when he had recommended taking Vitamin C before races. Twice I had to stop with a big lead until the feeling of stomach queasiness passed.

Browning eyed the salt tablets and said, "What are they supposed to do for you?" "He told us they would help us acclimate to the heat," I replied. "They gave them to us in the Navy, Browning continued. "All they did was give everybody the runs. I would flush them down the toilet, they won't be any help." I did.

Bonnie remembered, "I would watch a track meet on TV with dad and the announcer would say someone ran a certain time and my dad would shake his head no. They would invariably come back a few minutes later with the correction to the time. He always knew the correct time and wanted them to be accurate.

On a sunny, hot May afternoon, four runners remained after track practice wound down running additional quarter mile repeats under Browning's guidance. After one of the repeats, a runner looked at the bottom of his shoe and made a disgusted face, "Ugh! I just stepped on two of those tent caterpillars."

"I've been *trying* to step on them!" another runner answered. "What is it with these caterpillars, there are hundreds of them and they are all headed in the same direction across the track."

Browning smiled and said, "Well as long as they're not passing you on this lap you're doing alright! O.K., one more quarter in under 75." Knowing the runners were thirsty, Browning used his patented reverse psychology reinforcement, "I have some nice salty peanuts waiting for you when you guys are done!"

A few years ago, I interviewed many of the top running coaches in the country for a magazine article on "Positive Coaching." I noticed that Browning exhibited many of the positive coaching traits those coaches mentioned.

For example, legendary Coach Joe Vigil (19 National titles primarily at Adams State) mentioned empathy for his athlete's, and how much he liked Teddy Roosevelt's quote "People don't care how much you know until they know how much you care". Vigil also shared Browning's trait of never being late. I attended a coaching seminar where Vigil arrived days early to ensure he would still be early if there were travel issues.

Olympian and Coach Don Kardong, "I really think negativity comes into coaching from the military influence on our culture. There is that feeling that a coach has to yell or belittle their charges like a drill sergeant in the military. It doesn't make sense to treat a group of athletes that way. It seems like a good way to drive athletes away. I think positive reinforcement works better. Basically, criticism doesn't do anything other than tell you what not to do. Positive reinforcement rewards you for doing something well. It puts you on the right track to improvement." Browning served in the Navy during World War II, but only carried the trait of punctuality and not stern discipline from his military experience in coaching.

Coach Jack Daniels mentioned the positive trait of treating each athlete like an individual, "Many coaches don't really know what they are trying to accomplish with a workout. The coach must be able to say what the purpose of every workout is. The coach must be willing to tell a runner that a rest day can be more important than a workout day-- rest is part of the training program and can lead to more improvement than can work when conditions so dictate."

Was running with an Olympic caliber athlete an advantage for his runners? Mark Worthington was a 1976 graduate of Gloucester Catholic, one of Browning's best runners who attended and ran for Villanova. I mentioned to him that I thought running with Browning gave me a competitive advantage. I wasn't intimidated by the top high school runners after running and keeping up with Browning in practice. Mark had a different view. With a smile, he said, "I think running with Browning was a bit of a disadvantage for me. I thought, how am I going to beat the top runners when I had such a hard time keeping up with this 50-year-old guy in practice every day!"

BROWNING ROSS LETTER TO THE 1976 GLOUCESTER CATHOLIC CROSS-COUNTRY TEAM

To: GLOUCESTER CATHOLIC HIGH SCHOOL CROSS COUNTRY TEAM 1976

Our program must start <u>July 1st</u> if we want to improve on last year's record of 18 wins and 5 losses. NJSIAA rules prohibit me from meeting with the team during the summer months, thus you must run on your own (waiting until school opens is too late!) During the month of July everyone should run once a day. The distance should vary on ability: newcomers to the program start with three miles and try to add one mile to this a week. The veterans start at 4 miles and add one mile a week. In August, everyone goes on a two a day, a morning run of between three and five miles with a 5-8 miler every evening. All of this running should be done on grass if possible at no faster than 6:00-mile pace for the vets. All of you should try to attend my cross- country camp in Medford Lakes, N.J. during the last week of August. When school starts in September you should consider continuing the two-a-day workouts- either before breakfast or during gym, then again at 3 PM (3 to 5 miles).

My philosophy is simple; I believe that speed, strength, form and relaxation, all the necessary functions that make a good cross-country runner, are a direct result of miles. I've read with amusement over the years of the super workouts that many high school squads do. I am also well aware of their great high school success in cross country. However, it does not surprise me that runners from these schools, for the most part, never repeat any of their high school success. In fact, many of them fail to continue to run in college due to injuries or lack of interest. I'm well aware that many schools use workouts such as 30 x 440 in 70 seconds and ten x 880 in 2:12. I also believe that because we have never trained in this fashion that many of you will continue to train upon graduation (injury free) and will continue to enjoy and improve your running.

During cross-country season, we will never run on the track or do any intervals or pace work. The only speed you will be exposed to is some Fartlek running in the woods. I have never walked a cross-country course with my kids or given a mile or two mile split during a race. The only strategy I believe in is "keying on" another team. Through study and "scouting" we try to become familiar with the opponents and find out who will be our competition. Then you will be asked to "key on" the opponent's strong runners. Such things as shin splints, tendonitis and overtraining should be unknown to us with this program.

What I'm trying to say is this—my program will give you the opportunity to run. Interval training, speed, pace, correct form and super workouts will never replace fun and/miles.

Note: A couple of you have discovered that there are girls in this world & that they come first and your running second! Wrong—you have to exhaust every means you can think of to get them to run—we will have a girls cross-country schedule this year also.

Gateway, Eastern, Highland, Paul VI (teams in South Jersey) think about them now, not in September when it's too late.

If you want to test your condition run in our FUN Runs at Stewart Park behind the YMCA in Woodbury on Sunday mornings at 10:30 AM. We time and award certificates to everyone.

Training Diary— I have one for each of you. They are important and by studying back on your workouts when you have some bad races you should be able to determine why you ran so poorly.

Quote by Bill Rodgers, a 28-year-old teacher from Massachusetts who started the 1975 Boston Marathon as an unknown and finished at the winner who smashed the previous record of 2:10:30 and will represent us in the Marathon at the Montreal Olympics... "In high school, I did 95% interval workouts but when I went to college it was just the opposite—95% long distance that's when I started to improve. My feelings about running are that it's something I generally enjoy. Part of the time, I hate it but I'm always trying to find ways to fit it into my life more effectively and easier. I enjoy running and get along with all runners. It's an enjoyable part of my life. It's given me a lot of good things."

B. Ross

But I'm Not Here for the Money

Leroy Samuels of the Philadelphia Bulletin interviewed Ross during the height of his coaching career at Gloucester Catholic in 1976 in an article entitled "Now, It's Coach Browning Ross." Ross had led the 1975 Gloucester Catholic Cross-Country team to an 18-5 record and was in the middle of what would turn out to be a 19-4 season for the 1976 squad. Samuels went on to be inducted into the Nevada Boxing Hall of Fame in 2015.

Gloucester- A string of runners wound through the city streets, stepping onto asphalt and cement sidewalks and wherever they could find it, beds of grass. Browning Ross, the former Olympian from Villanova followed in his faded Volkswagen van and offered bits of encouragement to the stragglers.

Ross, now 52, has not run away from running and the athletes who pound the streets and want to develop stamina and strength. He has coached the varsity cross country team here at Gloucester Catholic for five seasons. For that and coaching the school's track and field team in the spring he will not make a great amount of money. "But I'm not here to make money," said Ross at the school the other afternoon. "I'm here because I like to take those kids without any ability whatsoever and help them."

If one measures success in wins and losses, Ross is a success. His team won 18 and lost five meets last fall. And Mark Worthington, who used to finish "in the 20's" among the runners as a sophomore, is now a Villanova Wildcat. "He (Ross) has never pressured any of us to run," says Jack Heath, Gloucester Catholic's No. 1 runner. "Some coaches want their kids to win so badly they get jittery and nervous and they can't do it. We don't have those sorts of problems. Everything, the coaching is a bit low-key and we like that."

The first time Heath ran against Ross the results were stunning. "I was a sophomore and he looked like an old man and I said to myself "how fast does he think he can go?" Then halfway through, he blew me off the course," said Heath. "Since, I know what he has done, how good he is." Twice, Ross was an Olympian. In 1948, he briefly led the 3,000-meter steeplechase in the London Olympics and finally finished seventh. In 1952 in Helsinki, he didn't make the finals of the same event. Instead, he made a hospital bed and a trial heat. "Before our flight left for Finland from New York, our team went to the airport restaurant and we ate hot dogs and hamburgers and all sorts of things," said Ross. "I had a stomach ache. The team doctor said it was appendicitis and when we landed, I was placed in a hospital. I didn't see the doctor again. And no one else was speaking English. Finally, when I was released I never got past the trial race."

He began running in Woodbury High in 1939 and continued at Villanova. He briefly coached at St. Joseph's College and in St Joseph's high in Camden and in 1954 his Woodbury high cross-country team was undefeated and Matt Singleton won the state title.

Now, Heath and juniors Mike Browoleit, Jim Plant and Alan Cipolone listen and absorb the advice and encouragement. For example, Ross on the basics of long-distance running: "You have to develop stamina and to do that you have to run a minimum of 50 miles a week. Heath ran 70 miles a week during the summer and now he is 30 seconds ahead of Worthington's pace.

Ross on form— "When you run those number so mile you are going to look for the most economical way- the way with the least amount of energy—and the form will arrive by itself. Believe me, I should know."

He should know because he has run thousands of those miles."

Barbara, Browning and Sis Ross visit Pete League on a trip to a sporting goods convention in Houston.

Sports East

BROWNING'S FIRST VENTURE SELLING SPORTING goods was called Blue Ribbon Sports, selling Blue Ribbon shoes out of his house and car. Next, he briefly opened up a store called Browning Ross' Woodbury Sports Centre, briefly going into business with Jack Pyrah, and then chiropractor Bill Heughan on the north end of Woodbury. When a bigger Sporting Goods store became available on the south end of Woodbury Browning and Bill Heughan purchased it and named it Sports East. Sports East was open from 1971 to 1991.

Bill Heughan recalled how a chance meeting led to a long-term friendship and business partnership with Browning and the partnership.

"I came to Woodbury in 1960, I used to smoke and I'd never run. In 1962, I got an itch to run from my house with a friend around Bell Lake. I would drop him off and run back home along the street on Delaware Avenue in Woodbury.

In 1963 a car pulled alongside me while I was running and the driver said: "Hey, where are you running to?" I'm going out to West Deptford to run if you want to come along." It was Browning. I got in the car and we rode out to West Deptford farmland (where Riverwinds Recreation complex is now). I started meeting Browning to run and we did a lot of running on trail courses through the woods, through farmland, and off the roads.

Browning started a "Run For Your Life" fitness program while he was working at the Woodbury YMCA and at Boat House Row in Philadelphia-- and I went over there with my two kids to help him, and I started running the Boat House Row races that Browning put on along with the track meets he put on at Woodbury High's cinder track.

Browning and I were the only two people running around Woodbury at the time with shorts on and people started to notice and remark about us running together.

Underwood Hospital (in Woodbury) put an annual comedy skit with their doctors and nurses in the 60's and one of their skits had the line, "it must be spring because the nuts are out-- those two guys running around town with nylon shorts on". They didn't mention any names but everyone knew who they were referring to!

In 1971, we started Track and Field Sports Center on North Broad Street in Woodbury.

There was also a regular sporting goods store in South Woodbury; it was mostly a fishing store. The owner was about to retire and we talked to him and he sold us the place. So, we got involved with the fishing supplies and hunting and fishing licenses he had along with our track supplies.

There was a Sports West running club on the West Coast where a lot of top runners ran so we figured we'd name the new store Sports East.

Browning and I went across the street from the store before we opened to the bank to get a loan in 1971. I stood with my back to the door while Browning sat in a chair next to the bank manager. We were talking to him about borrowing money to open the store when all of the sudden the door banged open and we heard "Freeze MF-ers!!"

When they said "Freeze," I turned around and looked. There was a sawed-off shotgun pointed right at me being held by a young black guy with big fake glasses. Another guy ran in with a red floppy hat and leaped onto the counter and then over the counter next to us. Browning was sitting there and he looked like he was in complete shock his face completely drained. We were both scared. The poor bank teller girls were scared to death. They handed over the money and the robbers ran into a car parked right outside and took off. We got the loan and opened up. We started with 2 types of Tiger shoes in inventory, one for training and one for racing.

Then we added the original New Balance leather shoes from England for the Pennsylvania Military College (which changed to Widener' coach, he loved New Balance for his team. (Pennsylvania Military College changed to Widener in 1972).

We loved the store. My wife and daughter worked at the store and they along with Browning and I were robbed a few times. What ultimately drove us out of business though were the big sporting good chains. The coaches used to come in and size the team up for shoes for track. We'd bring a van to their school and bring the shoes to the teams. Then the school budgets dictated that the coaches had to submit their orders the year before and they didn't know what they'd be ordering so we were losing business.

The Gateway (NJ) High School track coach, for example, would bring in old shoes from his team from the year before and trade them in for new ones. We'd do it, but of course, we wouldn't make any money on the exchange and it would be such a hassle.

I remember parents would bring in a kid for shoes who just went out for track and the shoes would fit but they'd say "Do these come in purple?" We couldn't offer the selection of the big chains. We'd have basic sweats and they could offer state of the art clothing.

"We forgot all about the robbery. After a while, the police got in touch with us and their lawyers told the girls from the bank, the bank manager, and Browning and I to report to Riverside (Philadelphia) prison. The lawyers there ran a lineup for us to separately identify the robbers. Everyone in the lineup was the same age, the same height and weight with the same identical orange clothing and all had shaved heads with no hat-- so the dress was nothing like what the robbers wore. Everyone guessed someone different as the robber. I couldn't positively identify anyone.

They told us later that one of the guys was killed in another holdup and the other was still in prison so from what they told us they did catch up with them.

We later changed banks and Browning went into the new bank to make a deposit. When he walked in that bank was being held up too."

Browning and Sis often went to yearly sporting goods trade shows to check out the latest line of sporting goods. In the early 70's they attended a trade show in New York City and Sis spotted Ted Williams in the corner. Williams was there representing a line of Ted Williams sporting goods for Sears-- everything from baseball equipment to weights to hunting and fishing gear. Sis wanted to meet him but Browning balked, wary of bothering the Hall of Famer. Browning said, "Sis marched up to Ted and said, 'Mr. Williams, you're the greatest hitter who ever lived!' Ted smiled and said, 'Ma'am, that's what they tell me.'"

Before the internet, Sports East was a meeting place for South Jersey and Philadelphia runners to catch up on upcoming races, race forms, results and running news. Browning produced a Sports East newsletter which was a condensed, local version of the Long Distance Log.

Dave Platt: "Sports East was like one of the old general stores you'd see up north where everyone gathered around the "pot-bellied stove" to talk. You'd walk into the store and see all kinds of iconic running people sitting there talking to Browning. The top runners all stopped in. The store had lots of race applications and a Sports East newsletter containing the results from his race series—the "Snowball Series," the "Summer Sizzler" etc. Those races would give you a real benchmark of your fitness because you could run the same course at different times.

Every year we have an end of the cross-country season spaghetti dinner (at Paulsboro High School) for the team the kids called the "Platt annual" I would go into Sports East and get prizes for the dinner—trophies, t-shirts, running magazines and books that Browning had in the basement of the store--even one or two of the old Long Distance Logs that he published."

Barb Knoblock,"I remember in the 1970's when gym bags were really popular, like backpacks are now. They were tough to get and sold out of most of the bigger stores sporting goods departments and my dad was able to get them and stock them in his store."

Browning started to host Friday night meetings for the Sports East Running Club he sponsored to discuss upcoming races.

Many runners also showed at Sports East on Friday nights to converse about running and other topics with Browning and a cast of regulars. One regular, Mark Kordich said, "If I could relive any moment in my life it would be those Friday night meetings at Sports East with Browning, just shooting the breeze."

Typical of the free-form discussions was a conversation about running and golf courses. Browning, "I've been running near the Woodbury golf course every day. I always find golf balls and pick them up for the Gloucester Catholic Golf Team." Someone present said, "It's a shame most of the best running areas in south jersey are all tied up with golf courses, and most of them have no trespassing signs."

Someone else added, "I had the cops called on me one time when I was running on a golf course at night. They actually said, "Freeze! Don't take another step or the police will be called!"".

Browning added, "Boy, sometimes you see the biggest cornballs on a golf course. They don't appreciate standing on the best running places around. They'll walk around in cleats and drive back and forth in a golf cart loaded with beer, at the same time keeping runners away; even though runners won't hurt the grass."

Another Sports East roundtable discussion focused on a million-dollar New Jersey lottery that was going to be awarded that weekend. The attendant runners discussed how they would spend the money if they won.

Browning said, "I wouldn't care to win a million dollars. I would be satisfied with a $100,000 jackpot. I could pay off my debts and give the rest of the money to Barry, Bonnie, and Barb."

Years before Yelp, the runners often traded restaurant reviews. When a runner remarked that they had a terrible meatball sandwich down the street recently Browning said, "Meatballs are the one sandwich I won't order out. You never know what they put in them, it could be sawdust!"

Another more somber discussion revolved around Jim Fixx's death at the age of 52 from a heart attack. One of those present noted that Fixx had outlived his father who also died of heart disease by 9 years. Browning said, "I think genetics plays the major role in our life expectancy. I also think each hour you run adds hours to your life."

I stopped in one Friday night in the 1980's. Browning put down a running newsletter he was reading and said "I don't think I've ever seen a bigger disgrace in track than this Coe-Ovett rivalry. They keep ducking each other and it really shortchanges the sport. They'll have to race each other in the Olympics, but imagine what they could have done to the record book and what interest that would have generated in track and field! It's a shame because I haven't seen this kind of rivalry in the mile since Gunder Haag and Arne Anderson in the 40's.

I just read where Ovett was on pace to break his mile world record and he slowed down in the last 100 meters because he has an upcoming race with a huge bonus for breaking the world record. He slowed up because he didn't want to lower the record and make it harder to break. You never know when you will get a chance to break a record with injuries etc." (Ovett never did run faster.)

Reuben Frank is one of the many writers who worked across the street from Sports East at the Woodbury Times who would stop in to talk to Browning. Frank now covers the Philadelphia Eagles for Comcast Sports Network and he recalled, "I was starting to seriously get into running and went to Sports East to buy shoes and talk to the older guy who ran the store. I didn't know his name but noticed he patiently listened to me describe my novice running exploits. Finally, someone at the Times said, "Don't you know who that guy is? He's Browning Ross-- a 2 time Olympian, gold medal winner at the Pan Am Games!" "I thought, Geez, what a modest guy, he never said anything about himself as I did most talking about my own running!"

"After that, I found out about all he had accomplished. One day I stopped in for a race entry blank and Browning also gave me a map of the race course so I was able to prepare for the race in Thorofare (New Jersey). About half way through the race Browning was standing in front of a closed fence by railroad tracks windmilling his arm, diverting runners to a detour. Someone had closed and locked the fence in the middle of his course, but he adjusted a new the course on the fly. Nothing seemed to rattle him."

One of the many top high school runners who stopped in Sports East was Keith Collins of Deptford, N.J. "I stopped in to get a pair of training shoes but the ones I really liked were a lot more than the money I had. Browning must have seen me looking longingly at the more expensive shoes because he said, "Do you like those?" I said I did but admitted I didn't have near enough money for them." "Do you promise to work out in them?" he asked. "I nodded and he said, "Go ahead, take them." I'll never forget his generosity." Collins went on to become a South Jersey track and cross-country official.

When I stopped in to see Browning at Sports East he was frequently putting together trophies or engraving awards.

His engraving machine resembled Thomas Jefferson's polygraph duplicator invention. He picked up and recycled trophies from different places including bowling trophies from the Goodwill across the street.

Vince Phillips: "I once saw him recycle a big trophy with a parachutist on the top; he replaced it with a runner for an award for one of his races."

One day I stopped into Sports East and Browning said, "Do you want to take a ride with me? I have to get this scarf embroidered. Some lady caught an Elvis impersonator scarf at a show in South Jersey and she brought it into the store to get it embroidered with the place and time of the performance. Boy, you'd have to be the world's biggest Elvis fan to embroider a scarf from an Elvis impersonator!"

Sports East also embroidered jackets and sold custom t-shirts, sometimes with mixed results. The manager of a nearby bar and seafood restaurant called

Captain Cats in Thorofare ordered a couple of dozen t-shirts. When they were ready Browning drove to the parking lot of the bar at 2:30 pm. He felt funny walking into the bar to deliver the shirts during the middle of the afternoon and noticed a patron about to enter the bar. Browning stopped the man and said, "Hey, could you do me a favor and bring these t-shirts into the bar and give them to the manager behind the bar?" A few days later Browning received a call from the bar manager asking when the shirts would be ready. The man had apparently walked in one entrance and quickly out another with the shirts.

Browning reprinted the shirts and personally delivered them in the bar the second time. He shook his head at the desperation of someone who would hustle off with a box of personalized bar shirts-- "What could he possibly do with them?" he wondered.

If you wanted to get an up-close look at Browning's sense of humor, there was no better place than watching his interaction with customers in Sports East. A small boy came in one day and asked for sneakers. Browning measured his foot and came back with a size 18 1/2 sneaker that he kept in the back. The boy's eyes opened wide and he shook his head that it wasn't going to fit. Browning said: "How do you know, you haven't tried it on yet!"

Browning always got a laugh when he gave his customers change and re-marked, "Here you go, 25 cents, that's lunch money for tomorrow."

After a mail delivery to the store, Browning said, "Well I see the mailman finally finished with my Sports Illustrated, it's only a week late!"

I stopped in the store on one occasion and Browning seemed especially glad to see me. "I'm glad you're here. Can you fix my watch? It's beeping every hour and driving me crazy!" He handed it to me. I set the watch, turned off the chime and handed it back to him. "Thanks, I was ready to bury it in the backyard!" he said.

He proceeded to tell me about a new keychain he had received. "When you whistle the keychain whistles back-- so you can always find your car keys," he said. "It works, but I do have one problem with it. The priest at St Patrick's Sunday mass has dentures that whistle every time he speaks, and my keychain whistles back to him!" "I had to turn around and pretend the whistling was coming from the guy behind me at church!" he said.

"Do you like Peanuts?" Browning asked on another visit handing me a can of peanuts. I opened the can and a toy snake sprung out of the can like a jack in the box. "A truck filled with them over turned out on Broad Street a few hours ago," Browning explained. "The driver picked up most of them and then pulled away in a hurry leaving half a dozen behind. I picked them up thinking they were peanuts and got the surprise of my life when I opened it!"

There were times when I headed to Sports East just to see Browning's reaction to something comical that had happened, like the Tic-Tac-Toe playing chicken. One day I stopped into Sports East just to tell Browning, "I was leaving Deptford Mall when I noticed a Tic-Tac-Toe Chicken arcade game. There was a real chicken inside the game, so I stopped to play." (The chicken must have been coached by a rudimentary 1970's computer because she never lost. After her human opponent would enter a move with a switch the chicken would instantly counter the move with the best corresponding X or O.) "How did you do?" Browning asked. "I lost 3 games and seventy-five cents to the chicken," I admitted. Browning started to laugh. "He did go first though," I added. Browning stopped and nodded in mock sincerity. "Sure, that's the only reason she beat you, she went first," Browning added helpfully before dissolving into hearty laughter.

Browning was a good source of information and equipment for track and cross- country coaches. His generosity was not always reciprocated. A new coach, from Eastern High School, came to see Browning in Sports East one evening. "I just got a teaching job at Eastern High," he said." "But the catch is I have to coach track and cross country to get the job. I never ran a step in my life and know nothing about either sport. Everyone told me to stop in and see you to get some information."

Browning explained the basics of both sports including how to score meets and went down to the basement returning with a stack of books. He handed the new coach score books and books on running fundamentals and track and field technique, along with some running and track and field magazines.

"How much do I owe you for all of this?" the neophyte coach asked. "Nothing, take them and good luck. Stop back in if you ever need anything."

Browning said "A few years later I ran into that coach at a coaches meeting. I said hello to him and he just looked at me like 'Who the heck are you?'" Browning continued, "A few years ago when he first stopped in the store he wasn't even sure which direction to turn running around the track, now he thinks he's Bill Bowerman! Well, that's not true. I met Bowerman and he was a pretty down to earth and humble guy."

Bill Heughan: "We made a big mistake when we were doing well and opened up a second store called Sports East 2 in Clarksboro, NJ in the 80's. The partners that took it over didn't make it."

When Sports East 2 went out of business one of the partners sold all of the stock and never paid Browning or Bill Heughan.

Jane Hoopes remembered, "I tried to tell Browning to declare the loss from Sports East 2 on his income tax but he wouldn't do it. Even though he lost a lot of money and thousands of dollars in stock from it, he didn't feel comfortable doing that. But when our sporting goods store Athletes Korner closed in Hammonton, Browning helped my husband Gene and I sell our leftover stock. He kept track of everything he sold on a little piece of paper and gave us the money for each item right to the penny."

Because of increased competition from the big box sporting goods stores, and the larger variety of sporting goods they were able to carry, the profits at Sports East dwindled in the late 80's and early 90's. Ironically, as Nike became a sporting good behemoth they later balked at supplying running shoes to small sporting goods stores like Sports East-- despite the early connection with Browning selling Blue Ribbon and the first Nike shoes. "I can't get running shoes from Nike unless I carry their full line of shoes, including wrestling shoes and a lot of other things that won't sell like javelin shoes," Browning said at the time.

Browning sometimes cashed checks for some nearby residents who didn't have bank accounts from the Sports East till. There were at least a few times I saw him trying to track down the check holders when their checks bounced.

Bill Heughan, "The big sporting outfits killed us. There were businesses in Chicago bidding on South Jersey school athletic accounts for shoe contracts that we had to compete against. Nike running shoes started the running clothing craze too. If you couldn't get Nike shoes like the big chains, you couldn't get their clothes either."

The robberies at the store were also becoming more frequent in the stores final years. One robbery made the front page of the Gloucester County Times. Under the headline, "Ex-Olympic runner chases thief from his store with a baseball bat," the story read:

"For the second time in a month, someone tried to rob the Sports East store on South Broad Street Sunday. But this time store co-owner Browning Ross chased the would-be thief out of his store with a baseball bat and ran after the man for about a half-mile before losing sight of him somewhere near the Woodbury Court Apartments police said. Ross had an advantage- in 1948 and 1952 he participated in the steeplechase in the Olympics and won the steeplechase in the first Pan-Am Games in 1951. He has also won eight national championships for long distance races and won countless races throughout the country. He wasn't quick enough to avert a robbery on Jan 14 by a man wielding a knife and gun. But on Sunday, police said that a man wearing a silk stocking over his head entered Ross' store and demanded money. The man was brandishing a folding knife. When Ross showed the man that the cash register only contained change, the thief reportedly asked for Ross' wallet. With that, Ross picked up a nearby Louisville Slugger and chased the man out of the store. Police found footprints in the snow that led to an apartment complex, but Ross could not positively identify the resident of the apartment as the man he chased. The incident is under police investigation."

Bill Heughan, "One time we were robbed, the guy pulled a knife on me and I threw a bat at him and missed, knocking off his hat and scaring him away.

Guys would come in and switch their old shoes for new ones while you were helping someone else. My wife had her pocketbook stolen while she was working here.

We even had people try to sneak into the store overnight through the air conditioner over the roof. I asked my lawyer if I could wait for them with a shotgun. He said absolutely not-- "Bill if you shoot them you will be charged with entrapment—by laying in wait with them with a gun. By the way, Thank God you missed that kid with the baseball bat and didn't injure him or you would have been liable for his injuries too!"

We came to the selling point in 1991; the store was a weight around our neck by then. We couldn't keep up with what was happening in the retail business. It burns me up what they were charging for the Nike shoes by that point-- we were one of the first to carry them, and knowing what it cost them to make them overseas— beans!"

Matollionequay and Ockanickon

In 1970 Browning started the Mid-Atlantic Running Camp in the YMCA camps of Medford, New Jersey. He once joked that if you could pronounce the names of the boys and girl's camps, Matollionequay and Ockanickon-- you must have stayed there.

The camps were located on 550 acres in the Pine Barrens in Southern New Jersey. The 1st Mid-Atlantic Running Camp ran from August 30 to September 4th, 1970. Browning was assisted by Co-directors Jim Hawkins, coach of Deptford, NJ, along with Robert Wirtz (Sterling High School) and Vince Siderio (Drexel University's coach).

The cost of the first camp was $60 with a $15 deposit. Browning would hold his camp in Medford every year but one for the next 20 years. His guest speakers at the first camp were a "who's who" of great coaches: Jumbo Elliott of Villanova, Jim Tuppeny of the University of Penn, Kevin Quinn of St Joseph's College, and Harry Groves of Penn State to name a few.

Many of the coaches brought along their top collegiate runners, and many Olympians and World class runners-- especially from Villanova (Don Paige, Marcus O'Sullivan, Tiny Kane, and Dick Buerkle) served as counselors at the camp over the years.

The first camp was for boys only but was held in the "girl's" camp at Matollionequay. Within a few years, the camp would become co-ed and utilize both camps. Most of the running campers had no idea that Matollionequay and Ockanickon were real people who had once lived in the area of the camps.

Ockanickon, a Chief of the Mantas Lenape Indian tribe in the mid-1600's, and Princess Matollionequay his wife, were both known for helping the first Quaker settlers in Western New Jersey survive. Ockanickon died in 1681, the same year that William Penn received a land grant that pushed the Lenape out of New Jersey and into Ohio. Chief Ockanickons' reputed last words were, "Be plain and fair to all, Indian and Christian as I have been."

At the first camp, Jumbo Elliott started his talk by asking how many of the campers ate cereal for breakfast that morning. Almost every hand went up. "Next time throw away the cereal and eat the box," Jumbo said. "The box is better for you." Jumbo also told the campers to "live like a clock" and have a running routine and to take a drink from every water fountain they pass during the day. He also repeated one of his favorite aphorisms, "Runners make runners."

Mike Fanelli remembers, "I went to the camp during the summer between my junior and senior year (summer 1973). Dennis Fikes the sub-four-minute miler from Penn was one of the camp counselors. Most of the top South Jersey runners were there, like Mike Elder (Haddon Township High) and the Marino Brothers (Williamstown High). Browning was almost 50 but I remember him still being able to run us into the ground every morning. We concluded camp with a barefoot beach race at Avalon. "

In the spring of 1975, Browning had the members of his Gloucester Catholic track team who were interested in attending camp sell "Olympic cookies" to defray the cost of the camp. Browning had bought cases of cookies in the shape of the Olympic rings earlier that year thinking they would make great prizes at these races. Browning had, in fact, bought too many cases and was thought this might be a good way to move some of the cookie boxes before their expiration date.

I remember standing in Gloucester City, across the street from Gloucester High school selling the cookies. It seemed that most of the people that bought them from us had a connection to either the Gloucester Catholic track team, or knew Browning.

Our next sale took place in Woodbury. We started off going door to door to slim sales and then Browning dropped us off in front of Underwood Hospital, telling us he would return in an hour to pick us up.

About 2 hours later it started to rain. One of the Gloucester Catholic track team members said, "Man, Browning must really want us to sell these cookies! We've been out here for hours!" Just then Browning's son Barry pulled up. "I think dad might have forgotten to pick you guys up, hop in the car and I'll take you home." Browning was apologetic for forgetting to pick us up when we saw him and said: "Well, I guess the only thing worse than Olympic cookies are soggy Olympic cookies!"

A few weeks later Browning said, "How would you guys feel about donating the money you made from the cookies to a girl, to help pay her way to the camp? She has a disease and it would mean a lot to her to go." Everyone was immediately in favor of the idea but one runner inquired, " Mr. Ross, is it a good idea for a poor young girl with a disease to be out in the middle of woods with runners in a running camp?" The girl had a mild non-contagious blood disease and enjoyed the camp which ended up not being held "in the middle of the woods" for the first time but at the Stockton State College dorms in Galloway. Stockton College (now University) while also in the Pine Barrens was 12 miles from Atlantic City.

Villanova Olympian Larry James, the Athletic Director at Stockton, had started co-directing the camp with Browning a couple of years before. The camp that summer also featured former World indoor mile record holder from Villanova Dick Buerkle and 1972 Olympic 800-meter Gold medalist Dave Wottle. Both had a great sense of humor and were down to earth and always accessible to the campers.

Wottle walked by a middle school aged camper eating watermelon at lunch in the Stockton cafeteria and joked, "Be careful not to swallow any of the seeds, or you'll get a watermelon growing in your stomach!"

For high school runners, the camps offered opportunities to run with and get to know world-class runners and take a leap forward in confidence. Browning and Larry James took most of the campers to run on the Atlantic City Boardwalk. Dave Wottle, Dick Buerkle, and Browning lead the runners on a five mile out and back run on the boardwalk. About five minutes into the easy run, Wottle and Buerkle asked if we would like to race a boat that was about cutting through the surf about 100 yards off the beach, parallel to the boardwalk.

The run seemed to go by in a flash and I noticed the top high school runners finished a few minutes behind. I know the workout was a turning point in my confidence. How could one be intimidated about a high school race after cruising through a workout with Buerkle, Wottle, and Ross?

The following year the camp was held in Medford, New Jersey again. The first thing a camper noticed when they drove down the "sugar sand" roads of the Pine Barrens to check into the camp was the loud calling of Blue Jays back and forth. If there was a breeze you could hear the sound of whispering pines.

The first night, just before dawn, campers also heard another sound-- a loud scream as one of the campers woke to find a squirrel, inches from his head eating the peanut butter and jelly sandwiches his mother had packed. In the still dark cabin, the squirrel looked a lot like a gigantic rat to a sleepy camper.

The first night of Camp Browning introduced a guest, a friend of his who was also a cardiologist, author, and runner who was going to give a talk to the camp, run the optional Sea Isle City Half Marathon race with some of the campers and then return to camp for another talk before departing. Doctor George Sheehan.

Browning held up a copy of his book "Dr. Sheehan on Running" as he introduced Dr. Sheehan. Sheehan talked about the "Magic 6 plus 2 stretches," and had the campers try them. Next, he talked about preventing injuries. He said most running injuries start at the feet and said runner's feet should be examined and treated first.

He recommended inserting a pad of surgical felt into the heels of running shoes to absorb shock and prevent injuries. He said, "Everything God made has a crack in it. If you have a structural weakness in your feet, it will probably manifest itself in lower leg injuries when you run."

Dr. George Sheehan returned after the half-marathon as promised with his hair stuck and plastered to his head, a result of dumping Gatorade handed out by race volunteers that he thought was water over his head as he ran.

I quickly found out that Dr. Sheehan, who asked us to call him George, was one of the adults without pretensions it was possible to meet through running much more frequently than other sports. Adults who treated teenagers as full functioning people, deserving of respect, as equals and not just children as we had met while participating in most other sports.

George Sheehan talked about the importance of play, and to always remember to treat running as play. Those who did he said would be lifetime runners. He also said "It's very hard, in the beginning, to understand that the whole idea is not to beat the other runners. Eventually, you learn that the competition is against the little voice inside you that wants you to quit."

Sheehan also talked about the runner's natural enemy, the automobile. "Don't assume the driver sees you; many drivers only look one way. My experience is if you see an elderly driver who is driving right at you, don't assume they will see you and reverse course in time, it's up to you to get out of the way."

(In October of 1993, I wrote to George and asked him a few questions for a magazine article I was writing. I received his reply a few days before he passed away, November 1, 1993. His philosophy was the same. "Too many kids are getting turned off to the great sport of running much too early by people putting pressure on them to win instead of treating their running as play.")

Some memories of the camps: One morning about a dozen campers gathered around an old weathered telephone pole using it to stretch before the first run of the morning. With a loud "Crack!" the telephone pole split in half and then fell to the ground. Browning standing nearby said, "See, that's why I never stretch!"

As we walked from breakfast after another morning run many of the campers stopped to feed a little piglet named Philomena, a resident of the camp called some cereal. Philomena became a camp favorite. Then one morning the little piglet was gone, returned to a farm. The camp breakfast that morning included pancakes and bacon, which no one touched. Browning saw the camper's reaction and said, "I don't think it works that quickly. He chuckled and said, "As far as I know you can't take the pig away and serve it as bacon an hour later!"

The camp was strictly analog. Without newspapers, television, radios, or yet to be invented cell phones the camps had a "Mayberry RFD" feel of quiet and relaxation. One of my favorite memories is rocking on a porch chair as Browning, with nothing much else to do quietly relayed stories of his past that I hadn't had a chance to hear. For example the time the US Olympic Team spent traveling to the 1948 Olympics on a ship; and coaching the 1968 World Cross Country meet in Africa against great runners such as Mamo Walde from Ethiopia.

Larry James and Browning often traded stories about Villanova and Jumbo Elliott. James an expert motivator, talked about his Olympic experience in Mexico in 1968. He talked about his 43.9 Penn Relays leg for Villanova in 1968 when he earned the nickname the "Mighty Burner".

When someone asked him if he got nervous he admitted to sometimes having a fear of falling while running at top speed. Larry James also mentioned the mental games the top sprinters in the Olympic camp played. "You'd go out to train in the afternoon and guys would look at you sleepily like "Nah, not today." Looking like they were just going to take it easy. But if you got up and out to the track at 5 am they were out there training like crazy."

James was a big believer in the power of positive thinking and his motto was "Your attitude determines your altitude." One thing Larry said in the camp always stayed with me. "You can't give more than 100%. Anyone who said, Man, I just gave 110% in that race probably usually only gives 80%. You can only give 100%; the trick is to consistently try to give that 100%."

Browning's camps offered a chance to train with top-notch runners. Many of the runners on the 1976 Villanova cross-country team including Tiny Kane and Steve Crook attended the camp asked me to go along on an "easy 3-mile run" one day. After an easy start, the pace gradually picked up. Trying to hang on, I looked at my watch and noticed 30, 35 and then 40 minutes had gone by. It seemed like we should have covered three miles and the pace was getting faster as time went on. Not wanting to get lost in the Pine Barrens, I managed to "hang onto the bumper" of the college runners until we made it back to camp.

I approached Browning rocking on the porch and said, "That's it! I know one thing for sure I'm not going to run in college. If that was an easy run forget it..."

Browning just smiled, knowing perfectly well what had just happened. The next day he told me some of the runners had approached him and said they thought I was going to have a good (high school cross-country) season because they had done their best to drop me and I had hung on.

The camps offered a chance to improve a young runner's confidence by running with those much better. Not many sports offer this opportunity.

Larry Kalb remembered getting lost on the sandy trails and finally finding his way back, "When I told Browning what happened he said, 'maybe you'd be better at track-- you just have to remember to keep making left turns!'"

I think this is one of Browning's favorite memories from his camps: One day a young camper approached Browning as Browning sat on the porch, with a camp brochure in hand. "Mr. Ross, can I ask you a question?"

"Sure."

"It says in the camp brochure 'there will be plenty of fun'. What time does the fun start? It says here there will be fun."

Browning laughed heartily. He would catch his breath, and start to laugh again his eyes watering. He loved that line and would sometimes approach me when we coached together; during a boring stretch of a track meet and say, "What time does the fun start? You told me there would be fun!" (He did approach the young runner before the end of that camp and asked if he was having fun yet and the boy answered that he was, with a good bit of enthusiasm.)

For a few afternoons of the camp, a former Penn AC friend of Browning's would show up with some family members to host an Olympics quiz. He would ask the camper's questions about the Olympics and reward correct answers with pins and other prizes.

After a few nights, Browning confided in me, "Do you know why he comes here every night about dinner time?" "No." "He lost his job, and he has eight kids. He's been bringing different kids with him each time so they can get a good meal."

The only thing I heard Browning say to the man at the end of the night was, "See you tomorrow."

Every Saturday night Browning would say to the gathered campers, "OK how many of you heathens want to go to church?" In a modern equivalent to the miracle of the Loaves and Fishes, he would squeeze everyone who wanted to go into his car for a trip to evening mass at St Mary's of the Lakes in Medford. Some years I counted 11 people in his car.

Jane Hoopes later remembered the camp, "The angels were always with Browning. A couple of times Larry James went back home to Pomona at the same time for a few hours, not knowing Browning was also leaving to go to mass. So the camp was unsupervised for an hour or so, but nothing ever happened. When Gene and I helped him with the camp the last couple of years we would help drive and he would say, "OK if any of you heathens want to go to mass we are leaving in half an hour. The boys can come with me and the girls, or boys who look like girls can go with Jane!"

I enjoyed the camp so much I went back for a number of years to assist Browning as a counselor. One year as we drove to camp Browning pulled into the Medford McDonalds. "Let's get some lunch, we aren't going to eat for another 7 hours." As we stood in line Browning said, "Look at that guy behind the counter. Doesn't he look like Boris Becker, the tennis player?" He really did. "He looks more like Boris Becker than Boris does," I said. When it was our turn in line Browning said, "Hi Boris, I'd like a Big Mac, an order of fries..."

One year before a college cross-country season at Rowan I attended both Browning's camp and then Ed Mather's camp as a counselor. Mather was an extremely successful coach at Mountain Lakes (NJ) and Bernard's High School winning dozens of New Jersey state championships in cross-country. He was also a bit of a curmudgeon. At the time Mathers was coaching with Mark Wetmore who went on to a great college coaching career at the University of Colorado, winning multiple national championships in cross-country.

Wetmore seemed soft-spoken and approachable and usually had a small group of runners surrounding him talking training and Arthur Lydiard. Mathers had invited me to the camp and approached me and started our first conversation by mentioning the names of a couple of world-class runners who had left his camp on the first day. Then he said, "You were Browning Ross's boy at Gloucester Catholic!" Then he walked away muttering.

When I returned from camp I went to visit Browning. He said, "So how is ol' Mathers?" I repeated our brief conversation and Browning laughed.

"Eddie's a character. I met him in the 50's when I was coaching at St. Joe's University. He ran all of our races."

Jack Pyrah remembered Browning helping a young Ed Mathers land a lifeguard job in Sea Isle In the early 1960's as well as putting up the Mathers family for a while at the Ross home in the summer. Browning confirmed it. "He called me looking for a job and I got him a job as a lifeguard in Sea Isle City and we let him and his family stay with us down there until he found a place to live. He started coaching in New Jersey and invited me to speak at his camp. A few years later when I started my own camp he called me up and told me not to do it, not to open a competing camp. I told him, "Jeez Eddie there's plenty of runners to go around. They won't be in competition-- I'm drawing mainly from South Jersey and you're drawing from further away, up in North Jersey. But it really seemed to make him mad when I went ahead and started my camp anyway."

Years later I asked Mark Wetmore about the camps and if he believed that was a reason for Mathers to possibly hold a grudge. Mark said, "I know that Ed Mathers loved Browning. Deep down he was probably appreciative for everything that Browning had done, but he was also ultra- competitive, and I could see him staying mad over something like that (starting another camp). Any other cross-country coach or coach of distance runners probably felt tested in their friendship with Ed. He was not often the most magnanimous loser (or winner).

I mentioned this camp and Browning's reaction to Joe Henderson and he said, "Sometimes Browning's kindness was answered with ingratitude. Luckily Browning was the type to just let such pettiness roll off his shoulders."

Jane and Gene Hoopes took over the Mid-Atlantic Running camp for a final year when Browning and Larry James decided to stop directing it in the mid-1980's. Browning cited insurance concerns as his primary reason for discontinuing the camp.

When I hear blue jays loudly calling back and forth, my thoughts always return to Browning's camps in the New Jersey Pinelands.

Jack Pyrah with the victorious Villanova 4 x 1 Mile Relay team, wearing black ribbons for Coach Jumbo Elliott at the 1981 Penn Relays. From left: Ken Lucks, Marcus O'Sullivan (Current Villanova Coach), Jack Pyrah, John Hunter, Sydney Maree.

Jack Pyrah

JACK PYRAH WAS ONE OF Browning's closest friends. Jack grew up in the Germantown section of Philadelphia and graduated from Germantown High in 1937. Jack was raised by his Uncle George who took him to his first Penn Relays in 1934 at age 16.

Jack would go on to attend 73 Penn Relays in a row. His first trip to the Penn Relays started in motion a lifetime love affair with running and track and field, and a lifetime of friendships with some of the greatest track-and-field athletes of all time.

Jack began his coaching career at Philadelphia's Shanahan Catholic Club in 1942 in Philadelphia. Browning first met Pyrah while running road races as a member of the Shanahan Catholic Club of Philadelphia in the 1940's before attending Villanova.

Jack's Uncle George passed away tragically and unexpectantly and Jack was on his own. He started to spend a lot of time with Browning and Sis Ross. Jack was introduced to his wife, Jean, by Browning and Jack and Jean married in 1957.

Jack said, "I told Browning you introducing me to Jean was the best thing you've ever done. More important than all of those trophies you won and all of the prizes like electric cooking machines you've won at races over the years! Before Browning introduced us, Jean's husband had been killed leaving her a widow with three small children. After we met and married it was great for us and for the kids who needed a daddy."

Jean recalled Browning and Jack's long friendship. "Jack was all alone in the world and Browning and Sis were the closest thing he had to family. In fact, I think he was there every night for dinner until we married. When Jack and Browning got together they could just spend hours talking about track and they would laugh about the smallest things. After we married, Jack went into business for himself opening an ice cream store in Gloucester City. Jack was so interested in track he would spend most of his time on the phone talking track while customers came into the store and helped themselves. Before Browning opened Sports East, Jack and he opened a sporting goods store on the other end of Broad Street in Woodbury. They took over the inventory of that store and I remember Jack and Browning had me counting fishhooks!"

Jack joined Villanova as Jumbo Elliott's assistant track coach and head cross-country coach in the fall of 1966 after meeting Elliott in the spring of 1965 on a plane on the way to a Knights of Columbus track meet in Cleveland. As Villanova Coach, Jack had a front row seat at the Penn Relays and witnessed an incredible 54 Championship of America relay victories by Villanova at the Penn Relays.

Jumbo Elliott once said of Jack, "That Pyrah has the mind of a computer when it comes to Track. He has heard more sad stories [from Villanova runners] than a bartender. He's so nice, so understanding that some of the runners call him 'Mother Pyrah." Pyrah won eight IC4A and an incredible four NCAA championships (1966, 1967, 1968, and 1970) as Head Cross-Country coach at Villanova. The 1970 title was famous because it was won after Irish runner Donal Walsh demanded that a film of the race finish be reviewed in order to prove that a Villanova runner had finished ahead of other point scorers and had been passed in the finish chute.

Jack coached 18 Olympians at Villanova including Eamonn Coghlan, Marty Liquori, Sydney Maree, and Villanova's present head coach Marcus O'Sullivan. Jack stepped in and became Villanova's head track coach in 1981 when Jumbo passed away on March 22, 1981. During his years as head coach, Villanova won three Penn Relays titles and the school's first Big East Conference Championship. When former Olympian and Villanova alum Charlie Jenkins was hired at the end of the season, Pyrah went back to his previous coaching duties of head cross-country and assistant track coach.

I interviewed Jack for Runners Gazette Magazine and asked for his favorite Penn Relays memory. Jack recalled Larry James winning the 1968 mile-relay at Penn, running a 43 quarter and beating a kid from Baylor who ran "only" a 45-second quarter mile. James, a Gold and Silver medalist at the 1968 Olympics in Mexico City ran on the World Record 4 x 400 relay team (2:56.16). In that interview, when I also asked Jack to name the best runner he ever coached he hesitated. "There have been so many. We've had guys who went on to world records and many Olympians, but I guess you'd have to put Marcus O'Sullivan and Sydney Maree at the top of the list. Marcus ran over 101 sub-4 minute miles and 83 equivalent 1500-meter races at sub-4-minute mile pace. Sydney Maree from South Africa ran a 3:48 mile, a 3:29 1500 meters, and held the American record (13:01) in the 5000 for a while.

Jack described Maree's first race on American soil. "Browning and I met Sydney Maree his first day in America (from South Africa). He ran in a 4th of July race Browning put on in Woodbury, NJ. After the race, Browning, Sydney, and I went out to eat at the Colonial Diner in Woodbury. "When the waitress took our order, she thought Sydney was pulling her leg when he ordered 'passion-fruit juice' with his meal. He said he always ordered it in South Africa but it wasn't on the menu at the Colonial Diner!"

In correspondence from Alberto Salazar, I was surprised to learn that Salazar almost accepted a scholarship to Villanova in 1977 because of Pyrah.

"If I didn't go to Oregon, Villanova would have been one of my top choices. My father liked Jack Pyrah best of all the coaches who recruited me and I really considered going there."

Of course, Salazar had a great career at Oregon winning the NCAA cross-country championships and setting the indoor 5,000-meter world record, but it also boggles the mind to think of Salazar attending Villanova during those years with Don Paige, Sydney Maree, Marcus O'Sulliva and the other Villanova greats of that era. Jean Pyrah recalled Alberto later stopping to visit Jack years later at their Gloucester Home while on a run when Alberto was in Philadelphia.

Jack was a voracious reader of anything sports related. Browning mentioned to me "Well I cleaned out some of the old magazines in my basement. I gave an old Sports Illustrated I had down there to Jack." "Was Eddie Matthews on the cover?" I asked. "Yes, he was. How did you know that?" asked Browning. "Because it's the first issue and worth a fortune," I said. Browning said, "Oh Crap! I've got to get that back from Jack!"

When Jack retired from Villanova in 1991 he was named Villanova "Coach Emeritus". Villanova presented Jack with a unique gift--the offer to accompany the Villanova track or cross-country teams to any meet in the country.

Jack took Villanova up on the offer often accompanying the Villanova track and cross-country team on trips across the country.

In his free time, he often came out to assist me with the Gloucester Catholic cross-country team. When he wasn't present at one of our meets, I was always amazed at Jack's ability to reconstruct a cross-country race from a one-inch result in the newspaper. He seemed able to visualize the race more clearly than I who had been there the day before: "So it looks like your number-one runner was a little slower than usual, was it at their place? This course might be a little long; they probably didn't measure it. Your number-two runner was further back than earlier in the year, right? Shame you can't get someone from the soccer team who is in shape and isn't playing. You could turn them into a better runner than your number-five runner who was pretty far back...."

I once asked Jack if anything disappointed him about our local South Jersey track scene. "One thing, it amazes me that so many of the area high school coaches never even heard of Browning. First of all, I don't think people realize just how good a runner Browning was. I first saw Browning when he was a senior at Woodbury High School. He ran in the AAU championships as a high school kid against grown-ups. He was New Jersey State Champ in the mile and cross-country. Browning was so humble but could always make you laugh; he had so many great sayings. One of my favorites is when he would console one of his runners with, "Well, you can't win 'em all. Yep you can't win 'em all-- especially since you just lost one!"

In 2006 Jack was honored in March at halftime of the Villanova-Syracuse basketball game in Philadelphia for his enshrinement in the National Coaches Hall of Fame, joining Jumbo Elliott. Jack received a long-standing ovation from the 19,000 fans present.

Jean Pyrah recalled, "When Jack became ill in 2007 he wrote out the Act of Contrition (A Catholic prayer) on different pieces of paper around the house in case he should become too sick to remember the prayer."

Jack Pyrah passed away in 2007 at the age of 88. The long-time Villanova coach had a gift for processing the hard times he experienced in his life into empathy for others. At Jack's service, Gloucester Catholic grad Jim Rafferty recalled Jack giving him a special pair of spikes from Villanova after finishing 4th in a high school track meet. "Give these a try," said Jack. To Jim, the shoes from Jack seemed to have magical properties and he easily vanquished the 3 who had beaten him in his next race. Jack also let the neighborhood boys including his son Bill Van Tassel practice pole-vaulting in his back yard. The boys frequently finished one-two-three in their meets for Gloucester Catholic and one of the boys, Jim Waters, went on to set the South Jersey Pole Vault record in 1967.

Marty Liquori, one of the best American middle-distance runners ever, ran for both Jack and Jumbo Elliott at Villanova as part of the legendary Villanova teams. He recalled Jack's impact on Villanova's great runners: "We all realize now that Jumbo had a real attention-deficit problem and it was Jack who kept everything on an even keel. He was the detail guy to Jumbo's George Patton. Some coaches may have been able to do both, but I never had one. As Jumbo said, 'I kick them and Jack kisses them.' Without either of them, Villanova in the '70s would not have been as successful."

Present Villanova Coach Marcus O'Sullivan recalled how Jack was always positive, and always had an encouraging word for his runners no matter their performance on the track. "Jack was a huge inspiration to me as a runner and a coach," Marcus said. "Jack's loyalty and dedication to Villanova were unmatched. I remember Jack leaning on Assistant Coach Jim Tuppeny out on the cross-country course because he was having some difficulty walking. Then when Jim Tuppeny got sick, I saw him leaning on Jack. It was a touching thing to see. I saw Jack's great gift after I became coach at Villanova- his gentleness and positive outlook and limitless patience." With a smile, Marcus also recalled Jack's gift for gab. "Jack would call while you were making dinner to chat and the next thing you knew it seemed like it was time to get the kids ready for school."

When Marcus O'Sullivan went on a recent recruiting trip to Kenya, he met former Villanova distance great Amos Korir. Marcus said, "Amos's first question was 'How is Jack doing?'" Jack was Amos's coach at Villanova.

Another former Villanova runner, Tom Donnelly, the longtime Haverford College track and cross-country coach, was a key member of Jack's championship teams in the 1960s. Donnelly's runners have earned close to 100 cross-country and track and field All-American awards since 1980 including 24 individual NCAA championships and a NCAA championship relay team. Tom remembered, "Jack was both loved and respected by every single athlete, male and female, who came into contact with him at Villanova. He was the soul of that program for a third of a century. In his understated way, Jack Pyrah had an enormous positive influence upon hundreds of young athletes. They and Villanova are richer for the experience."

Herb Lorenz succeeded Browning as the top runner in the Southern New Jersey and Philadelphia area in the '60s and early '70s and then became one of the top Master's runners in the country. He recalled similar memories of Jack: "My fondest memories of Jack include late-night phone calls and lengthy conversations about running. In 1964, I had just moved to South Jersey (from Germany) and after meeting Jack I realized that he was the person who knew the history of South Jersey running dating to the days of Browning Ross as well as where track and field meets were held and where to go for top-notch competition. It really is a shame that in today's world there are very few people the likes of Jack. He never was in the sport for the money but for the pure love of it. Jack was truly an icon, one who should be immortalized for his quiet manner and his pure love of the sport. The South Jersey running community lost one of its biggest fans and supporters when Jack passed away and he will be sorely missed."

Tom Osler recalled Jack and his impact on the Philadelphia running scene: "Jack was certainly one of a kind. His contribution wasn't any great coaching theory but the way he dealt with people. Jack was a true gentleman. When I met him in 1954 he was "coach" of the Shanahan Catholic Club. They had a large clubhouse on Lancaster Avenue close to Fairmount Park. He was instrumental at that time in sponsoring the Shanahan Marathon in late January of every year from 1954 to about 1964. So Jack was an originator of the Philly Marathon which I suppose is now over 63 years old. Jack was a great friend, and I shall miss him so much."

Mike McIntosh, the former Canadian National Junior Coach, recalled Jack's influence spreading to Canada: "Coach Pyrah developed a Canadian pipeline (secondary only to the Irish pipeline) of track and field athletes who he was mainly responsible for recruiting to Villanova's scholarship program. Jerry Bouma was the first Canadian athlete to receive a scholarship to Villanova with much more to follow including Glenn Bogue the 400-meter bronze medalist at the 1978 Commonwealth Games.

Bogue commented that Jack Pyrah was the kindest man he had ever met and at the same time one of the most knowledgeable people he knew in track and field. Throughout the years Coach Pyrah and I enjoyed many great moments together with family and friends; his fantastic wit and humor were enjoyed by all that knew him. I will always treasure his friendship and the many memories we shared over the past 33 years."

Jack Pyrah Jr. recalled, "My dad found his vocation- coaching track athletes and cross-country runners. "He was a peacemaker and a born leader in his own way. I remember hearing so many times that he was like a father away from home for so many of those boys at Villanova. Not too many people have a career that allows them to be called that.

"One of the things that we all have to do in this world is find out what we are here to do. My father was a man who did that."

Jack was inducted into the Villanova Wall of Fame in 2001.

An indoor track meet, the "Jack Pyrah Invitational," was named after him and is held the first week in December.

Browning Ross directing one of his many races.

One Man Running Boom

AFTER STARTING THE ROAD RUNNERS Club of America in 1957, Browning decided to address the dearth of road races in the Philadelphia area by hosting his own races.

In the 1920's through 1950's almost all of the road races held were handicapped runs where runners started at different intervals or "handicaps"—the fastest runner started from "scratch" and was the last to start.

The handicaps were determined by judges before the race, and often published in newspapers the day before the race. Tom Osler recalls, "During those years almost all the road races in this area were handicaps.

When Browning started the Road Runners Club in 1957, the RRC could hold its own races under the umbrella of the AAU, this changed. Quickly only a few handicaps remained."

Before the RRCA formation, most races also required runners to pass a mandatory doctor's pre-race examination by one or more onsite physicians. Runners, who "failed" this exam, although often completely healthy, were denied entry to the race.

For example, on January 1, 1930, Jim Elkins was examined by three doctors and failed the pre-race exam. (The incident was reminiscent of Clarence DeMars losing six prime years of his running career due to a failed physical examination). One of the three doctors denied Elkins entry to the West Philadelphia Business Men's Classic right before the start believing his "heart could not stand the strain of the run."

After a long conference, two other onsite doctors overruled the verdict and Elkins was finally permitted to run. Elkins' heart was obviously up to the challenge as he used a furious kick to take over the lead at the four-mile mark and win the race by more than 100 yards in front of over 10,000 spectators, one of the largest crowds to witness a race up until that time in Philadelphia. The pre-race physicals faded out with the AAU.

Tom Osler recalls, "Races were considered regular sporting events until the running boom with starting times like a football or baseball game of 1 o'clock in the afternoon. Later, when the races got more popular, considerations were given to traffic and people's schedules and moved to weekend mornings. Until 2012 the Jonas Cattell 10- mile race was one of the last races to keep its Sunday afternoon starting time. I first met Browning in September of 1954. That year, and probably before that there was a ten-mile race in Woodbury, NJ that started and finished on the Woodbury High School track during a Saturday football game that Browning set up. In the 1950's he also teamed with Ed League of the "Inlet and Social Club" of Atlantic City, NJ, Atlantic City to put on many races.

In the summer of 1957, I recall that Ross put on a 6-mile race in Farnham Park adjacent to Camden (NJ) High School. The race became known as the "Bob and Ray" race, after a comedy team popular in the 1950's because almost everyone in the race got lost. A reporter from the local Courier Post newspaper covered the race and was heard saying "Why are they finishing running in different directions?" and "Why is that guy running over that bridge way over there?"

When the RRC formed in late 1957, the races quickly became more frequent, usually weekly. Of course, Browning was responsible for these."

Browning frequently put on races at the Boat House Row on the East River Drive in Philadelphia.

Registration and the start and finish were usually held at Plaisted Hall, a Boat House built in 1881 (and demolished in 1992) along Philadelphia's famous "Boathouse Row". Runners could smell liniment when they entered Plaisted and usually saw Joe McIllhiney, or Browning Ross sitting in a chair at a small race table for registration. Runners usually had to walk around a public basketball court and go up rickety stairs to use the boathouse's bathroom or showers. The races were often held weekly and wound along East River Drive in Philadelphia in the 50's through the early 70's. Later the races were held in South Jersey-- predominantly at Cooper River in Pennsauken New Jersey.

Then Browning moved the races closer to his home putting on a summer and winter series of races held every weekend in Woodbury or West Deptford, New Jersey.

Dave Platt a Woodbury neighbor of Browning's and a coach for over 30 years at Paulsboro, NJ High School first met Browning as a teenage runner in the early 1960's. "As a senior at Clearview high school, Browning sweet talked me into running for his club Penn AC. One race that I vividly remember was one in which I ran with Dave Patrick, the great Villanova miler as my teammate.

It was an out-back course and I remember Patrick encouraging me (way in the back as much as he was way in the front.) Thinking back on that experience...a 17-year-old hardly more than a few years of running having the opportunity to run with a "stud" from Villanova. Browning opened some significant doors for me I will always be grateful to him for that.

For a South Jersey Boy, those races on Boat House Row were an entry into the whole Philadelphia Culture. Jack Kelly, brother of Actress and Princess Grace Kelly was a runner (and said to be a relative of Browning's wife's Kelly family).

We got gray "Jack Kelly for Brick Work" shirts for running the race that absorbed sweat. The shirts were precursors to the race tech shirts with advertising that came much later. No one had them at the time they were designed for the brick worker to use while working. A few days after President Kennedy was assassinated I remember being in the Boat House after a race and seeing Oswald shoot Jack Ruby on the TV in the Boat House.

Browning directed and ran in many of the races when he was still a national class runner in the late 1950's through the mid-1960's. Since he was the race timer he had to run fast enough to finish first and recover quick enough to call out the other runner's race times.

This multitasking of running and timing proved a dilemma when other top runners started to catch and surpass Browning in his 40's. Neil Weygandt ran in 45 straight Boston Marathons and most of Browning's races in the 1960's and remembered, "Browning was still winning races, beating runners who were younger and faster who should have beaten him by his competitive experience and wiles."

Herb Lorenz, a 4:03 miler and 2:17 marathoner during that time explained, "Browning put on a 5-mile race in the Wenonah Woods. No one knew the course and Browning led the whole way. He kept a good pace but I was reluctant to pass him until I saw the finish. Suddenly he stopped dead right in front of me and said, "That was the finish!"

Tom Osler, "There were no course markings or signs on Browning's course in the Wenonah Woods. One time he got lost on his own course. We really had a lot of fun razzing him when that happened. One of the landmarks on the course was a big landfill or dump. You were supposed to turn there, but one time I tripped on a log or something and went head first right into the garbage dump!"

Browning transitioned from primarily running in races to putting on races in the 1960's. Moses Mayfield, a school boy from Philadelphia was one of the top runners in the area, winning races at a variety of the local races at distances up to the marathon despite being considered legally blind.

Moses would later become a member of the US World Cross Country team in 19 coached by Ross and would win the Philadelphia Marathon in 1970 and 1971. Mayfield said: "Browning Ross literally kept running alive in the Philadelphia area from the late fifties through the early seventies until the running boom. He was the only one putting on races—if he didn't do it, who would have? There would have been almost no races without him."

Some of the unusual races Browning put on included a "4 event quadrathlon". Each participant would do four events within a short time. The four events usually consisted of a 100-yard dash, a mile run, and a 2-mile cross-country run and a fourth event, usually something like a race walk.

Browning's reward for directing the Philadelphia Marathon in 1966 and 1967 was a suspension by the AAU for permitting a woman, Susan Morse to run the 1966 and 1967 Philadelphia Marathon. Browning scoffed at his suspension as being inconsequential but said "I often wondered what happened to that poor girl (Morse) after the race. Banning her served no purpose, it just ended very talented athletes running career."

While most of the media were focused on Roberta Gibbs 1966 "crashing" of the Boston Marathon and Katherine Switzer's 1967 crash into Jock Semple, (Browning's friend and Navy teammate whose preferential treatment in being selected for races had frustrated Browning) Morse received little press for her groundbreaking race. Browning's encouraging Susan Morse to run showed the courage it took just to let a woman participate in races in those years.

Browning remembered a Philadelphia marathon finish in the 1960's, waiting for a straggler to finish, it was approaching the time Sis expected him home for dinner. "There was a woman at the finish line waiting for the lone runner to finish. I handed her my watch, showed her the elapsed time and said, "I have to go, can you give him his finishing time when he finishes? Give him the watch as a prize."

For all of the thousands of races and the hundreds of venues Browning chose to put on races, he remarkably, rarely seemed to have problems with local authorities or with fickle runners. I can recall a race when there were issues with both.

Browning put on a five-mile beach run in Avalon, NJ for over 30 years. For the last 6 years or so he asked me to go with him to help put on the race. He really did not need any help putting on the race but I was glad to go, and I think he was happy for the company. We would get to Avalon about 4 o'clock for the 6 o'clock race when most of the beachgoers had left for the day.

We would both run the five miles of the course along the waters' edge. I would run barefoot and he occasionally would do the same depending on how his toe felt. He had stubbed his toe years before running on the beach. The toe had turned black and blue, and he was certain it was broken at the time. He didn't seek treatment and it never regained flexibility. In his sixties, in the hospital for another procedure, he had calcium deposits scraped from the toe and an artificial toe joint inserted but it did not improve the toes flexibility.

After the run, he would remove cones from the trunk of his car and set them up on the beach near a pier in Avalon for the finish line. Then he would remove a card table and chair from his trunk to register the arriving runners. He was just kicking out the legs of the table with his foot when a police car pulled up. The policeman got out and asked what was going on. The tone of his voice suggested that he was anticipating Browning's answer that he was setting up for a race. The officer then asked if he had a permit.

Browning calmly responded that he'd been putting on the race for over 30 years and had never needed a permit. The runners were just running on the beach and no lifeguards or town services were needed.

The policeman said, "You need to come with me to the police station; you can't hold the race without paperwork and permission." We got in the police car and were taken the few blocks to the nearby station. On the way, I asked Browning if he'd ever done any "hard time" for a race before. He gave a quick laugh and said "not yet"-- but I could see he was worried.

Browning asked if I could go back to the registration table. He was worried that quite a few runners would arrive to register with no one there to tell them what was going on.

He quickly returned with the permit and a vow never to hold the race again. As he was registering runners, one man asked him, "Is a banquet provided with the six-dollar entry fee?" Browning and I laughed but the middle-aged runner was serious.

Browning had noticed the Avalon Community Center sign that they were holding a clambake that night on the way drive into town. He didn't hesitate. "Banquet? Yes, there is, just go to the Avalon Community Center after the race." Browning provided directions to the Community Center.

After the race before heading home to go to a pool party at Villanova Track Coach Jack Pyrah's house, Browning stopped to buy us two jugs of apple cider at a farm stand. Stopped at a light we were swigging from the jugs when a driver in a car next to us rolled down his window to ask directions. He took one look at us drinking from jugs and said, "Forget it!" pulling away at the light at the sight of what must have looked like two moonshiners.

At Jack Pyrah's party, Browning and I laughed about the driver who thought we were drinking moonshine. Browning said, "Boy, that's the last time I drink that much apple cider, I forgot that stuff is just like prune juice!"

Jim Crossin also had some fond memories of Browning's Avalon races. "I was a college student at St. Joe's. There were about 40 of us toeing the line in the sand at the fishing pier where the race started. Browning looked at us, hesitated and then said, "Does anyone have a watch?"

I gave him mine, which had a sweep hand, and he counted down as the second hand neared its apogee... "Five, four, three, two, one, GO!" And of course, he simply called out our times as we finished. That was it."

"One year the race went off during a northeaster or a bad thunderstorm. My younger brother took a picture of me leaning into a 45-50 mile per hour wind! Some people were mad that he held it and some would have been mad if they drove all the way down there and he canceled it.

Another year I drove down to Avalon from Philly to run the race and as I started walking towards the beach, running shoes in hand, I watched as the pack disappeared down the beach! It turns out Brownie had changed the time to an hour earlier, (probably due to the tides) but this was pre-email, the internet, text etc. I wasn't on the inside and had no idea it had changed. I think I did catch a few people once I got my shoes on."

Browning put on a variety of races but Ken Kling was most impressed by the track meets Browning put on by himself. "They usually didn't have every event like a high school meet does but they had quite a few events and he put them on usually without any help. He did that for years pretty much every week in the summer primarily at Woodbury, Deptford or Gloucester County College's track.

The entry fee was usually a quarter and he got the best talent in the area to enter. There were a lot of great South Jersey high school milers in the 60's and 70's and I think the opportunity he provided to be able to run those track races was a factor in why they ran so fast."

Tom Osler remembered, "Browning put on a track meet every Fourth of July in Woodbury with the Woodbury Jaycees. One year, in the 1950's he had enormous trophies for the mile. He kept pushing the mile back in the order of events because he was waiting for an outstanding runner that he coached at Woodbury, Matt Singleton to come. He never did come and I ended up winning the mile and the huge trophy. I wouldn't have been able to beat Singleton."

Ironically the Woodbury Fourth of July race was Irish Olympian John Joe Barry's last race and Villanova world record holder Sydney Maree's first race on American soil.

Ed League, "One of the events Browning put on was at YMCA Camp Carney where he was the director. I remember it being a ten-mile, two-person relay, with each runner running legs of a mile or so up and down some hills. It was pretty rugged as I recall. It seemed as though I barely had time to catch my breath before my "team-mate" came around to tag me for my next lap. I don't recall if Browning and I were teammates or not that evening. I suspect we were. In August 1961, I was home on vacation from a stint in Thule, Greenland where I worked for RCA and entered a race that Browning put on that started and finished in a "traffic free course" in a Cemetery in Woodbury.

He continued to put on AAU all-comers track meets through the mid-1970's at Woodbury and Deptford High School that coincided with a golden age of South Jersey distance running. The Deptford AAU meets featured distance aces Larry Schmelia of the University of South Carolina, Larry Rush of the University of Clemson, and Mike Butynes a sub 9-minute two-miler from CW Post running against the top high school runners in South Jersey in the mile and two-mile every week.

Those races and Browning's running camp had much to do with the number of Division 1 scholarships awarded South Jersey high school runners at that time. As Jumbo Elliott often said, "Runners make runners."

Many remember a similar story year's later when the Water Street track complex was long gone, involving Clearview, (NJ) High School schoolboy sprinter Peanut Gaines. Gaines became a national sensation in 1967, after running 9.3 in the 100-yard dash to better Jesse Owens national high school record of 9.4 set in 1933. Gaines reported to one of Browning's all-comers meets in 1967 or 1968. Gaines was told about and paid the low meet entry—possibly 50 cents at that time to compete. Browning would continue to put on all-comers track meets by himself into the 1990's.

In the 1970's during some bad winters, Browning put on outdoor high school winter track meets for Gloucester Catholic in December and January. Instead of using the track which was covered with ice and snow, Browning measured distances in the visiting schools parking lots which were both paved and lit. I remember running in 3 dual meets with other schools. I've never seen anyone else do anything similar since.

Many of the unique races Browning put on are documented in his "Long Distance Log. For years he put on Married Men vs. Single Men races where total points were added cross-country style to declare a "championship" team.

Browning also hosted and participated in "pentathlons" consisting of five running events spread through the course of a day. They were frequently held near Atlantic City near Bader Airport and consisted of events and a point system from 100 yards to 3 miles. The event distances would sometimes change according to the venue. The race was grueling and awarded versatility. Browning was still winning some of the pentathlon's which usually consisted of a 100, 400, 800, mile and 2 or 3-mile race against younger runners when he was in his 40's.

Many runners remembered participating in a race Browning held that finished with a length in Publisher George Braceland's pool. Braceland was the publisher who had printed Tom Osler's pamphlet "Conditioning of Long Distance Runners." He remained an active runner into his 80's.

Browning got together with runner Jim Latz, the owner of Atlantic City's prestigious restaurant the Knife and Fork Inn for a series of races on the Atlantic City Boardwalk just as the casinos were developing. The post- race dinner featured steak and lobster from the restaurant in Latz's backyard.

Browning also hosted many "Devil Take the Hindmost" track races in which the runner who was lapped had to drop out until only the winner remained. Each runners distance was recorded.

Browning also hosted a number of two and four-man relay races, often with college or high school teams, many were held in Atlantic City. These races are rarely seen today.

It is ironic that while the "explosion" of races and participants after Browning started the Road Runners Club of America in 1957 helped end the practice of handicapped races held up to that point, it was Browning who helped bring the handicapped races back again.

He would host at least one handicapped race among the series of races he put on including races at East River Drive and Belmont Plateau and in his long-running summer and winter race series.

Browning would try to give the biggest trophy (often recycled from one of his own races) to the youngest runner. Everyone who ran his race won a prize of some sort. From the 1970's to the late 1990's the race entry fee stayed around $5, $6 for his Avalon race.

The highlight for most runners was the eclectic assortment of prizes Browning laid out after the race, and of course the freedom of picking out one of the prizes.

Runners selected their own prize from among the books, magazines, socks, clothes, jackets, bags of produce, watermelons, cookies and other items were prizes besides the standard medals and trophies.

For my first road race, he picked out a prize for me, a biography of his close friend, Ted Corbitt.

For my second race, he also selected my prize, a bulky wristwatch radio that was an early forerunner of today's Apple Watch. I remember running with the watch while listening to Phillies games.

I accompanied Browning on some of his shopping expeditions to pick up the prizes. I was surprised at how much thought into the selections paying no attention to the cost. "I'll bet Larry would like this sweatshirt," or, "I think Ed would like this Eagles hat..."

There was no guarantee that the person would attend the race but the prize would make some runners day. All runners got much more than their five-dollar entree fee in prizes.

Tom Osler, "I don't remember when the tradition of Browning getting those unique race prizes started. I know that I ran the Philadelphia Marathon one year and stopped at an Army Navy store before the race and loaded up on everything from ash trays to clothes for prizes and the runners went crazy when they picked out their prizes after the race."

In the 1970's Browning started many of his Sunday 5-mile races at Bell Lake in Woodbury. Tom Osler," I remember one race when a really good runner from New York showed up. He bolted out to a big lead at the start and kept going. We never saw him again.

After the race, we drove around the streets of Woodbury looking for him but we never found him."

In 1976 Browning ordered cases of Olympic shortbread cookies to give out as prizes. Because they were perishable, Browning brought them to every race to give them out as prizes. Browning laughed when he heard runners start to grumble, "Not those cookies again!" "OK, first place is a box of Olympic cookies, second place is two, third place three boxes..." he said.

Browning was still giving out boxes of cookies in his fall races after the Olympics when he overheard one runner grumble, "The last time I got a box of one of those cookies it had a worm in it."

Browning stopped and said, "Huh, that's funny, I didn't think worms would go for them!"

Walt Pierson remembered Browning's quick reactions when something went wrong in one of his Bell Lake races. "One 5-mile race I was in the car with Browning and we were driving next to the lead runner who was really flying. I asked Browning what his time was and he reached down and looked at his stopwatch, which had stopped. In a Solomon-like reaction, Browning asked the lead runner if he had the race time on his watch. When he said he did, Browning asked if he could borrow it and then he stopped his car, jumped out, caught up to the runner and grabbed his watch on the fly-- just like a baton handoff. Browning calmly drove back to the race with the watch and everyone including the winner got their times."

Browning was also often the first person called by anyone wanting to put on a race who didn't know where to begin.

After agreeing to help, he would drive to the race site to do an informal analysis to see what the race needed. He would then measure a course (usually with his car), and provide timing trophies and whatever the race needed at no cost to the requestor.

Most of the people who called him for help were unaware that race directors and timers usually charge for timing races and other race services like course measurements and for providing trophies. Browning never brought it up. He took care of the details from A to Z and the requestor or race beneficiary only noticed a successful race. It was usually a thankless job; his cooperation and assistance were always granted purely for the love of the sport-- he thought it was the right thing to do.

Browning was involved with what many runners consider the "best race of all time"-- the Gloucester Sportsmen Athletic Club's free four-mile race in Gloucester NJ. Every June for close to 20 years the Sportsmen AC sponsored a free race and provided the shirts, trophies, hot dogs, and soda (or beer for those of age) to runners and families after the race. The race was strictly word of mouth and runners showed up at the Athletic Club on a Saturday morning in June and since Browning knew all the area runners, he would sign them in on a clipboard.

He would double check their ages for age group prizes, "Jeez you're forty already? What does that make me?" was typical of the pre-race banter.

Browning would time the finish of the race, and oversee the awards ceremony. The race always attracted some of the best runners in South Jersey. For a decade Larry Schmelia had a long string of victories in the race, including a year when he had such a big lead he was the only runner to beat a train that passed through the course with a half mile to go.

The rest of the field gathered together to wait for the train to pass and then engaged in a mass sprint for the finish. Browning was obligated to sort out the blanket finish. Luckily, he knew most of the runners making the finish order easier to record. Gloucester City's other running legend Dave Williams participated in the Sportsmen AC race in his 60's in the "Year of the Train."

One year I witnessed how Browning's unsung dedication to the sport could sometimes be taken for granted. Race directors asked him to assist with the Jonas Cattell 10 mile run every year since its inception in 1969. The race was a tribute to Jonas Cattell, a revolutionary war hero who ran 10 miles from Haddonfield NJ to Red Bank Battlefield (National Park, NJ) to warn the American forces of the British approach to Red Bank.

Cattell was briefly captured, questioned and then released by the British before successfully continuing his run. His warning was a success, and the American Revolutionary Forces were able to aim their cannons at the road and fire on the approaching British army. (Most amazingly, Cattell then ran the ten miles back to work in Haddonfield after delivering his warning.)

Browning provided timing for the race and often stopped at the midpoint of the race in Westville NJ to cheer on the runners and give out splits. He would then drive to the finish to record times and give out trophies from Sports East that he had engraved for the race. He would call the results into the Gloucester County Times and also print them in his Long Distance Log.

Browning had female trophies made and brought to the race before there were any female finishers. One year Jonas Cattell had two female finishers so Browning had 3 female trophies made the following year. That year there were four female finishers. The coach of the fourth-place finisher started to rant and rave

about the injustice when he saw his runner did not get a trophy.

Browning said, "It looked like he was going to hold his breath until I did something about it so I offered to get drive off and get another trophy from the store and give it to his runner. He said that wasn't good enough, it should have been there now."

Browning had donated his time and all the trophies, and he finally told the coach, "Look, every finisher wasn't guaranteed a trophy. There are a lot of men who ran great and didn't receive a trophy either. That's what competitions is all about-- come back next year and try to do better."

The coach came back for subsequent Jonas Cattell races to monitor the number of awards but never offered to contribute anything to the race. Browning felt bad enough about this to mention it to me months later. I thought it ironic that Browning had to put up with the complaint after he had always done so much to support and encourage female runners.

There were numerous instances where Browning would measure a course for those requesting help with a race and then provide the traffic control during the race and finish line timing after the race. He would then quietly slip away, unsung and without compensation, after the races awards ceremony to go back to work at Sports East or to officiate a track meet.

Browning would often not hear a thank you or have any contact from the race organizer until shortly before the following year's race when they would call him and ask "Do you think you can give us a hand with the race again this year?"

Browning seemed to be involved in almost every race in South Jersey in the 1970's and 80's in some capacity.

When the Camden YMCA race was in danger of stopping for the first time since 1922 in the early 1980's Browning stepped in to save the race which he had won many times alive by moving it to nearby Cooper River.

In the 1980's corporations looking to hold races in South Jersey to publicize their opening reached out to Browning to help them put on races. Browning helped AMC theaters put on a race when they opened their Deptford, NJ location. The course ran through a combination of parking lots adjacent to the new 8 movie theater. All of the runners received movie tickets. At the time, it seemed like the mega movie theaters were taking a chance with most large South Jersey towns still having single movie theaters open.

There was another corporate opening that didn't go as well. Chili's in Deptford also chose a Browning hosted road race as their public relations grand opening a short time after AMC, and a short distance away. Browning used almost the same course. At the races finish Chili's management refused to let in any of the sweaty runners. Browning was angry enough to call the corporate Headquarters when he found out. Chili's promised to welcome runners inside with free drinks and food and they honored their word in their next South Jersey opening.

Browning put on a race each year in Oldmans Township near Pedrickton, NJ. Browning led the race of 100 entrants through town with his car and when some bystanders asked what was going on he responded, "They've all escaped from the nut house, I'm leading them back!" The look on the faces of the spectators as they stepped back showed little doubt he was telling the truth. The next year there were more even spectators waiting for the race and watching the runners from their front steps.

Setting the pace with his car once again Browning called out, "Hey, it's a five-dollar fee if you want to watch!" The spectators quickly ducked inside.

Browning was enough of a South Jersey historian to know there was a 200-year-old precedent for his joke. In 1793, Jean-Pierre Blanchard a French aeronaut sold $5 tickets to a curious crowd at Philadelphia's Walnut Street Prison (later Independence Mall) to witness his balloon flight, the first in the United States. President George Washington was among the crowd to watch as Blanchard successfully flew the balloon to a safe landing in an astonished farmer's field in nearby Deptford New Jersey.

In the 1990's, Browning put on most of his races in West Deptford. Ian Stevenson of Mount Laurel NJ was a frequent participant, "I grew up in Edinburgh, Scotland before moving to the USA in 1981. I chose to run cross country in high school as a way to avoid playing rugby! When I came to the

US I joined the Pineland Striders and discovered Browning's weekly races in the 80's. I thought he was a nice older gentleman who liked running enough to put on "I had run quite a few of the races when they told me, "Do you know who that polite man gentleman is? It's Browning Ross and he is an Olympian and 8-time National Champion runner!"

"For months, I couldn't figure out how he was able to start the race, get to every mile to cheer us on, and give splits, and get to the finish in time to get our times. I thought he must have had the power of teleportation like Star Trek. Then I finally figured out he had laid out the course in such a way where the mile, two-mile, three- mile, four-mile points and finish were really close to each other."

Many runners would schedule their summer vacations around Browning's race series so they could race as often as possible. For reasons unknown, maybe to keep things fresh, Browning would often alter the course half way through the season bringing mock protests from the runners.

One winter race was won by an excellent out of town runner. He picked out a barrel of pretzels for his prize. He was surprised when Browning started to call out the other prize winners, "First place 18 and under..." and reached over and unscrewed the top of his pretzels, reached in and took a couple and continued with the awards ceremony.

The races often took place under bitter cold or scorching hot temperatures. I sat in Browning's car before one Sunday winter race when the temperature struggled to reach the low teens. The Eagles and Cowboys were scheduled to play a playoff game later that afternoon. No one had come to sign up for the race. Browning said, "Geez if no one comes we can get out of here and watch the game." "You don't think anyone will come?" I asked. "No, they'll be here," Browning said. Minutes later the first of 30 runners arrived, shivering to keep warm as they signed up to run in sub-zero temperatures. Browning missed scores of those Sunday games.

Fran Masciuli: "I was a freshman in High School at Paul VI High School in Haddonfield in 1969 when I ran my first road race. I remember all the old timers at East River Drive in Philadelphia. Browning was directing the race and was just as welcoming as could be. I couldn't believe that he would take the time to make me, just a freshman in High School, feel welcomed. I'm still running more than 47 years later thanks in part to his encouragement when I started"

I was visiting with Browning in Sports East one day when he handed me an article written about his summer race series held at Gloucester County College. The writer estimated both the number of times Browning had run around the world (in multiples of 24,000 miles, the earth's circumference) and took an attempt at guessing the number of races Browning had put on in his lifetime, arriving at a "conservative number of 1,800, maybe more" track, cross-country and road races up to that point.

I asked Browning if that number sounded accurate. He thought for a moment and then shrugged. "I really have no idea, most years we were able to put on a race almost every weekend. Runners complained there were no winter races, so we started the snowball series."

Whatever the true number of races, it is hard to imagine anyone in the world putting on anywhere near a comparable number of races.

Barb Knoblock: "I sold sodas at Dad's races a lot during the summer, starting when I was about 9 or 10 years old. There was no Gatorade or bottled water back then, and he wanted to have something available for the runners, especially on hot summer nights to drink.

We would go to the Acme and buy cases of the store brand cola, grape, orange and lemon-lime sodas and ice them down in a cooler to bring to the race. He enticed me by allowing me to sell them for 25 cents more than he paid and keep the profits. We would load the cooler into the car with his folding table and all of the prizes and trophies he would award that day.

It doesn't surprise me a bit that he had specific runners in mind for some of those prizes. I remember spending the time waiting for the runners to finish, playing in the long jump pit making sand castles.

The runners always seemed really appreciative of those sodas, and Dad said they were disappointed if I wasn't there. Little did he know, I needed no encouragement to go anywhere with him, especially the races.

I loved watching them and getting to know all the regulars and still, do today at the memorial races. But more importantly, it was the time we got to spend together that means the most to me. I know that is what he had in mind when he came up with the idea. Going to the races was a chance for him to share what he was passionate about with me, a gift I am glad I rarely passed up.

As you know, Dad continued holding races right up until he passed away, and as often as I could I would bring my girls to West Deptford Park on Sundays to watch. He was so happy and in his element putting on the races. That is how I always want to remember him."

Coaching With Browning

IN SEPTEMBER OF 1981, I stopped into Sports East to visit Browning on my way home from a class at Rowan University. After a few minutes of chatting Browning said, "How would you like to coach cross-country with me this season at Gloucester Catholic?"

The offer took me by surprise. I knew he definitely didn't need any help with the team and was flattered at the offer but I had no plans on coaching.

"No thanks," I said. I told him I was looking forward to finishing up my eligibility running for Rowan, and then training and racing on my own. "Browning nodded. "I'll swing by at 3 tomorrow to pick you up for practice," he said.

"What?" I said out loud, thinking he must have misheard me.

"Thanks very much, but I'm not interested, besides I'm only a few years older than the kids on the team. I'm not sure they would even listen to me…"

He nodded slowly and this time I knew he had heard me clearly. His next words took me by surprise, "Ok, I'll swing by your house at 3:15, that will give us plenty of time to get to practice." I felt like throwing up my hands in disbelief, but figured after all he had done for me I should go for one day just to humor him.

Browning knew better than I did what was good for me. He stopped by the next day to pick me up and I saw coaching with him was not only not too bad, it was easily one of the best things I had ever done in my life.

I am still coaching 35 years later because he would not take no for an answer. For most of the next 18 years, we would coach together in 3 different spans. Coaching with Browning was rewarding because his personality made every practice and every meet enjoyable. I instantly remembered why I had enjoyed running so much under his tutelage when I got to work with him every day as a coach.

A week into my first season as a coach, I rode with Browning to an Olympic Conference coaches meeting at Overbrook High School in Pine Hill New Jersey. Browning picked me up and I was surprised at feeling butterflies driving over to the meeting. I could not remember the last time I'd felt any apprehension before running in my own races, or why I would feel them now, but this was new territory. I had probably run against most of the coaches we would be seeing, and their teams only 4 years before. This was the unknown of a new role.

The Chicago song "Does Anybody Really Know What Time It Is?" came on the radio and Browning turned it up and said, "That's really true isn't it?"

"As I was walking down the street one day
A man came up to me and asked me what
The time was that was on my watch, I said
Does anybody really know what time it is?
Does anybody really care(about time),
If so I can't imagine why (Oh no, no)
We've all got time enough to cry."

We pulled up to Overbrook and Browning was relaxed and still singing the song. Seeing how relaxed he was comforted me, and I relaxed. I was glad he was there. This is routine I thought-- probably even going to be a little boring.

As we walked into the classroom, where the cross-country meeting was held we heard loud swearing in the back of the room. One coach was trying to choke another coach, and other coaches were scurrying to break it up. The moderator apologized for the altercation and things calmed down.

While driving home, I turned to Browning and said, "Wow, did you see that? Why would that one coach grab the other coach? What could have provoked that" Was he drunk?"

Browning smiled and said, "We don't know what happened, who knows, maybe it was justified."

Browning knew both coaches, and he was never quick to jump to conclusions.

One cold, windy and rainy March day the school was closed during Easter vacation. Browning, another coach and I waited in his car for a 12 o'clock practice to start and for the first athlete to show up. It was a few minutes after 12 when a car pulled up letting out the first member of the track team.

"I saw him first!" Browning exclaimed, quickly jumping out of this car. "I've got someone to coach; not sure what you other guys are going to do!"

At another practice during and off day, Browning teased a runner who had missed the previous day's practice, "Mike, I haven't seen you since March!"

"Ah Mr. Ross, I only missed one practice. I overslept yesterday."

"You slept past noon?" Browning asked. "Well, sleep while you can. Once you get in your late 60's, you'll pop out of bed at 6 in the morning every morning with your eyes wide open and won't be able to get back to sleep."

While waiting for a track practice held at the school, Browning noticed a female "student with good size" as he put it, walking through the halls of the school. He approached her and asked her if she would "like to come out for the track team and throw the shot?" "I would" she replied, "but I'm 28 years old and have been teaching here at the school for 6 years, I'm not sure how much track eligibility I have left."

Browning walked away sheepishly and started to laugh, "Well she was good natured about it, that's what I get for trying to recruit someone I don't know."

Browning combined a mix of humor and perspective. As we drove together on the way to a Meet at Kingsway High School one day Browning asked, "Do you see that cemetery on your right?" I nodded yes.

"It's filled with people who thought the world couldn't do without them." he said.

Browning had the best rapport with teenagers that I've ever seen. He really enjoyed the give and take of coaching and always kept things loose with his sense of humor. His method of discipline was to good-naturedly tease if someone missed practice, never to scold.

When someone complained about the training method of the upcoming practice, "We're doing hills? I *hate* hills! "Browning would say, "That's funny because hills speak highly of you!"

Browning often told runners asking what to do for minor aches and pains before a race to "just rub peanut butter on it." They would reply: "Just peanut butter?" Eventually, the runners stopped complaining knowing that would be his response, and you could often detect the faint whiff of peanut butter among the first-year runners along with the aroma of atomic balm.

Years later I couldn't believe my eyes when I read an Australian sports medicine study that recommended rubbing peanut butter on sore muscles to speed recovery. After rereading the article, I cut it out and brought it to Browning at one of our practices. He took the article, glanced at it briefly put it in his pocket and said, "See, I told you!"

When occasions when someone on the team started to provide a detailed and dramatic excuse for something, Browning would hold up a finger asking for a moment's pause, remove his handkerchief, and then ask them to continue as he pretended to dab the tears from his eyes in mock sympathy. One reliable runner was worth a multiple of runners on our small team.

To frequent excuse makers he would say, "Boy, you've got more excuses than Carter has liver pills." The exact meaning of the analogy was usually lost on his young athletes but they got the idea.

Browning's favorite expression on coaching came from Yankees Manager Casey Stengel, "The secret of managing is to keep the five guys who hate you away from the four who are undecided." Of course, no one disliked Browning.

At one practice Browning said, "Sometimes you have to tell the kids "this is going to be a tough workout," their confidence will increase when they successfully create the workout." I noticed however that this pronouncement from the mild mannered, low key Browning often led to an expression on the runner's faces of something close to fear, they looked like they were being sent into battle. He would then diffuse their apprehension with humor.

Mike Kain, one of his runners remembered, "After Browning said this is going to be a tough workout everyone but one or two runners looked scared to death. He looked at me and repeated, "This is going to be a tough workout. You have a nice watch. If anything should happen to you in this workout, can I have your watch?"

Browning's knowledge of training and racing strategy gave any runner who asked a unique advantage. You had to be interested enough to ask him first. He was a firm believer in training over the summer on your own, and running road races in the offseason to improve and to develop a racing strategy. It was surprising to me how few runners we coached would do either.

Every year his runners were surprised to find out his first name was not Browning. He would provide his first initial and then get a kick out of hearing the kids trying to guess what name the "H" stood for. "Henry, Herbert, Harold, Hal, Hank, Horace..." were typical of the many incorrect guesses. Occasionally someone would remember or land on the correct choice, "Harris".

Browning always liked to discover new places to run and would sometimes call me to check out a potential course. "Do you want to take a ride down to Thorofare (NJ) to see if we can get 3 miles out of that loop along the Delaware?"

Before a cross country meet with crosstown friendly rival Gloucester High one of our runners approached me and asked what the consequences would be if Gloucester Catholic lost the meet.

Both teams and their coaches were good friends, but I said to the runner in jest, "If we lose this meet I hear there might be a big cross-country coaching shake up." The runner looked a little rattled, and I turned around to see Browning with his hands in a prayer-like supplication of "make it happen".

We would sometimes practice at Proprietors Park. The Park, on the Delaware River, had been the site of so much of Gloucester's history. The Park had also once held the pool building where Browning had met Sis at a dance.

Browning was 58 and moving quickly to swat late fall bees that were swarming as the runners warmed up. One of the runners said, "It's approaching winter, and these bees really go after you when they're on the way out." Browning continued to swat the bees away and said, "I'm on the way out too, and I'm not going after anybody!"

At one of our cross-country meets I was trying to count and add the places of the Gloucester Catholic runners as they ran by when I noticed Browning a few feet in front of me to the side, really studying every runner going by.

I asked him if he was able to mentally calculate the runner on every team and their place as they went by. "Heck no, I'm just counting their shoes. I'm trying to get an idea of what to carry in the store. It looks like Asics are really selling. There seems to be a lot of Saucony this year too."

During this time, the school bought the uniforms and they were collected and redistributed after the season. Some of the athletes held on to the uniforms tenaciously, often in inverse proportion to their contribution to the team it seemed.

One season when the supply of uniforms on hand was especially low Browning walked into a thrift store in Gloucester and bought back some uniforms that had found their way into the store.

Browning knew South Jersey so well that we often practiced on other locations besides our home cross-country course.

Browning took the team to train in a variety of places. Some days we ran the 4-mile round trip over the Ben Franklin Bridge into Philadelphia. Other days we ran through abandoned farms along the Delaware River in West Deptford, land which later became the West Deptford Riverwinds athletic complex.

The New Jersey State Cross Country Championship is held in Holmdel NJ, an hour and a half ride from Gloucester. Browning read a quote from a local coach that caught his attention.

"We expect to do well in the state meet because we've gone up to Holmdel ten times since the summer. The more you go up there the better you'll do," the coach said.

Browning said, "That's ridiculous. Imagine dragging kids up there for at least a three-hour round trip ten times? Once you know the course you'd be much better staying home and training or getting some rest than traveling up there!"

The one constant was Browning's sense of humor win or lose, whether the team was strong or weak. Almost daily he cut out and presented me with a comic from the daily newspaper such as "The Born Loser," "Frank and Ernest" or "Drabble," right before practice or a meet. One of the characters in the comic would invariably be labeled as "Ross" and the other "Heath". He would get a chuckle as he watched me read the comics.

I kept most of the comics, and remember a Frank and Ernest that was typical. The character named "Ross" remarked if "Heath" had "gone the extra mile, he must have made a wrong turn." I was amazed that he managed to find a relevant and funny comic almost every day.

He would also find headlines in the paper that contained either of "our names" and cut them out and gave them to me. I remember him handing me clippings that said "Ross bowls 300 game again" or "Browning pitches a perfect game." "I just wanted to give this to you because you seemed a little skeptical when I mentioned to you that I was a good pitcher." he joked.

The pitcher, of course, was Tom Browning of the Cincinnati Reds. It was surprising how many of those headlines Browning, an inveterate newspaper reader was able to find.

I was somewhat surprised when I started to coach with Browning how often the kids on the team were unaware of our schedule. "Coach, who are we running today?" Browning would always provide the same answer, "Little Sisters of the Poor."

Browning often loaded up his car to take every available runner to the meets. On the way to nearby Camden County College for a meet, Browning loaded the maximum number runners into his car. As he pulled up to the first red light, a car in the next lane beeped and waved. Browning gave a slight wave back and the kids in the car whooped back, "Hey how's it going!"

Browning continued to drive and a car going in the opposite direction beeped and waved, as did another car as we entered the Freeway. One of the runners in the back said, "Mr. Ross, you really know a lot of people around here." Another runner added, "Well, what do you expect, if you coached as long as Mr. Ross and were as well known a runner, you'd know a lot of people too, duh!" As we slowed down and approached the parking lot of the college a departing car beeped and pointed at us. Kids in the back gave the thumbs up.

We arrived and as Browning got out of the car he said "Jeez, there's a gym bag on the top of my car! I don't know how the heck it didn't fall off, which one of you guys in a hurry to get in left it up there?"

A year later, I was in the hallway one day waiting for the dismissal bell to ring and practice to start when the Gloucester Catholic Principal, Joe Martelli approached me and asked if I would like to teach Computer Science at Gloucester Catholic after I graduated Rowan.

I told him that I hadn't majored or taken any classes in teaching. I had studied business and computer science. (You do not have to be state certified to teach in Catholic schools.) "That's ok. I've heard good things about you as a coach, and we'd like you to be our first computer teacher." "Think it over." Principal Martelli said. Browning was standing a few feet away and noticed my hesitation.

He said, "If I were you I would take it. It's hard to get teaching jobs. You know the subject and will catch on (to teaching) quickly. I taught for years. Plus, it will help you for coaching and you will have a better opportunity get to know the kids. It's a heck of a lot easier to get kids out for the team when you're in the school!"

I took the job, but the following year Browning decided to resign as coach to give me the opportunity to take over as the head track and cross-country coach. He would later come back to coach with me for many years.

My first year of coaching by myself produced mixed results. The team lost a number of close meets; we were sometimes winning until losing the race in the last 100 yards as our runners were outkicked.

I was surprised to see him come out to one of the losses and for some reason felt like I owed him an apology that I might have let him down. He waved me off, "Well, like I always say, "You can't make chicken salad out of chicken shit."

Browning managed to put things into perspective and of course gave me a boost.

A few years later Browning came back to coach. I was assisting him in track and brought my two-year-old son Sean to a practice he was holding on the 800-meter track at Johnson Boulevard in Gloucester. The team was heading out for an 800-meter loop when my son broke away to accompany them.

I went to grab Sean to hold him back, and Browning said, "Let him go. He'll only go as far as he can. I believe in never discouraging a kid from running," he said with a smile. To my surprise, my son ran with the team for two laps and then collapsed in mock exhaustion in the grass as the team started to run 100-meter sprints.

Browning never forced anyone to run track races against their will "for the points" believing it would only discourage them from sticking with the sport. His goal was to encourage lifetime participation. It always seemed to work out as his track teams seem to overachieve.

Coaching with Browning, I was amazed at his in-depth knowledge of the technique of every track event. It was only later that I saw the correspondence he had exchanged with Bob Richards, Bob Matthias and other track greats in his files about the fundamentals of each of their events.

One of the things that made Browning such a good coach was the fact that he had actual experience trying every track event and then had sought how to knowledge directly from the best athletes about how they trained. He had gathered similar distance running schedules as editor of the Long Distance Log.

When he coached me I only saw his expertise with sprinters and distance runners but coaching with him you could appreciate his depth of knowledge and ability to convey knowledge with humor. I watched him explain the javelin technique to the team one day. "You might be able to throw it further with a spin but it's illegal. In 1956 a Spaniard named Felix Erausquin broke the javelin world record by 14 meters with a spin method-- similar to how you throw the discus. I was at Franklin Field for the Penn Relays when Erausquin's throw went awry; it was hard to control and landed in the crowd. Soon after they banned the spin method for the javelin. So, this is the way you gotta throw it." He then gave an example.

When one of his throwers subsequently threw a javelin that landed tail first he joked, "Maybe you should turn it around with the tail leading!"

Browning Ross officiating his hometown Woodbury Relays.

I'll get the next 24

BEFORE THERE WAS A CERTIFICATION program for track officials, Browning became one of the first "official" track officials in South Jersey and Philadelphia through his involvement with the AAU and his international racing experiences. He officiated at the finish line of the USA-Russia Meet in 1959, the Penn Relays every April, and also at other major meets including the "Dream Mile" between Marty Liquori and Jim Ryun on May 16, 1971, in the Martin Luther King Games at Franklin Field in Philadelphia.

When the Southern New Jersey Track Officials Organization began admitting members and assigning them to meets, Browning joined that organization as one of its charter members. He served as the informal Official for many of the track and cross country meets we ran for him in high school, and of course as both official and meet director for the thousands of races he put on.

Tom Osler, "There really are no independent track meets today there are too just many events and the permissions, logistics etc. are too difficult for anyone to manage. Browning routinely directed hundreds of meets where he also officiated by himself.

Browning was coaching Gloucester Catholic's Cross- Country team against his alma mater Woodbury High in 1995 and also officiating when he witnessed what he would often call "one of the craziest things I saw in a cross-country meet".

The race featured two of the best high school runners in South Jersey-- Woodbury's JP Carter and Gloucester Catholic's Damian Gallagher, a native of Ireland. Before the firing of the gun, both began to jockey for position. Neither runner wanted to concede any advantage in what was expected to be a close race. The two quickly pulled away from the pack, but continued to jostle and then to shove and to curse.

The pair were far enough in front of the lead pack that the trailing runners from both teams did not notice what happened next—the swearing increased and then the two stopped and started to square off to exchange blows on the Woodbury soccer field. In a strange twist, the two were quickly disqualified by a coach or official in a different sport-- soccer and told to walk back to the start.

As they did the distant third place runner to his surprise went on to win the race as the two dejected rivals slowly walked back to the start. "Browning said, "The most amazing part was what came next, after being disqualified the two of them walked back together to the finish line chatting, shaking hands, friendly as can be, models of good sportsmanship." The race took on an air of myth over the years as stories spread of the combatants pushing each other into the Woodbury Creek and helping each other out and other tall tales. Walt Pierson, also an official, stood with Browning at the finish. "I asked Browning what the protocol was for the two disqualified runners. Was there going to be paperwork to be filled out, a report made to a central office, would they get in trouble for the rest of the season? It all seemed like overkill because both runners were now buddy-buddy." Browning said, 'Well, I didn't see it so there's really nothing to report.' Which was true."

When I started coaching with Browning I would take the teams to some track meets like the Woodbury Relays where he was officiating. He stopped over to check in with me before the relays began and I told him we only had 3 runners for the 4 runner shuttle hurdles relay. Browning looked at the runners present and asked, "Where's Julie?" Julie was a hurdler who had run on the team the previous year.

One of the girls answered, "She got a job, and she's working at the Roy Rogers across the street." "Can we get her?" Browning asked. So, we did. We drove down to Roy Rogers and Julie clocked out with the permission of her manager. She changed out of her Roy Rogers uniform, into a track uniform ran the third leg of the shuttle hurdle and then returned to work.

When I was coaching at all day relay meets it was hard to leave to get something to eat or drink because athletes would be looking for you the minute you did. Browning would get my attention from the infield of the track when he was officiating and stop over carrying a drink and hot dog for me from the Officials tent. It was extremely thoughtful, and I do not think many others would have even thought to do it.

Chet Dirkes remembered timing with Browning at a South Jersey track meet. Chet remembered, "It was a freshman mile race and there were about 25 kids entered. Browning told me to "just get the winners time." He said he had a new watch that could get 99 splits and he would get the next 24 places. I was watching the winner come across and I just clicked on his time when I heard Browning say "Oh, crap! My watch stopped!"

What happened next was amazing. As each kid came across the line Browning gave him a time and lined them up in order against the fence. "5:40, 5:43, you were 5:45!" Each kid got a time and it must have been close to what they usually ran because no one complained. Talk about grace under pressure!"

Browning also had a way to ease the pre-race tension for young runners when he was officiating. Dave Platt remembers, "One time everyone was edgy on the line before the start. Browning said, "Relax, this isn't the Olympics."

Two things impressed me about that moment. First, it seemed like everyone did relax and second, he *was* in the Olympics, so who would know better than him?"

John Stratton remembers another instance when Browning's sense of humor helped break the pre-race tension but a runner wished he hadn't. "Dave Miller was a great hurdler and 400-meter runner from Woodbury who grew up with Barry Ross and me. Dave had a job caddying at Woodbury Country Club in the summer. The golfer he was caddying for lit up a cigarette took a couple of puffs and put it down on the grass to putt. Dave immediately stomped on the lit cigarette and rubbed it out with his foot. The golfer went ballistic and started screaming at Dave. Well, Dave told Barry and Browning found out about it.

Later Dave is on the starting line of a championship meet, full of concentration waiting for the race to start and Browning is the official. Dave hears Browning calling him "Dave, Dave!" but doesn't want to look up. Finally, he does, and Browning is pantomiming stepping on a cigarette and stomping it out, of course laughing the whole time. Dave tried not to look at him but of course, he had to laugh.

Ken Kling, "I officiated dozens of meets with Browning and he always made the long meets fun. He was down to earth and looking out for the best interests of the runners. A few of our fellow officials seemed to like to boss around the runners; or spent the whole time looking for an infraction. Maybe a uniform not matching exactly, or a singlet not tucked in, so they could disqualify a kid for example. Browning never did that.

Browning would joke with the kids and relax them. He showed them the sport of track and cross-country could be fun.

Before he'd start a race, he would say something like "Good looking guys in front," if he knew one of the kids in the field that he could joke with, maybe one of the kids he coached he'd add "and you so and so, you can get in the back!" Everyone would laugh and it would break the tension.

Of course, most track officials were school teachers or officials. I spoke to Tom Osler about some officials infatuation with rule enforcement. Osler offered, "I think obsessing over rules is a function of academia. Sometimes before our staff meetings with the Mathematics Department, they will spend an hour going over the rules before the meeting even starts!"

I recall Browning officiating a grade school CYO meet when he noticed a worried look on a young runner at the starting line. "What's the matter?" he asked. "*They* made me do this, it wasn't *my* idea, and I really don't want to be here!" she answered. Browning smiled and said a few words to help relax her while getting a kick out of her honesty.

Bill Thompson also officiated many meets with Browning, "I officiated a lot of meets with Browning and before each meet he would hand me a folded-up slip of paper and tell me to put it in my pocket until after the meet. It was his prediction for the meet score. Even though he hadn't seen either team before and had no connection to the teams his predictions were uncannily close. The final scores were usually within a point or two.

I remember his ability to make the best of a bad situation and see the humor in it. One time four of us (South Jersey Track Official's) officiated a winter track meet together at Widener University, Pa, one freezing cold day. The temperature was in the single digits and the wind was howling and I was driving, Browning was in the back seat.

Of course, the heater in my car was broken, it seemed to be just sucking in cold air and blowing it around making it even colder. I looked in my rearview mirror and Browning was shivering like crazy in the back, his teeth were chattering. I felt bad for the guys in the car. When I stopped to let him off at his house, Browning stepped out haltingly and said, "Thanks a lot Bill for trying to freeze us to death, you almost succeeded, I've never been so cold in my life!" My wife and I would see Browning and Sis in church and we laughed about that for years. I'd offer to give him a ride home from church and he'd say no thanks! Browning's sense of humor made those cold and bad weather meets go a lot quicker."

One memory shared by many of Browning's runners of different generations involved Browning officiating at the Penn Relays.

Browning seemed incapable of lying or even exaggerating and this made this memory especially interesting to his runners. Browning officiated the

Penn Relays almost every April for decades. Years of officiating meant an impressive collection of Penn Relays hats.

At some point, Browning would approach his favorite runners on a team he was coaching and say, "Why don't you go to the Penn Relays Saturday? Just wear this official's hat and they should let you park and let you into Franklin Field, probably even to the official's buffet after the Meet. Like all the other generations of Browning's runners, the vintage Penn hat got me into the Relays but subjected me to strange looks and a line of questioning. "Say, aren't you kind of young to... never mind, go ahead."

The magic Penn Relays Hat got us the full Penn Relay experience up to but not including the buffet. For some reason, we must have only looked too young to participate in the Officials buffet and were usually closely scrutinized and shown the door at that point.

Mike Fanelli remembers, "I still have some of those Penn Relays hats he gave me!"

I interviewed Browning for an article in "American Runner Magazine" in 1996 about his thoughts on officiating. Browning said, "I think colleges should strive to bring back dual meets instead of big meets every weekend. This would encourage rivalries, and take up less time. I just finished two days of officiating the Big East Meet at Villanova and even I was bored.

People do not want to spend 8 hours at a track meet."

Twenty years later Track and Field News editorials also called for shortening track meets.

Browning Ross holds his iconic London Olympics picture 45 years in a picture taken for Running Magazine.

Bad News Bears and a Trip to Oregon

BROWNING WAS ALWAYS INTERESTED IN the movies. Woodbury had two movie theaters that he frequented in his youth, and he watched probably close to a thousand movies in the Navy.

I remember not liking "Network" the 1976 critical favorite and Browning teased me about my thumbs down review for that and a couple of other movies.

"Are you saying the critics are wrong?" Browning asked with mock indignation. "You're going to put the movies out of business with these bad reviews! The critics all said "Network" was supposed to have an important message, did you get whatever the message was?" he asked. I told him the only message that had gotten through to me was that nothing lasts forever except a bad movie.

Browning laughed and then a few weeks later said, I think I saw a movie last night that you would like-- the "Bad News Bears." The 1976 movie about a down on his luck former minor leaguer (Walter Matthau) who coaches a team of misfit baseball players remained one of Browning's favorites for years.

Browning got to coach his own team of Bad News Bears when he accepted the cross-country coaching position at Rutgers-Camden in 1980. The Rutgers-Camden Athletic Director Pony Wilson was a fellow track official and friend of Browning's who had long tried to recruit him to Rutgers-Camden to start up a cross country team. Browning's Rutgers team featured six runners of every nationality, and the team had an air of the Bad News Bears or "Welcome Back Kotter."

Because it was difficult to train in downtown Camden near the Rutgers campus, Browning often took the team in his van to soft surfaces places to train. Browning invited me to come along with his team on an off day (from Rowan University cross-country practice) to run along Mantua Creek. There was a sewer line that ran for seven miles along Mantua Creek from Mantua to Glassboro that he liked to run to get the team to train away from asphalt and traffic.

Browning picked me up and I got in the front seat next to him as he drove to Rutgers to pick up the rest of the team. When we arrived I noticed his team was lined up but seemed reluctant to enter his van. I also noticed that the team looked like a United Nations with every ethnic group represented.

Browning said, "All right, let's go everybody in the van!" Before the team climbed into the van someone yelled, "All right honkies in the back! Another runner said, "No, Puerto Ricans in the back Juan! Eventually, they all got in the van whooping and hollering in the process. Browning rolled his eyes, "I've talked to them about that. They do this every day," said Browning. "Anyone watching them would probably keel over, but they really like each other and get along. They are friends outside school and the team. They are all also really good students. At first, I asked them to knock it off, but I think they enjoy the getting in van routine as much as the practices."

Browning continued, "We had to go to a banquet for Rutgers Sports Awards and none of them owned any ties! I had to lend them my ties and I ended up tying all their times for them at my house. Hard to believe there is a whole generation (in their late teens and early 20's) who never had to tie a tie, isn't it?"

Browning joked with my Rowan Coaches Bill Fritz and Oscar Moore about making a "trade" offering to send some of his Rutgers runners to Rowan for me so I could run for him again. The farcical "discussions" went on for a while with Fritz asking Browning to throw in some javelins and track equipment from Sports East to seal the deal.

Browning coached for a couple of years at Rutgers, coaching track with Dave Brier, who was a director of the Philadelphia Jewish "Y" and the race director and founder of the Philadelphia 8.4 mile loop race that started in 1972. Dave Brier, "Our teams at Rutgers weren't very strong. There was no recruiting, whoever came out for the team was what you had to work with. Many of them hadn't competed in high school, Browning made the whole experience fun and worthwhile for those who did came out for the team." Browning then left Rutgers and returned to coach at Gloucester Catholic with me.

After I graduated college, Browning handed me a graduation card. It read, "After a careful examination of your skills, abilities, and experience our computer recommends the following career for you..." I noticed Browning had a big smile on his face as he watched me open the card. "Shepherd is the ideal career path for you." There was a picture of a shepherd and staff with his sheep. Browning laughed and I both laughed heartily. Browning also enclosed in the card a newspaper clipping from one of the major races he had won in the 1950's. It was a treasure for me.

Soon after I was in Browning's house and noticed an extremely large potted plant. "That's from Cyndi Lauper," he said. "She's good friends with Bonnie. I don't like much rock music, but I really like Cyndi. Bonnie met her through being a nurse in the Red Cross and appeared in some of her music videos. Bonnie mentioned that there is a big demand for costume jewelry now and that she and Cyndi picked up some costume jewelry they found at flea markets in their spare time and have been selling it, it's in so much demand it sells out as quick as they get it!"

In her autobiography, Cyndi Lauper mentioned Bonnie and gave a nod to the possible family relationship with Betsy Ross.

Bonnie, "I helped introduce Cyndi to some songwriters from Philadelphia, and after they wrote a hit song together Cyndi was kind enough to send me royalty checks for 10% of the song royalties. I sent my mother and father a check for 10% of the royalties I received, so that is probably one of the reasons they liked Cyndi so much!"

Browning's youngest daughter Barbara would be getting ready for school every morning about the same time Browning would be returning from his three-mile run.

"Dad would come back from his run all sweaty and say 'How about a nice big hug?' I would tell him I'd have to take a pass until after his shower!"

In 1983 Browning had an artificial toe joint put in a toe he had stubbed on a run on the beach years before. He had little mobility in the toe and it had stayed black and blue for years before the surgery. In his excellent profile of Browning in the Runner magazine, Hal Higdon wrote about Browning:

"Yet he hasn't lost his competitive edge, at least where personal goals are concerned. Following the operation that gave him the artificial joint, he was virtually immobile, yet he would plead with his wife to help him out of his chair so he could limp, aided by a walker, several times around the dining room table. At the age of 59, he is still doing laps."

In 1990, I was coaching with Browning and finishing up my MBA at Rutgers. I was surprised to see Browning mentioned in my textbook for the MBA's Capstone class for a case study of the 1974 Onitsuka Blue Ribbon Sports lawsuit. Browning had been flown out to Oregon to testify in the case which Bill Bowerman called "win or die" for Blue Ribbon Sports.

In 1973, Blue Ribbon Sports and Phil Knight filed a lawsuit in federal court in Portland against Onitsuka which had been Blue Ribbon's partner in the USA, allowing Blue Ribbon to sell Onitsuka footwear, especially a running shoe called the Tiger, alongside the shoes Bowerman designed.

The lawsuit alleged that Onitsuka had breached the contract with Blue Ribbon by soliciting new distributors and demanding Phil Knight sign over his control of Blue Ribbon for the right to distribute Tigers. Knight alleged that Onitsuka had infringed on Blue Ribbons trademark by selling the eight models that Blue Ribbon had registered in the United States. After a tense game of brinksmanship, Knight and Blue Ribbon signed the settlement papers and the case was decided in Blue Ribbons favor. Blue Ribbon received two big steamer trunks full of $100 bills from Onitsuka as a settlement. The Onitsuka lawyers explained the unorthodox payment method as the result of the difficulty of transferring money out of Japan.

In the late 70's Blue Ribbon became Nike and of course was in the right place at the right time to ride the crest of the running and fitness boom.

I thought I would get an inside scoop on the case for my MBA class and excitedly showed the textbook to Browning. "Look, Browning, you're mentioned in this case, on a couple of the pages! What do you remember about the case?"

Browning casually glanced at the book but didn't seem too interested in reading about the case. "All I remember is they flew me out there and I testified, but I'm not sure whether my testimony helped anyone. The main thing I remember is I got to run on some great trails in Oregon for a few days."

Barry Ross said, "I remember my dad being excited about getting a free trip to Oregon for the trial. Blue Ribbon was Tiger's distributor and when they offered dad a five state protected territory in the northeast, my cousin Gerald and I took a trip down to Virginia to try to get some sporting goods stores to carry the shoes. We were unsuccessful-- not even getting one sale for a weeks trip. That was the end of our sales career.

When Blue Ribbon became Nike, dads territory was reduced to just PA and NJ. That's when I remember dad saying to me, "Well, the running boom has peaked. There are a hundred people coming out to races now. It's never going to get any bigger than this!" That's when he got out of the Nike shoe thing. Not too good of a prognosticator for sure. I don't think dad liked being on the road too much either. He had three kids and we must have been driving mom crazy."

Bonnie remembers Browning and Sis also briefly considering a move to Hawaii for a job in shoe distribution in that period. "We thought we were going to move, but mom and dad thought about it and decided against it."

While waiting together for a track practice to start in 1993 Browning said to me,"My class reunion is tonight."

"Are you going?" I asked.

"Nah, there will too many old people there!" he said.

Larry Delancy, "Browning's sense of humor was present in every conversation. When you interacted with him it was always enjoyable. He saw the humor in everything he was involved with and that made it a lot more fun for everyone else."

What Am I Going to Do with All of These Berries?

In the 1980's many races started to give out interesting prizes and Browning, in his 60's returned to competition. He won his age group in a number of major races in Philadelphia often winning the master's division outright and beating runners 20 years younger. He won the master's division in the Bar Diabetes 10k race, as well as the Terry Fox race where his prize was an overnight stay in the fanciest Philadelphia hotel.

I asked Browning how he and Sis enjoyed their stay and he said, "The hotel was nice but the breakfast cost us as much as the room would have!"

Barry Ross, "Dad ran in the Margate 10 mile in his late 60's and was still able to run about 6-minute mile pace."

One day in June when I stopped into Sports East, I mentioned to Browning that I was going to run the Whitesbog, NJ Blueberry 10k the following day. "How about if I go along with you?" he asked.

Whitesbog was an old blueberry farm that pioneered blueberry cultivation. It was being rehabbed deep in the New Jersey Pine Barrens, and featured sandy trails that got extremely hot. The course also featured a stream in the middle of the course that runners had to leap to cross, or scamper down and embankment and back up the other side. You could hear men and women swearing when they came to the obstacle. I immediately thought of Browning's World Cross-Country meets in Africa.

We both won our age groups and our prizes included an electric pencil sharpener and a flat of blueberries. Each flat contained 12 pints of blueberries. When I pulled up in front of Browning's house he said, "Jeez, do you want to take these blueberries? I never told Sis I was going to run a race and she'll wonder where I got them all." I told him I didn't think I could eat all of the blueberries I had so he reluctantly bid goodbye.

For the next couple of weeks, we compared notes on all of the ways we ate blueberries—including on pizza so they wouldn't go bad. I'm sure a couple of pints were welcome prizes in his races.

In the late 1980's the City of Camden started a 10k race through the city ending in the newly renovated waterfront on the Delaware. The new race had no connection with the long time Camden Y street run, but it seemed to end those races close to 70-year run. Browning and I ran the first couple of Camden Street Runs and Browning won his age group in the first race but finished second in the second. We were sitting on steps waiting for the awards ceremony after the race and Browning said, "Well, that's it, that's my last race." I asked if he meant forever and he nodded yes. "Why? You still ran great, you got second in your age group by a little bit to a much younger runner," I said.

"Nah, I'm done racing. I'll always keep running of course, but it's not worth racing anymore if I can't even win my age group!" He said it with a smile, but it was the last race he ran.

It's a Great Life

IN THE 1990'S AFTER BROWNING sold Sports East, he was still involved in as many facets of running as ever. He was putting on his series of races almost every weekend, coaching track and cross-country at Gloucester Catholic, and officiating track meets when he didn't have a coaching meet or practice. Barry Ross, ""Dad went with me on a Mission trip to Jamaica and we visited boys home back in the hills in Hanover called New Beginnings. We were there for less than an hour when dad organized a track meet right out in the cow pasture. Kids were running barefoot with cow poop all over the place. I think we had the 100, 200, 400, mile and high jump. I remember one kid in particular because he won every race—scholarship material for sure!"

I was coaching track with Browning and brought my two-year-old son Sean to practice to watch. When the team took off on a mile warm up I tried to stop him and Browning said, "Let him go! It's good for him to run." He accompanied the team for a mile and a half, and half dozen strides before collapsing in mock exhaustion on the grass. I realized I had just witnessed Browning's philosophy in action—never discourage anyone from running.

Browning and Sis scheduled their annual short vacation to a warmer climate around the snowball series races schedules he directed. A couple of times when his family was not close by I picked Browning and Sis up on a Saturday night returning from the airport. He had to return Saturday night to be on time for his Sunday races.

We drove back together after coaching the Gloucester Catholic cross-country team at the state meet in Holmdel in November of 1997. It was always a tiring four-hour round trip, but I was worried because I thought Browning looked especially tired on the way back from the meet.

About 10 days later, Thanksgiving Eve, I got a call from him and he sounded great. "Hey, would you like to go to Berwick with me tomorrow? They invited me up there and it would be great if you could come along."

I almost said yes, but remembered some minor family obligations I had for our Thanksgiving dinner. I regretted that I couldn't go on such short notice, but would be glad to go the following year. "Sure," he said. "We can go next year. Happy Thanksgiving!" As soon as he hung up I regretted not saying yes. There would never be another opportunity.

On March 11 of 1998, the South Jersey AC running club held a testimonial dinner for Browning in Westmont, New Jersey that brought back many of his friends including Harry Berkowitz, Tom Osler, and Jerry Nolan, and runners from throughout South Jersey. I was seated next to Browning and when he accepted a plaque from the organizers my first thought was of the hundreds of plaques he had won or engraved to give out as prizes. He looked at me and read my mind, "It's the thought that counts," he said. "We'll if you could pick a prize what would it be?" I asked. "Probably a gift certificate to a restaurant to take Sis out to eat" he replied.

In his witty address to the hundreds of runners and friends gathered Browning was humble and mentioned being surprised and honored to see so many friends at the tribute.

We coached track together that spring and he called me on a weekend in April to tell me he was officiating at the Penn Relays and to remind me of the following week's track schedule including a Meet with Williamstown High School. He also joked about his upcoming birthday and asked if I had time to pick out anything "expensive" yet for a birthday gift. We both laughed and I wished him a happy birthday before I hung up.

On April 27, my phone rang at home. As I went to answer it I told my wife, "That's probably Browning calling to remind me about today's track meet with Williamstown." Instead, the voice on the other end of the phone identified themselves from the Gloucester County Times, said a brief apology and asked if I had a comment about the news that Browning had just passed away. I was stunned. The reporter went on "He was found in his car after a run at parked near the apartments near the Woodbury Park. It looks like an apparent heart attack."

The phone soon started ringing— everyone stunned, unable to speak; in complete shock.

Years later, everyone close to Browning had the same memory of the world dark for days after his death. Besides being a close friend, he was more than a mentor-- literally the sun around whom the whole South Jersey running world revolved.

At Browning's service the most common reaction—"What are we going to do now?" Tom Osler, "I saw more grown men crying at Browning's funeral than I have anywhere else in my life. I was much too grief-stricken to speak at his service at St. Patricks's in Woodbury. I wish I had been able to say something but the grief for me like many others was just too much."

One of the grief-stricken in attendance at the service was a truck driver who had run in Browning's races in the 1960's. He had stopped at a rest stop in Virginia, read Browning's obituary in the New York Times and immediately turned north to attend the service.

To get through the service I kept hearing Browning's voice in my head saying,"It's a great life if you don't weaken," and the positive encouragement I had heard during my races for so many years, "Attaboy Jack." I especially remember seeing the look of sadness on Ted Corbitt's face; a good man grieving for another good man.

The Gloucester Catholic track team dealt with their grief by donning their track uniforms after the service and accompanying Browning one last time, running the mile alongside the hearse for over a mile from St. Patricks Church to the Woodbury Memorial Park Cemetery.

Gloucester County Times columnist and Browning's long-time friend Bob Shryock wrote, "And while the hearse was delivering legendary Browning Ross to his final resting place, members of the Gloucester Catholic High School track team he coached so proudly jogged alongside the hearse in a tear-provoking, gut-wrenching tribute."

One of the Gloucester Catholic runners, Sean McClenachan wrote a poem called "An Ode to Browning":

Everything we know, we learned from you.
How to run, How to Train, even what kind of shoes.

You saw the world and accomplished many feats;
The people you ran against said you couldn't be beat.

When you were done you came to GC,
The lowly track team is where you wanted to be.

Each and every year, a sad new bunch of guys,
Who weren't even fit to touch one of your prizes?

At the park or on the boulevard,
Never were your practices too hard.

You were never without a smile on your face.
No one will come close to taking your place.

Never was there a humbler man,
No mention of the awards or the meets that you ran.
The people you knew, the lives that you touched,
How badly *we* ran never seemed to matter much.

In our hearts and minds, you'll always be number one,
We'll be thinking of you each and every time you run.

They're calling you now, calling you by name,
The Angels know that they're running with fame.

We know that you now watch us from Heaven above,
We all just hope that you know you were loved.

We loved you dearly, we cared for you so,
If only right now wasn't the right time to go.

We'll miss you much, much more than you know,
We'll run in the light of the path you have sown.

All the things in this world I would surely give up,
Just to hear once more "Has everyone had their warm up!

Many running clubs and runners go out for a run to celebrate the life of a close running friend after they have passed away.

For a couple of weeks after Browning's passing, I did not feel like running. A gloom seemed to cover everything, especially running, because he was no longer in the world.

Then I thought back to a conversation with Browning one Friday night when I sat with him in Sports East, a few weeks before I sold the store. He said, "If I passed away after a run, would you keep running?" Taken back, I answered: "I don't think running itself actually causes our death, it's just the activity you happened to be doing, the place you happened to be at when you died."

I remembered Browning continued looking at me. I hadn't answered the question. Would *I* keep running if *he* died after a run? "Yes," I answered. "I would. I think running probably extends our lives even if it's where we are at when we pass away.

I know running adds quality to our lives, and that's how I look at it. I would keep running." He seemed satisfied with my answer. I thought about that conversation and finally went out for a run for the first time in over a week. Still, it took a long time to find enjoyment in running. I know Browning would not have wanted it that way but the running-related things I had done with him like looking for new running places, coaching, officiating and going to races were never as much fun without him.

For years I wanted to call him up to let him know about a great race I had just witnessed on television, a run or race, or a running related story in the newspaper. I still dearly miss getting his call about all things running related. I know many, many other runners felt the same loss.

Tom Osler recalled later, "There is a Greek maxim I thought about after we lost Browning, 'Those whom the god's love die too young'. I was inducted into the Gloucester County Sports Hall of Fame in 1998 after being nominated by Browning. This was his last gift to me after a lifetime of giving. His memory lives on in those who were fortunate enough to know him personally. He was the first runner I ever met, and no other runner has influenced me more. He was a mentor and a friend whom I shall miss dearly. Part of him became part of me, and I am the better for it."

National Distance Running Hall of Fame Class of 2002: Doris Brown
Heritage, Bill Bowerman, John J. Kelley, Browning Ross.

Afterword

BROWNING WAS INDUCTED INTO THE fifth class of the National Distance Runners Hall of Fame in July 2002 along with Bill Bowerman, Doris Brown Heritage, and John J. Kelley. Many of his family and friends made the 5 ½-hour trip from Woodbury, NJ to Utica, New York for the induction. Frank Shorter, Bill Rodgers, and Kenny Moore were among the runners in attendance.

He was also honored with the MarathonFoto/Road Race Management Lifetime Achievement Award in 2016 for his years as a race director.

Rosemarie "Sis" Ross passed away in April 2004 at the age of 79, almost six years after Browning. Bill Heughan passed away in 2016. Dave Williams was honored as the first member of Gloucester Catholic's Military Wall of Fame in 2016.

Derek "Ringo" Adamson, an Olympian and coach at Rowan University continued Browning's snowball and summer sizzler series of weekly races on Sunday at Rowan University. He also continued the tradition of low-cost entries with Browning type prizes. The Woodbury Road Runners keep his spirit alive by encouraging runners of all ability levels to run. The Woodbury Road Runners and his hometown of Woodbury also honor Browning with their annual Browning Ross George Benjamin race in Woodbury in June.

Gloucester Catholic High School has honored Browning with an annual Browning Ross Bob Kupcha 5k and 1 mile for ten years. (George Benjamin was the mentor instrumental in starting Browning's running career and was killed in action in World War II. Bob Kupcha was one of Browning's track athletes at Gloucester Catholic and also a veteran, an Orthopedic Surgeon, and a close friend who passed away in 2001 at the age of 42).

St. Mary's Parish in Gloucester City, NJ, and the Knights of Columbus NJ started a race to honor Jack Pyrah in 2017.

After a few years researching and writing this book, I was at an impasse with the book just short of the finish line. I received an email from Browning's long-time friend Ken Kling, "I know you still miss Browning, we all do. And I know you are at a standstill (with the book) because you don't want to write about his final days as the ending for the book. Think about this:

Browning left us much too soon and unexpectedly and it still hurts because we never got to say goodbye. But look at it this way. Browning was also fortunate in how he left us. Most of us do not get to pick how we will spend our last minutes on earth, but he passed away right after *finishing* a workout. He also wasn't sick and didn't suffer. Who could pick a better finish to their lives than that? I think you should think about the ending to Browning's incredible life story with this thought-- since we never got the chance, what would you like to say to Browning now?"

I welcomed this advice and would obviously thank Browning for getting me started in a lifetime of running. I would also thank him for encouraging me to coach. He knew better than I what was best for me and I've been running and coaching since his encouragement in both pursuits. I know hundreds of runners would also thank him if they could for encouraging them to run and for all of the hundreds of races he put on. (In this case "put on" seems more accurate than directed since he handled every facet of the race himself.) As Tom Osler has said, "The people you meet through running are really special." I've met a lot of them thanks to Browning.

Browning's influence remains with me every day. In one of the first meets I coached without him I noticed safety pins laying in the grass. I remembered him always stopping to pick up safety pins and saying, "You never know when you will need these." I always do the same.

An April 2017 study by Progress in Cardiovascular Disease reported that running added about three additional years to a person's life compared to nonrunners. Browning would have been very interested in the studies findings that an hour of running statistically lengthened a runner's life expectancy by seven hours. This was very close to the benefits of running on life expectancy that he had taken an educated guess at many years ago in Sports East. If the study is close to accurate, one can only wonder at both the quality of hours and additional hours given to us by running, through ambassadors such as Browning.

Gloucester Catholic English teacher Dave Coghlan once told his classes, "If you can do something well you have an obligation to do it. You don't have a choice." I believe Browning embraced this same sense of duty in the many contributions (sometimes involving personal sacrifice) he made to American Distance running.

Browning Ross turned his love of running into a lifetime of giving back to the sport. Hopefully, his gift and generosity will have ripple effects for those that knew him or those who never met him but will follow in his footsteps.

Running Pioneers: Ted Corbitt and with John A. Kelley

Olympians Remember Browning

SOME OF THE MOST INSIGHTFUL reflections about Browning were provided by his fellow Olympians.

Johnny A."The Elder" Kelley was a two-time Olympian best known for his two Boston Marathon wins in 1935 and 1945, and for his 58 Boston Marathon finishes. In 1998, he wrote to me about Browning, "Browning was my roommate in the 1948 Olympics. He was an easy-going guy with a great sense of humor. Besides being a great runner, I mostly remember what a true gentleman he was. I couldn't have had a better roommate in London." In the same correspondence Kelley also lamented what he saw as the diminishing coverage of distance running in the sports sections of newspapers in favor of off-season coverage of the major professional sports such as the Celtics. Kelley finished 21st in the 1948 Olympics at the age of 41 and was the second American finisher. Browning ended Kelley's streak of four straight Berwick Marathon victories with his first victory in 1946

Ted Vogel was the first American finisher in the 1948 Olympics in 14th place. Ted Vogel was also a life-long friend of Browning's. Vogel, a World War II Navy veteran, first met and befriended Browning at the 1944 Boston Marathon.

"In 1948 Browning borrowed a bicycle from a youngster who lived across the street from the Olympic Stadium. He accompanied me on the marathon course in the actual race, the entire way right up to the Stadium's entrance and the races finish. "Art Rosenbaum of The San Francisco Chronicle reported what happened next in an article Vogel provided to me. "After the winner, Argentinean Delfo Cabrera and several others had entered the stadium to receive the plaudits of 82,000, there was a time drag while awaiting the arrival of the slower runners. To utilize this time, officials signaled for a victory ceremony, and to the top of the stand leaped 17-year old Bob Mathias to receive his decathlon gold medal. The American flag was hoisted on the highest pole. The British band began to play The Star- Spangled Banner. Eighty-two thousand persons stood at attention, facing the north end.

At the band played, "…twilight's last gleaming" a lone figure churned, slowly, into the stadium from Olympic Way. He was Ted Vogel, 14th man to appear but first from the United States. The band played on, the stadium remained at attention as Vogel struggled his solitary way around the red tiled track for this last turn. At the strains of "Oh say does that Star-Spangled Banner yet wave". Vogel reached the finish.

Others before him had dropped in exhaustion, but Vogel in crisp military fashion about-faced and turned to the North, stood erect at attention as the band finished… "O'er the land of the free, and the home of the brave". As the last strains of our National Anthem died away, Vogle went limp. Friends leaped in to hold him up. Rubber-legged and seven-eighths unconscious, he was "walked" around on the infield to avoid leg cramps. Ted Vogel had run

2 hours, 45 minutes, 27 seconds over 26 miles 385 yards—but he knew "our flag was still there"."

Ted also provided a letter Browning sent to him in 1984 which Ted said he treasures. It offers a great snapshot of Browning's thoughts and life in that year,

Dear Ted,

It was a pleasure hearing from you and to confirm that I actually did ride that bike over the Olympic course behind you. Imagine trying that today! I turned 60 on April 26th. Like you I run once or twice a year in a race. Ran yesterday in the Phila. Bar Diabetes 10k race (about 2000 runners) and won the over 60 division (I won a Dolfin Running Suit). Hit 38.56, can't believe the number of runners ahead of me including young ladies!

We have 3 kids (Bonnie 33, Barry 30 and Barb 21), none of them run although Barry 2:02 for the 890 back in high school. Bonnie is a nurse over in Philly, Barb is a senior at Glassboro State and plays shortstop on the college team. Barry played soccer in college and is now a good golfer.

I taught school for a dozen years or so and worked as a physical direc-tor the YMCA for 15 years, then opened our full-line sports store in 1971. In fact, had two stores for a while but sold the second one to a husband-wife team last year. I've run a summer running camp for about 14 years or so, it comes up again in August. We have a lot of fun with the kids.

I can still remember seeing Zatopek for the first time—running quarters on the Uxbridge track. I stood there for an hour in awe (or amazement!) Seems so long ago!! Recently heard from Fortune Gordien (1948 Olympian in the discus and also later an actor in the "Cisco Kid"). He is a great guy. Got to know him in the service we competed in service meets together before the 48 Games.

I was looking through an old scrapbook the other day and found a snapshot I took of you and John Kelley, Fred Schmertz, and Mrs. Semple at the Uxbridge. Johnny was 41 and looks so young than compared to photos I see of him today in magazines. He is amazing, to say the least.

While running yesterday's race I had to turn around and smash a tiny snail on the ground behind me. Darn thing had been following me around the whole route! Best Regards, Brownie Ross!

At age 75, Ted Vogel set an age group record for 5k in his home state of New Hampshire.

Horace Ashenfelter was the 1952 Olympic Steeplechase Gold medalist in Helsinki, setting a new world record of 8:45.4. Horace's Steeplechase gold medal victory is probably one of the biggest surprises in American Track and Field history along with Billy Mills 10,000 gold medal in the 1964 Olympics in Tokyo. He won fifteen national AAU titles and 3 national collegiate titles and was also a five-time Millrose indoor two-mile champion. Living nearby in Pennsylvania and New Jersey, he competed frequently against Browning at various distances, indoors and outdoors including of course the 1952 US Olympic Trials and Olympic Games.

Ashenfelter also finished sixth in the 1956 Melbourne Olympic Steeplechase and finished second in the 1955 Pan Am games in the 5000. Ashenfelter was a Penn State grad who went out for track at the urging of Penn State alumnus and 3 time Olympian Curtis Stone. He was also an FBI agent. He made his home in Glen Ridge, NJ and like Browning has a race named after him in his hometown.

"Browning was one of the most gifted distance runners of our day. My experiences with him were from 1948 to 1956. During this period, we ran against each other at least 10 times, but we were at the same meets a lot more than that. He was a cheerful person, great sense of humor, fun to be with but always a serious competitor. We competed against each other once at the Berwick "Marathon," numerous cross-country events (5,000 to 10,000 meters). We also competed in several 3,000 Steeplechases and a few indoor and outdoor miles, and a few street runs.

Larry James was a gold (1600 relay) and silver medalist (400 meters) and world record holder (1600 relay) in the 1968 Olympics. James, also a Villanova Hall of Famer, was the Head Track and Cross-Country coach and Athletic Director at Stockton College. He was also Browning's partner in his Mid- Atlantic running camp for over a decade.

Browning and Jack Pyrah both said they considered James' 43.9 anchors 400 leg in the 1968 Penn relays to make up a large deficit against Rice University the greatest relay leg they ever witnessed.

Larry James remembered, "I put on a five-mile race at Stockton (Pomona, NJ) and asked Browning for some help as I had no idea what I was doing. He came down and helped me set everything up. About 10 minutes before the race was to start Browning asked me about the prizes. I mentioned that I had gift certificates to the Smithville Inn for age-group prizes. He said, "Then I'm going to run!" He proceeded to get changed to run the race and I started to panic because I wasn't sure if all of the runners knew the course, and Browning wouldn't be there to help me if he was in the race. Sure enough, he ran the race. At the finish, runners were coming in from five different directions and I was going crazy! Browning won his age group and the gift certificate.

The thing I remember about Browning from working with him at camp was he was low key but he always kept that world-class runner mentality of "guilt if he wasn't training" thing even when he got older. He told me he had a three-mile course in his house he would run if the weather got bad. He could have been pulling my leg but I believed him!"

Ron Delany was the 1956 Olympic 1500-meter gold medalist in Melbourne. Delany, a native of Arklow, Ireland was the seventh man to run a sub-four-minute mile. He also excelled at Villanova where he won three NCAA titles, broke the world indoor mile record three times and had a 40-race indoor meet winning streak. Since Delany was one of the most famous members of "Villanova's Irish pipeline" I asked him about Browning and the pipelines' origin. It was really George Guida (the 1948 400 meter US Olympian from Villanova) who was most responsible for starting the Irish "pipeline" of runners. Guida met with Jimmy Riordan, Irish Olympian in the athlete's barracks designed for World War II troops after the London Olympics and talked up Villanova and Jumbo. Jumbo offered him the scholarship to Villanova. I think Browning was probably most responsible for Irish Olympian John Joe Barry attending Villanova. Barry was, in turn, a big influence on my decision to attend Villanova.

Browning Ross was a dominant road runner before I got to Villanova and while I was there (1955-1958) and I think is well deserving of a book that tells his story."

Curtis Stone was another Pennsylvanian born, a 3 time Olympian who ran in the 1948, 1952 and 1956 Olympic Games 5,000 meters and tied with Browning in the 1951 Pan Am Games in the Steeplechase. Judges were forced to break the tie and awarded the gold medal to Stone.

"I first met Brownie in 1942. There were four of us from Penn State who had been on the NCAA championship team, Norman Gordon, myself, Gerald Carver and McClain Smith who decided to try for the National AAU title. Our fifth and sixth men were average runners so we decided to add Dave Williams who ran for Georgetown and Shanahan Catholic Club of Philadelphia as our fifth runner, and a young high school runner from Shanahan Catholic named Browning Ross. All of us college runners including Dave Williams were in the Enlisted Reserve Corp, going to college and simply waiting to be called up (to the service). McClain Smith had abdominal pains and finished 12th just behind Ross. They were our 5th and 6th team members. Thus, Brownie had a national championship team membership while still in high school. The six members all ended up in various places during the war-- four in Italy including Browning, myself in England for a couple of years and McClain Smith on Okinawa.

I next saw Brownie at the AAU Championships in San Antonio in 1946. He still looked young and ran in several races in both junior and senior AAU championships—everyone was just trying to get back in shape after the war. This was the first time the AAU meet was held south of the Mason-Dixon Line. Most runners from the east were on a special train which started in NYC, and then after St. Louis was completely segregated from the rest of the train. A few of the black runners tried to get served in the dining car. I met with Barney Ewell for breakfast and the waiters tried to get me to change to another table... finally, they put a screen around Barney and me. Barney refused to go to the dining car after that and I had to run out at train stops to get him candy bars and cookies to eat.

The next time I saw Brownie was at the NCAA championships in 1947 at Salt Lake City. At the end of the meet, the meet directors had the bright idea to have a final mile relay race with east vs. west. No quarter-miler was still available to run a leg, so everyone called on Brownie as we knew he was a good quarter-miler. Brownie ran a good leg, didn't lose any ground but the west won in a close race.

The following year, 1948 was an Olympic year and Brownie was the #2 runner for the US in the steeplechase. Bob McMillen was #1. (Bob fell in the water jump in his heat, and swore to return in 1952 which he did with a silver medal in the 1500) Brownie won the NCAA Steeplechase that year prior to the Olympic trials. He was the only US runner in the Olympic final and finished 7th. I think Brownie borrowing the bicycle and following Ted Vogel in the Olympic marathon was an early indication of his extreme interest in street runs. The Winetki article says that Browning stayed in Europe after the Games and started the Irish pipeline to Villanova while running in Ireland. Hogwash! He didn't start the pipeline at that time. I think the prime reason many of the Irish runners like John Joe Barry were attracted to Villanova was because they were interested in coming to the US to run the indoor track season.

Browning went to the Pan American Games in 1951 and won the 1500 meters and was second to me in the Steeplechase. There were only 4 American distance runners and one of them was a marathoner who also won the 10,000 meters. The other three of us tried to cover all the races. At the end of the week, we were pretty tired. John Twomey was 2nd in the 5,000 meters, but otherwise, we were able to win the 10,000, the Steeplechase and the 1500. So Brownie had a Pan American championship in Argentina in the 1500 for the first Pan Am games. Browning and I ran into the finish together in the Steeplechase, not holding hands as the newspaper article said and the judges made me the winner. I thought one championship (10,000 meters) was enough so I didn't press the last 150 yards and Browning refused to sprint ahead as he could have. Browning must have decided I should be the winner and refused to pass me. A sorry thing we both regretted I am sure. At the end of the 1500 meters, Brownie engaged in a little fisticuffs with the second place finisher. Brownie was incensed over being fouled. I was really surprised to see him angry enough to fight. The officials had to separate them.

I recall now that any cross country running in Philadelphia seemed to start at one of the boat houses and trails through Fairmount Park, but mostly on paved roads. Brownie usually won these races. He simply thrived on hard cement roads. I did beat him once at the Berwick Marathon. I usually avoided this race as I never liked the hard roads. I paid dearly for beating him as I was still sore for the AAU cross country race about 10 days later. He gained revenge in 1950 and beat me in the AAU cross country race on a windy day in Boston- preceding a hurricane.

Brownie thrived on street runs of over 4 miles. I can recall running with him for five miles or so in Canada on several occasions, and after about five miles he simply went into another gear and ran away from everyone. This seems unusual because he had extraordinary speed for every short distance on the track. I think the Sao Paulo midnight run was just too short for him to win. In indoor 1000 yard runs he always placed well and was always close to the winner if he wasn't quite fast enough to win. I don't think Brownie was ever particularly as fond of the track. The Steeplechases were his championships (in track) and I don't think they are wholly track and field. The AAU would tell him to run a track race and he would ignore them and go and run and win a street run instead.

The nine to ten-mile distance, like Berwick, probably fit Brownie's athletic strengths the best.

I have a newspaper picture of the Middle Atlantic AAU Cross Country with Browning, Herm Goffberg and me in 1949 I suppose. The three of us were leading, then later Browning and I were leading, I suppose I could have left Brownie, but we just ran together until somewhere near the finish, and Browning said, "What are we going to do? And I said we'll wait until the last 200 meters and I will say go. Of course, Browning won as he did in the AAU Cross Country in 1950 in Boston during the beginning of a hurricane.

Brownie also made the 1952 Olympic Games in the steeplechase but soon after arriving in Finland, he went to the hospital with stomach pains. There was a language barrier and he was gone for several days. When he returned he lay on his bed and kept us in stitches as he read the time's other competitors had run and moaned about his chances (after missing so much time). He was not in condition to advance in the heats of the Olympic steeplechase, but later in Norway, he ran really well. He came back from one trip up north in Norway and revealed he had won several races including 200 meters!

After the 1952 Olympics I took a teaching job in Smethport, Pa. hoping to end problems I was having with exercised induced asthma. Brownie would take a plane from Philly to the local airport in Bradford, Pa. I would meet him there and we would drive to Canada, a little over 100 miles away. Brownie had made contacts there, people liked him, and the races were well marked, well policed, lots of merchandise as well as trophy prizes, etc. I dropped him off for his flight back to Philly one day. He was carrying a trophy about 4 feet high, and he wandered off to his flight moaning that his wife had told him she would kill him if he brought home another trophy. It was during this period that Brownie won the Around the Bay race at least one. It was during this time I recognized his unusual ability to compete in street runs over four miles.

Brownie was quiet but amusing and gregarious. Despite his nonchalant attitude, he was really quite alert and really perceptive about racing, training, and people in general. Brownie could find humor most anywhere. He had a great sense of humor that was also most often self-deprecating.

Later in the 1950's Brownie started running track meets in Woodbury, NJ. I went there a couple of times and he would always offer me some of his trophies that he was using for prizes. I wish now that I might have taken some just to learn where he had won them. It would be great if someone would have cataloged all of this medals and trophies. Surely there was a world record there of some sort!

In the summer of 1957 Brownie, I and my wife and young daughter took a trip to Atlantic City to interview for coaching positions there. Brownie was apparently looking to begin coaching as he arranged the trip. We both were offered coaching contracts, but not for our own sports! A strange experience but it illustrates Brownies interest in coaching."

Oscar Moore- was a 1964 Olympian in the 5000 meters in Tokyo where he finished 8th in 14:24.

Ted Corbitt called him the "great Oscar Moore" because of his smooth-running form and dominance from 2 miles to 10,000 meters during the first half of the 1960's. Browning called Oscar "the smoothest runner I've ever seen." Oscar was one of the elite American distance runners who moved to Echo Summit in California for altitude training and testing with Coach Jack Daniels before the 1968 Olympics. The athletes Oscar moved from Southern Illinois with Bill Fritz to take the Glassboro State Head Track and Assistant Cross-Country position. He was also the top-ranked master's runner in the country for a time while coaching at Glassboro (now Rowan University).

Oscar remembered his first meeting with Browning, "I had heard a lot about Browning Ross and about his Long Distance Log magazine from Ted Corbitt. I went to meet him at this store (Sports East) and Browning told me about his series of races, and that he had one coming up in Medford, NJ that weekend at his camp. I ran his race in the Medford, NJ Pine Barrens. I think it was called something like "Camp Chippewa" (Camp Ockanickon). I had a big lead but got lost! Nothing was marked. At the end of the race, Browning was smiling and joking and took out a lot of different prizes from the trunk of his car, enough prizes for everyone in the race, including gym bags-- which I won. Browning was really a good guy. I still have some Long Distance Logs with results from the races Ted Corbitt and I ran in the 1960's."

Ted Corbitt was a US Olympian in the 1952 Olympic marathon, a member of the New York Pioneers running club, a physical therapist and one of the founding fathers of US distance running. He was the third president of the Road Runners Club of America and the founding president of the New York Road Runners Club. He was also an American pioneer of ultramarathon training and racing and a good friend of Browning. Oscar Moore recalled long training runs with Ted. Oscar, "One time I ran with Ted around the island of Manhattan, starting at Yankee Stadium, I made it about 25 miles to the U. N. building and I ran out of gas. I called my sister for a ride because I was embarrassed to get a cab ride home wearing running shorts." Ted was also humble and soft spoken like Browning. Browning really respected Ted, who was the third president of the Road Runners Club of America, Ted was also an accomplished writer who often set the record straight on occasions when a running writer would omit Browning's accomplishments.

Ted's son Gary passed on some of Ted's correspondence about Browning, "Chances are that few of today's road runners have heard of Ross, but they owe him a lot just the same.

My favorite story about Ross was from a race in New Jersey and a young runner-- who was apparently too naïve to know that he could not keep up with Ross in a race.

Ross' shoestring came loose during this race and Ross had to stop and re-tie it. The kid, instead of racing on out in front alone, also stopped and trotted in a circle around the kneeling Ross. This annoyed Ross to no end and he said, "Get away from me!" I believe the young runner had also been gabbing away to Ross as they raced along and Ross was moving. Ross then took off. This was told to me by the late Jack Barry (at the time one of the top marathoners in the country)."

In a previous chapter on the Berwick Marathon of 1956 Ted not-ed Browning's tough battle with New York Pioneer Club teammate Rudy Mendez, and how Browning's strong will to win helped him prevail in a tough race. In 1998 Ted nominated Browning posthumously for the Abebe Bikila Award for contributions to the sport of running. Corbitt won the first award in 1978. He listed Browning's extraordinary accomplishments including his two Olympic appearances as well as starting Road Runners Club of America and the first national running magazine the Long Distance Log among justification for the award. Browning was not selected and has still not received the Bikila Award as of this books printing.

Jerry Karver was among the top runners in the country in the 1940's and 50's and came as close as you can get to an Olympic berth without making the team. He was a frequent competitor of Browning.

During his high school career, Karver won a combined six state cham-pionships in cross country and track while never losing a race in three years. Serving in the Air Force as an officer in World War II 1945, he also won the Allied Forces mile in Paris and European-Mediterranean 1,500-meter cham-pionship in Florence, Italy.

Upon returning to Penn State after World War II, Karver won the IC4A, National Intercollegiate, and National AAU mile titles in 1947. Karver was NCAA mile champion in 1947 and won numerous mile, 1500 meters and 3-mile races in his running career. He finished fourth in the 1948 Olympic Trials, missing the team by one-tenth of a second.

During his collegiate career at Penn State, Karver won the IC4A Cross-Country title as a freshman.

In 1949, the Pennsylvania Catholic Interscholastic Association started the Jerry Karver Invitational mile as a way to honor Karver's accomplishments. The Karver mile attracted world- wide attention every spring as it invited the top 8 milers in the country and paid their expenses to the meet.

As a Villanova Sophomore in 1948, Ross made national sports page headlines by upsetting Karver, the reigning National Champion, in the AAU Mid-Atlantic Championship in Harrisburg, Pa. (Browning's brother Babe finished third in the race.)

Ross's time of 3:57.8 eclipsed the AAU record set in 1934 (4:03.2 set by Ernie Federoff). Browning and Babe a freshman at Tennessee, both ran for the South Jersey Track Club in the June meet.

Karver said, "Brownie ran in at least three of the Karver Miles, against the best competition in the country. You could be certain if Brownie was entered in a race, the race would be thrilling." I ran in a couple of "street runs" with Brownie for Brownie's Shanahan Catholic Club coached by Jack Pyrah."

Browning's Training Schedules

AFTER I GRADUATED FROM COLLEGE, Browning wrote a year's worth of training schedules for me by hand on index cards. Many of these schedules are reprinted here and can be adopted in part or whole by runners of different abilities with just a bit of modification. Browning said these schedules were based on his own training and modified for me.

In a nod to the popular Fred Wilt "How they Train" books Browning placed a note "Jack, How he Trains!" at the top of a couple of the training cards.

In the 20 years he wrote and published the Long Distance Log, Browning had access to and printed almost every successful distance coach and runners training schedules in the Log.

Tom Osler, "Browning was such a naturally talented runner, I don't know if he was a proponent of any one training method. I couldn't train with him; his natural training pace was very fast. He stayed in shape year- round, and was able to race extremely well on a small amount of mileage."

In our discussions on training, Browning most frequently mentioned being in agreement with Arthur Lydiard and his training methods.

Browning recommended hard/easy days and two endurance building periods a year and at least some speed work year- round. These schedules are similar to what Browning used in his own training and are based on trial and error and what worked for him. Distances are in yards.

Two Endurance Building Periods a Year- winter and summer.
One long run a week- no more than one-third of your weekly average mileage for the week (i.e. if you are running 45 miles a week your long run should be 15 miles; 30 miles- 10 miles).

One of every 4 weeks should be a recovery week that is 50% of the weekly average for the prior three weeks during your build-up.

To avoid stress, use hard day/easy day running to avoid strain and injury.

The long run will be one-third your total mileage for the week. Another one-third should be split between another two days over the week. The remaining one-third should be distributed over the remaining four days with the back to back recovery days coming before the long run. This will ensure that the <u>recovery</u> days are <u>short</u> runs. DON'T GO TOO FAR ON THE RECOVERY DAY because you feel to do so little seems to be a waste.

Sample weekly training schedules in endurance building phase:

	Sun	Mon	Tues	Wed	Thurs	Fri	Sat
1. 25 mpw	8	2	4	2	5	2	2
2. 30 mpw	10	2	5	2	6	2	3
3. 35 mpw	12	2	6	2	7	2	3
4. 15 mpw	5	1	2	1	3	1	2 (rest week)
5. 35 mpw	12	2	6	2	7	2	4
6. 40 mpw	13	3	6	3	8	3	4
7. 45 mpw	15	3	7	3	9	3	5
8. 20 mpw	7	1	3	2	4	1	2 (rest week)

Winter Training Schedule November to March
Mon- 12-mile roads and grass 7:00 to 7:30 pace
Tues- easy 4-mile run. Swim or bike (stationary).
Wed- 3 x 660 at 1:50   6-mile steady run 6:30 to 7:00 pace

Thurs- Same as Tuesday
Fri-long steady run 8 to 13 miles at comfortable pace, accelerate the last mile.
Sat and Sun- Same as Tues & Thursday

April Training: (Assuming Sunday race)
Mon- 6 miles at 7:00 pace
Tues- 4x3 laps (1320) at 3:30 pace with 440 jog interval. 3 miles slow on track at 7:15 pace finish with
6 x110 at 7/8 effort on grass.
Wed- 4 miles easy.
Thurs-Intervals 8 x220 in 30 second clip (all with 220jog);3x660 in 1:42; 1x440 in 64 seconds; 1x330 in 46 seconds. 2x 110, 3 miles easy warm down grass or track.
Fri- Same as Wed.
Sat-easy 3-mile jog 7:30 pace on grass or track.
Sun- competition or easy 15 miles or 10 miles (1st 5 miles 10 intervals of 4 telephone poles, second five at 7:15 pace.)
Every AM before breakfast 3 or 4 miles easy 7:00-7:15 pace.

June
Mon- Easy 15 Mile Run (in hills if possible).
Tues- 4x 1320 at 3:38 with 440 jog interval. 3-mile easy at 7:00 pace   6 x 110 at 7/8 effort.
Wed- 3-mile jog on grass 3 x 220 at 30 seconds 220 jog interval recovery.
Thurs- 3 x220 at 30 seconds with 220 jog interval; 3 x660 (1:49), 440 (66), 330 (52), 220 (30)
6 X110 with 220 in 90 seconds, between each run. 2-mile warm down.
Fri- same as Tuesday.
Sat- Easy 3- mile jog (7:30 pace) on grass.
Sun. Competition.

JULY
Warm up with 1 ½ miles easy jogging. (About 9 min mile pace.) 3 easy 110's.
Monday- 4 x 880 -220 interval 6 miles at 7-minute pace with some hills easy.

Finish workout with 4 x 165 at 7/8 effort.

Tuesday- 4 miles easy.

Wed- 3 x 660 at 1:45- 1:4:8 with 220 intervals. Repeat Mondays 6 miles.

Thurs- Same as Tuesday.

Friday 15 5o 18 miles at 6:30 pace or whatever feels comfortable.

Sat- Easy 3-mile jog 7:00- 8:00 pace on grass.

Sun- Race.

August

Monday- 5 or 6 miles steady 6:45 pace.

Tuesday- 10 miles (1st 5 hard with 10 surges for 4 telephone poles, 2nd 5 easy 7:15 pace)

Wednesday- 6 miles steady 6:45 pace.

Thursday 8 x 220 at 30 second with 220 jog interval; 3 x 660 (1:43); 440 (64); 3 mile warm down.

Friday- easy 3-mile run if race on Sat. If race on Sunday run for one hour.

Alternate summer training plan for 33:00 10k

One day a week 4:58 pace

3-6 x 800 or 8 to 12 x 400m 3- minute jog between repeats

September (Fall training Sept to Dec for 10k and up)

Assuming Sunday races.

Monday- 4 x ¾ mile 3:45 with 440 jog (about 3 min. interval) easy. 6 miles (on grass if possible) 4 x 165 yds. (Sprint 55 yards, float 55 yds, sprint 55). 110 interval, finish with 880 jog warm down.

Tuesday- easy 4-mile run

Wednesday- 3 x 660 at 1:45 – 1:50 with 220 interval; 6 to 10 miles easy.

Thursday- easy 4-mile run.

Friday- 15 to 20 miles at 6:30 a mile pace or whatever feels comfortable. 4 x 110 at 7/8 effort.

Saturday- easy 4 miles.

Sunday- race.

October

Same as September.

If not racing on Sunday:|

16X 330 with 110 jog interval

4 x 165 (sprint, float, sprint)

6 miles steady run 6:30 – 7:00 pace

Mile Training

Monday- Easy 5 miles incorporate 10 x 50 yards

Tuesday- 40-30 drill (Run as many laps as you can until you are totally exhausted 220 in 30 seconds.

(35 seconds if you can't handle 30) and the next on interval rest in 40 seconds. Run until you can't run 30-35 second 220's, or you have to go slower (or longer) than 40 seconds to recover. You will probably only be able to do a couple of laps like this at first. Perhaps you should do 35-45 seconds.

This teaches you what race pace is right for you.

Wednesday- Fartlek run in woods jog between faster runs don't walk.

Thursday-6 x 440 70 seconds each. Jog in between.

Friday- 3 or 4 miles easy.

Saturday- race

Sunday- long run

Vary the program- Do different sets of intervals, different distances and experiment with a recovery time that you can handle.

Run two miles and stretch a bit before interval workouts.

The way to progress with interval training is by cutting the recovery phase as you get stronger and (hopefully) faster, the recovery intervals become shorter and quicker.

Browning wrote down what he called "two general theories of running," possibly for future use in one of his weekly running columns in the Woodbury Times, or his Sports East newsletter.

1. Running will not prolong life. We are all born with an "age quotient." Some of us have a longer quotient than others due to heredity.

Stress is the big factor in early death, not lack of exercise. By eliminating stress, one may expect to live closer to his/her allotted quotient. "Play" for an hour, at least, every day. The effort at work tends to make for a high risk of heart trouble, while effort in play tends to lower the risk.

2. Supports in shoes- Most of us have some little structural defects of the foot, and distance running tends to exaggerate it. 30 miles per week causes the foot to strike the ground 20,000 times per week. 30 miles a week is the critical amount for a runner. That is the volume at which problems start occurring in most runners.

   Supports bring the ground up to the foot and prevent the foot from rolling over to the inside or to do something else it should not. 75 miles a week (50,000 foot strikes.)

   Avoid tilts in the road- feet don't get a nice flat surface to run on. Cortisone eases the pain, but irritation starts as soon as you run again so get supports made for those feet if you have foot problems!

ACKNOWLEDGEMENTS

I would like to thank Browning's children, Bonnie, Barry, and Barb for their indispensable help and patience in every stage of this project. They shared their memories and their father's scrapbooks, pictures, letters and his remarkable accomplishments with me; and this is the framework of this book.

This book contains but a survey of Browning's many race wins. Browning had bins of scrapbooks filled with newspaper clippings of race wins and correspondence. Each scrapbook contained dozens of articles between its pages that Browning had saved and then forgotten about. It quickly became apparent that to include all of this information would have created a book equivalent to William Manchester's multi-book series on Winston Churchill, overwhelming all but the most rabid track fan.

Thanks to Browning's brother Forest "Babe" Ross and his wife Reggie Ross for your kindness and sharing your memories of Browning.

I would also like to thank Tom Osler and Gary Corbitt for their assistance. I owe both a debt of gratitude. Ted Corbitt and Tom were two of Browning's closest friends who shared much of the history in this book with him.

Special thanks to Browning's close friend 3 time Olympian Curt "Stoney" Stone, for his patience in answering questions about races long ago. Thanks to Horace Ashenfelter, Ted Vogel, Alex Breckenridge. Ronny Delaney, Sir Roger Bannister, Amby Burfoot, and Jeff Johnson. Thanks to the Dave Williams family, especially Alexandra and Marcella for all of your help, including pictures and loaning a scrapbook from Browning's friend Jared Hoch.

Thanks to the Villanova Sports Department for permission to use their pictures and for their support. Thanks to the Press Enterprise for the wealth of information on the Berwick races.

A major thank you to Bob Shryock, who interviewed Browning probably more than anyone for the Woodbury/Gloucester County Times and to Tim Kelly, Neil Weygandt, Jean Pyrah, Dave Platt, Moses Mayfield, Ken Kling and Dave Brier.

I would be remiss without acknowledging posthumously some of the people I interviewed over the years about Browning who have passed away and are greatly missed: Jack Pyrah, John A. Kelley, Larry James, Dr. George Sheehan, Herb Lorenz, Kathy Osler, Jerry Scharff, Chet Dirkes, Bill Heughan and Harry Berkowitz, Jane Hoopes, Jerry Nolan, Dr. Ted Berry, Captain Tom Gallagher, Bill Fritz, John Stratton, and especially Dr. Dave Coghlan for starting the whole wonderful experience in motion.

Special thanks to the late great writer William Zinnser for his encouragement and direction. Thanks to Track and Field News, especially Jon Hendershott for your assistance helping me confirm times and races from long ago.

Thanks to the Sports Information Department at Villanova, and to Marcus O'Sullivan, Marty Liquori, Tom Donnelly, Don Bragg, Ilene Lee and Jim DeLorenzo.

Thanks to Freddi Carlip of Runners Gazette and Jim O'Brien of American Runner for publishing my magazine articles about Browning. Interest in those articles led to this book. Thanks to Bill Cleary and Cleary's Notebook. Thanks to the Press-Enterprise for your assistance with pictures of Browning in Berwick.

Thanks to Sean McClanachan, Dave McCollum, Mark, Pete and Paul Worthington, Jim Plant, Mike Browoleit, Tom Lutz, Mike Kain and all my teammates and the people who ran for Browning over the years. You know who you are.

Thanks to Ed Dodd, Fran Masciuli, Reuben Frank, Walt Pierson, Norm Ostrow, Ian Stevenson, Ann Warsing, Dave Jenkins, Ken Underwood, Warren Walker, Jim Flanagan, George and Margie Morris, Linda Lutz and to all of the people who ran Browning's races every weekend for decades. Thanks especially for your encouragement to finish this book on Browning.

Thanks to Pete League, Pat Avis, Don Sanderson, Norma Beard, James Shea, Dave Johnson, Oscar Moore, Jack Daniels, Vince Phillips, Irma Lorenz, Mike Fanelli, Jim Cheney, Bob Romansky, Mike Glavin, Mike Fanelli, Jim Crossin, Mark Wetmore, Kevin Quinn, John Carter, Bill Kile Jr. and Sr., Dr. Ron Ferguson and Mark Kordich. Thanks to Drew Desher and Family for loaning grandfather John Glaziers scrapbook of Camden Y races from the 1920's to the 1970s.

Thanks to Joe Henderson and Hal Higdon for your contributions and fabulous coverage of our sport for so many decades. Thanks to Dr. Tim Noakes, Ken Young, and Alberto Salazar.

Thanks to Fran Carver for his willingness to talk about memories from long ago. Thanks to Tom Heinonen for his memories of the US World Cross-country teams. Thanks to Bill Thompson, Keith Collins and all the officials who spoke to me about officiating with Browning.

Thanks to Gloucester Catholic High School for giving Browning and my-self the opportunity to coach such great people over the years; special thanks to John Colman for all of his support over the years. Thanks also to Mike and Caroline Dougherty who also coached with Browning.

(Videos of Browning running and directing races can be found on the Gloucester Catholic Cross-Country Website: http://www.intactest.com/GC_Heath/BrowningRoss.html)

Thanks to all the unsung, and uncredited writers and photographers for their great coverage of running in the newspapers-- especially in the 1950's and 60's.

Thanks to my parents Jack and Eleanor Heath for their love and support and rides to and from practice. Thanks to my son Sean for his assistance with the cover.

And finally, thanks to my wife Maryanne Heath for her encourage-ment and patience while I worked on this labor of love. "Is it done yet?" Yes, it is.

BROWNING ROSS BIBLIOGRAPHY

Bannister, Roger. "The Four Minute Mile" Lyons and Burford, 1989.

Barry, John Joe. "The Ballincurry Hare" Athletic Publications, Inc. 1989.

Berry, Theodore and Elliott, James. "Jumbo Elliott: Maker of Milers, Maker of Men" St. Martin's Press, 1982.

Chodes, John. "Corbitt" Track and Field News, 1978.

Erby, Earl. "Around the World and Then Some on Foot" Philadelphia Bulletin, November 28, 1958.

Henderson, Joe. "Father Ross" Running Commentary, June 1998.

Higdon, Hal. "Renegade Ross" The Runner Magazine, December 1983.

Holland, Gerald. "Here Comes Jumbo" Sports Illustrated, January 2, 1962.

Kelly, Tim. "Ross Helped Pave Way for Running Boom of '70's" Courier-Post, June 3, 1992.

Kiseda, George. "Browning Ross a Pro?" Philadelphia Bulletin, May 7, 1969.

Kiseda, George. "Ross Runs to Relax; Still wins at 40" Philadelphia Bulletin, March 18, 1964.

Lester, Michael. "Browning Ross Berwick Run for the Diamonds"

Press-Enterprise, November 23, 1995.

Morrow, Art. "Barry Heads Villanovans in Inquirer Track Meet"

Philadelphia Inquirer, January 7, 1951.

"Browning Ross wins Pan Am Gold" New York Times, March 6, 1951

Osler, Tom. "Serious Runners Handbook" World Publications, 1978.

Phettepace, Ed. "Browning Ross Symbol of the Olympic Athlete" Sports of the Times, September 1956.

Pollock, Ed. "Browning Ross Likes to Run 10 Miles Daily to Escape Colds." Philadelphia Bulletin, February 17, 1961.

Robbins, Charlie "Browning Ross, the Most Versatile Runner of All Time" 1955

Samuels, Leroy. "Now It's 'Coach' Browning Ross" Philadelphia Bulletin, October 20, 1976.

Shryock, Bob. "Browning Ross Never Slowed Down" NJ.com/South-Jersey, July 28, 2015.

Telander, Rick. "Nobody's Bigger Than Jumbo" Sports Illustrated, March 10, 1980.

Will-Weber, Mark. "Run for the Diamonds." Breakaway Books, 2008.

PHOTO CREDITS

Front Cover and Villanova cartoon and photos courtesy of Villanova University Sports Information Department.

Browning Ross and Sir Roger Bannister courtesy of British Pathe.

Amateur Athlete Magazine courtesy of Mike Fanelli.

Berwick Marathon Photo Courtesy of Press Enterprise.

Boston Marathon Photo courtesy of Jeff Johnson.

Browning and the Police cartoon from the Philadelphia Bulletin.

Browning Ross Road Shoe Courtesy of Coach Phil Scott and Cedarville University Track and Field Shoe Museum.

Atlantic City Boardwalk Photo Courtesy Dave Brier.

Other Photos Courtesy of the Ross, and Williams Families and Pete League.

Made in the USA
Middletown, DE
14 May 2018